T5-AQR-230

FAMILY PSYCHOLOGY II

Theory, Therapy, Enrichment, and Training

Luciano L'Abate
Georgia State University

UNIVERSITY
PRESS OF
AMERICA

Lanham • New York • London

Copyright © 1987 by

University Press of America,® Inc.

4720 Boston Way
Lanham, MD 20706

3 Henrietta Street
London WC2E 8LU England

All rights reserved

Printed in the United States of America

British Cataloging in Publication Information Available

ISBN: 0-8191-6680-4 (pbk. : alk. paper)
ISBN: 0-8191-6679-0 (alk. paper)

All University Press of America books are produced on acid-free
paper which exceeds the minimum standards set by the National
Historical Publication and Records Commission.

Acknowledgments

I am grateful to the publishers and editors who have consented to the reprinting of many of the chapters in this collection.

Chapter 1 was published in The American Journal of Family Therapy, 1987, 15, 19-33, and is reprinted here with the permission of the publisher, Brunner/Mazel.

Chapter 2 has been submitted for publication.

Chapter 3 is in press in The American Journal of Family Therapy, 1987, 15, and is reprinted here with the permission of the publisher, Brunner/Mazel.

Chapter 4 was published in The Personnel and Guidance Journal, 1981, 59, 263-265, and is reprinted here with the permission of the publisher. Copyright American Association for Counseling and Development. No further reproduction is authorized without the written permission of AACD.

Chapter 5 was published in Integrating Sex and Marital Therapy, edited by Gerald R. Weeks and Larry Hof (New York: Brunner/Mazel, 1987). It is reprinted here with the permission of the editors.

Chapter 6 is the outline of a workshop given at the Midwinter meeting of the Florida Psychological Association, December 7, 1986.

Chapter 7 was published in Innovation in Clinical Practice, VI: A Source Book, edited by P.A. Keller and S.R. Heyman (Sarasota: Professional Resource Exchange, 1987), and is included here, in a modified form, with the permission of P.A. Keller, editor.

Chapter 8 was published in Family Therapy, 1983, 10, 37-45, and is reprinted here with the permission of the editor, Martin Blinder, MD.

Chapter 9 was published in The American Journal of Family Therapy, 1984, 12, 12-20, and is part of a chapter in L'Abate's Systematic Family Therapy (New York: Brunner/Mazel, 1986). It is reprinted here with the permission of the publisher, Brunner/Mazel.

Chapters 10 and 11 are published here for the first time.

Chapter 12 was published in the International Journal of Family Therapy, 1983, 5, 39-53 and is reprinted here with the permission of the publisher, International Universities Press.

Chapter 13 is published here for the first time.

Chapter 14 was published in the _Journal of Psychotherapy and the Family_, 1986, 2, 117-128, and is reprinted here with the permission of the editor, Charles Figley, and the publisher, The Haworth Press.

Chapters 15 and 16 are published here for the first time.

Chapter 17 was published in _Family Relations_, 1985, 34, 169-175, and is reprinted here with the permission of the publisher, the National Council for Family Relations.

Chapter 18 was published in _Family Relations_, 1984, 33, 245-250, and is reprinted here with the permission of the publisher, the National Council for Family Relations.

Chapter 19 was published in the _Journal of Psychotherapy and the Family_, 1986, 2, 59-67, and is reprinted here with the permission of the editor, Charles Figley, and the publisher, The Haworth Press.

Chapter 20 was published in _Professional Psychology_, 1981, 12, 761-768 (copyright by the American Psychological Association). It is reprinted here by permission of the publisher, the American Psychological Association.

Chapter 21 is published here for the first time.

Chapter 22 was published in _The American Journal of Family Therapy_, 1985, 13, 7-16, and is reprinted here with the permission of the publisher, Brunner/Mazel.

Chapter 23 is published here for the first time.

Chapter 24 was read at the 1982 annual meeting of the National Council on Family Relations and is published here for the first time.

Chapter 25 was published in _The Family Coordinator_, 1977, 26, 61-64, and is reprinted here with the permission of the publisher, the National Council for Family Relations.

Chapter 26 was read at the 1983 annual meeting of the National Council on Family Relations, St. Paul, Minnesota, and is published here for the first time.

I am appreciative of Marie Morgan's editing of the chapters published here for the first time and the word-processing of Marti Hagan (Word Wizards).

List of Contributors

Hilary Buzas
Private Practice
Chicago, Illinois

Guiseppe Colondier
IBM
Rome, Italy

Elaine Gibson
The Link Counseling Center
Atlanta, Georgia

Edgar Jessee
St. Mary's Hospital
Knoxville, Tennessee

Trudi B. Johnston
Counseling and Psychological
    Services Department
Georgia State University
Atlanta, Georgia

Gregory Jurkovic
Department of Psychology
Georgia State University
Atlanta, Georgia

James Kochalka
Private Practice
Tampa, Florida

Michael Levis
Family Psychology Program
Georgia State University
Atlanta, Georgia

John Lutz
Family Psychology Program
Georgia State University
Atlanta, Georgia

Sherry McHenry
Pershing Point Counseling Center
Atlanta, Georgia

James Metts
Private Practice
Atlanta, Georgia

J. Brien O'Callaghan
Southern Connecticut
    State University
New Haven, Connecticut

Gregory T. Samples
Cross Keys Counseling Center
Conley, Georgia

Sadell Sloan
Private Practice
Atlanta, Georgia

Frederic E. Stevens
Morningside Emergency Shelter
Brattleboro, Vermont

William C. Talmadge
Private Practice
Atlanta, Georgia

M. Lyn Thaxton
William Russell Pullen Library
Georgia State University
Atlanta, Georgia

Victor Wagner
Salesmanship Club
Dallas, Texas

Contents

Acknowledgments

List of Contributors

Introduction

Section I: Theory and Theory Testing

Section II: Therapy

Introduction

Since the publication of an earlier collection of writings on family psychology (L'Abate, 1983), a great many changes for the betterment of the family in general and of family psychology in particular have taken place. Family psychology has received a certain degree of status and legitimacy by the creation of a separate division (Division 43) within the structure of the American Psychological Association. This recognition is being implemented by a variety of parallel improvements, for instance, (a) the formalization of training programs in family psychology; (b) the creation of a forthcoming journal, one that will not imitate the field of family therapy but will define the issues that beset the creation of a whole new field of study and practice and a new profession; (c) publication of a two-volume set that will, I hope, help define the field further and serve as a base for increased progress and even greater differentiation (L'Abate, 1985).

As far as the betterment of families is concerned, many other changes have taken place that indicate an ever increasing interest and deserved attention. If there is one theme that pervades this collection, it is the concept of verifiability in theory construction, in effectiveness of therapeutic delivery, in prevention, and in training. This is perhaps the very concept that distinguishes family psychology from family therapy. While family therapy is characterized by a veritable hodgepodge of unverified and unverifiable concepts and techniques, family psychology strives (albeit slowly) to couch theoretical concepts and therapeutic methods in verifiable terms.

Section I reflects the fact that theory and theory-testing have been receiving much greater attention in the literature than they did in the past. A critical review of family theory and therapy indicates the need for quantifiable measures for concepts such as competence and intimacy.

Section II presents the tenuous and optimistic possibility that family therapy and the fields of prevention and psychoeducational programming, which have been going along with practices that are mutually exclusive, have reached a rapprochement, a position that will, however, take years to be reached fully.

Section III shows that prevention is becoming more and more differentiated, producing at least three additional and ancillary specializations: (a) enrichment (L'Abate & Weinstein, 1987; L'Abate & Young, 1987); (b) psychoeducational programs (Levant, 1986); and (c) social skills training (L'Abate & Milan, 1985). The vigorous growth of this field, based on a more empirical stance than is family therapy, may well become the next mental health movement, supplementing earlier movements (psychoanalysis, behaviorism, humanism, and family therapy).

Finally, the issues of training family psychologists need to be considered within the whole context of professional specialization in clinical psychology as well as in psychology as a science and as a profession (Section IV). Again, the emphasis is on reproducible methods of training rather than on the one-of-a-kind, sleight-of-hand, seat-of-the-pants approaches used in family therapy training.

References

L'Abate, L. (1983). Family psychology: Theory, therapy and training. Washington, DC: University Press of America.

L'Abate, L. (1985). Handbook of family psychology and therapy (2 vols.). Homewood, IL: Dorsey Press.

L'Abate, L., & Milan, M. (Eds.). (1985). Handbook of social skills training and research. New York: Wiley.

L'Abate, L., & Weinstein, S. (1987). Structured enrichment programs for couples and families. New York: Brunner/Mazel.

L'Abate, L., & Young, L. (1987). Casebook: Structured enrichment programs for couples and families. New York: Brunner/Mazel.

Levant, R. F. (Ed.). (1986). Psychoeducational approaches to family therapy and counseling. New York: Springer.

SECTION I.   THEORY AND THEORY TESTING

CHAPTER 1

THE EMPEROR HAS NO CLOTHES!
LONG LIVE THE EMPEROR!
A CRITIQUE OF FAMILY SYSTEMS THINKING
AND A REDUCTIONISTIC PROPOSAL

LUCIANO L'ABATE
Georgia State University
GIUSEPPE COLONDIER
IBM, Rome, Italy

Family systems thinking is too abstract to be testable and too discontinuous to be related to the field of psychology as a science and as a profession. Its basic untestability might be necessary, but it remains insufficient to account for behavior in the family. After a detailed discussion of these and other shortcomings, a reductionistic proposal submits three major dimensions of family behavior. The major dependent one is development, which is a function of two process functions: the ability to love and the ability to negotiate power. Much published evidence tends to support the present proposal; however, it will be the purpose of future research to question whether two major process functions are necessary to describe behavior in the family or whether additional and/or different functions will be necessary.

This is the first paper of a critical series focused on the theoretical, professional, and clinical practices of family therapy (L'Abate & Jerkovic, in press). This paper specifically argues that a great deal of so-called family systems thinking (Dell, 1985; Hoffman, 1981; Keeney, 1983; Tomm, 1984) may be *necessary* to understand and predict behavior in the family. However, this thinking, as presently understood (Amerikaner, 1983; Buckley, 1968; Churchman, 1979; Gray et al., 1969; Hansen & L'Abate, 1982; Levant, 1984; Sauber et al., 1985), is *insufficient* to do so, because

Luciano L'Abate, Ph.D., is Professor of Psychology at Georgia State University, Atlanta, GA 30303. Dr. Giuseppe Colondier is in charge of professional training at IBM. This paper was written while Dr. Colondier was on temporary assignment to IBM in Atlanta.

of inherent shortcomings in its high level of generality and abstraction, its discontinuity from the field of psychology as a science, and ultimately, its untestability. It may work well as a metatheory but it fails to meet substantive criteria for qualifying as a theory (Howard, 1985).

In order to start with a clear understanding of terms, it is important to define "theory" and "hypothesis." The term "theory" has at least two different meanings: (a) a coherent set of generally accepted, more or less verified and established propositions used as principles of explanation for a specific class of events or variables; and (b) a proposed explanation based on still provisional and conjectural principles or hypotheses. An hypothesis is a conjecture put forth as a possible explanation of certain events or relations, which serves as a basis of argument or experimentation to reach consensual agreement from a variety of different and disparate sources. Given these definitions, one would argue that family systems thinking fits into the second meaning of the term "theory." The reductionistic proposal submitted here, on the other hand, attempts to fit it into the first definition.

A SUMMARY OF FAMILY SYSTEMS THINKING

Family systems thinking emphasizes concepts like: 1) complexity (at the expense of simplicity), as made up of hierarchical structures and organizations (Sauber et al., 1985); 2) circularity, as derived from equipotential and equifinal views of causality; 3) wholeness, i.e., the whole is greater than its component parts; 4) boundaries separating component parts; 5) size and strength of component parts (like the individual's contribution to the whole family); and 6) miscellaneous concepts, like stasis, homeostasis, etc., related to the state of equilibrium in the system.

1) *Hierarchical organization* or structure in which component parts or superordinate or underordinate components are subsystems, i.e., sets of interrelated variables, factors, or functions. Note, however, that the properties of systems are the same at any level of the hierarchical structure, that is: the properties of individuals as systems in their own rights are the same as the properties of their families as superordinate systems. These properties are:
2) *Complexity,* characterized by *circularity* or the ability to feedback information reflexively into the system and *multiple causality,* where equifinality (different causes may produce the same result) and equipotentiality (same cause may produce different outcomes) make prediction and control much more difficult than in a view of causality according to linearity (one cause, one effect).
3) *Wholeness,* that is: component parts work together in an interrelated unit, where the whole is greater than the sum of its parts. This property is due to the synergistic or multiplicative effects of interactional interrelatedness, that is, all the parts working toward a common goal. By the same token, this multiplicative relationship could become division if and when one component part or the relationships among parts fail to work in concert and in unison.

4

4) *Boundaries*, or the limits where one component part ends and another begins. These boundaries could be vague, rigid, permeable, impermeable, porous, or diffuse, producing fusion, diffusion, and confusion at one extreme of openness or rigidity, isolation, and compartmentalization at the other extreme of relative closeness.
5) *Size or strength* of each component part, that is: the individual contribution that each part brings to the whole, as assessed by time and energy expenditure, involvement, commitment, etc., in human terms, how helpful or hurtful each part is to the functioning or dysfunctioning of the entire system.
6) The state of *equilibrium* in the system and its ability to change and to resist change is described through terms like "stasis," "homeostasis," etc.

All of these characteristics of systems are acceptable, provided we keep a few distinctions in the forefront: (a) these concepts are mostly meta-theoretical, that is, they serve as working assumptions and, like most assumptions cannot be directly tested; (b) they are not nor should they be considered as replacing individually derived concepts from which definite and specific predictions about family functioning-dysfunctioning can be made; (c) individuals are also systems, and as such behave like systems; however, systemic functions are not sufficient to account for all of the behavior in the family. We need to rely also on developmental concepts to understand how families function or fail to function well.

Consequently, one would argue here that:

1) *A great deal of what goes for family systems thinking is mostly a metatheory that is unrelated to the field of psychology. It may be vaguely related to it but it is not connected. It lacks specificity.*
2) *A great deal of what goes for family systems theory is untestable, or at best, an unrelated set of unverifiable hypotheses, some of them without substance.*
3) *A great deal of what goes for theory is methodologically sterile and vacuously unproductive. In short it lacks empirical productivity.*

THEORY OR METATHEORY?

Most of what goes for theory is unrelated to practices of most therapists, or, to put it another way, it is practically impossible to demonstrate a link between the theory and the practices of most family therapists. As has been demonstrated in the individual psychotherapy field, one's theory and one's therapeutic practices are not always matched (Garfield & Bergin, 1978). Since what is talked about (theory) is so widely separated from what is done (practice), one is led to conclude that theory fails to link itself to actual behavior, or it is so generally and vaguely stated that it fails to link itself to specific therapeutic practices. If there are links, they are weak, that is, they are either too vaguely and abstractly stated or practically nonexistant. Thus far, to our knowledge, no one has been able to deduct specific propositions that may lead and link to specific therapeutic practices or consensually validated conclusions. One theorist's word is as good as another's. As long as one's therapeutic practices can be "explained" by a variety of different theories, there is no way one can state that one theory is "better" or superior than another. The problem, then, becomes one of *specificity*: Can one theory predict or produce therapeutic changes that another theory cannot predict or produce? Without specificity, it is difficult to compare and contrast different theories, and ultimately to arrive at any conclusions of comparative superiority of one theory over another.

This metatheory may serve as a general paradigm of a cosmological nature (Dell, 1985), but at that level of discourse, it is too distant from actual behavior, either in families or in therapists, to make any visible or substantial difference. It is destined to remain a seductive, interesting, and even exciting metatheory, but it does not make an iota of difference to how family therapists behave. It goes beyond a specific theory of how human beings (therapists included) behave inside their families (L'Abate, 1986).

THEORIES: TESTABLE OR UNTESTABLE?

As long as a theory is stated in very general and abstract terms, it will be difficult to test. In fact, family systems theory is indeed untestable, and that is where the major trouble lies. One needs to ask why it is practically impossible to test this theory? Most of the antiempirical bias in the field of family therapy theories can be traced to three major therapeutic emphases that have been derived from family systems theory (Gurman, 1983):

1) *An antireductionistic bias with a corresponding emphasis on emergent overconstructivism*. What does that mean? It means that there is a strong tendency to avoid simplification and instead to stress complexity. This tendency is evident in at least three different practices: (i) stress on the dialectical and the aesthetic at the expense of the pragmatic and the demonstrative (Keeney, 1983); (ii) emphasis on circularity at the expense of linearity (Hoffman, 1981); (iii) emphasis on metaphorical communication and abstract symbolism, as evidenced by therapeutic claims of theorists in the experiential area (Satir, Whitaker, etc.) at the expense of simple and concrete therapeutic methodologies (L'Abate, 1986). Not one single shred of evidence has ever been abducted by these theorists-therapists to support the validity of their position, a common practice in the field (Hansen & L'Abate, 1982).

There is no question that family systems thinking has been a decided conceptual and pragmatic advance in the evolution of our interventions (Gray et al., 1969; Marmor, 1983). By the same token, to consider reductionism, or all forms of reductionism as defective and fallacious would put us in the kind of digital self-defeating either-or position that we find so distasteful and dysfunctional in the very families we treat.

Consequently, if a reductionistic position is taken here, it is to correct the rampant and exaggerated tendency toward emergent constructivism

6

that seems to characterize the field. Hence, the present position needs to be reiterated to make sure that no misunderstanding will take place, and that is: family systems thinking may be necessary but it is not sufficient to relate the field of family therapy to the rest of psychology as a science and as a profession. As Howard (1985) notes, in regard to values in science, predictive accuracy, internal coherence, external consistency, fertility, and simplicity are among its most crucial values. Among these, the third is the more relevant to the arguments and thesis of this paper, and that is: "theory must be consistent with other theories and also the general background of scientific expectation" (Howard, 1985, p. 257). Here is where systems thinking falls down, no empirical evidence seems to exist, since most of the concepts derived from family systems thinking are untestable even if plausibly seductive.

2) *An overly antiempirical stance with a parallel emphasis on overimpressionistic biases*, as evidenced by at least three different practices: (i) the alleged irrelevance of empiricism (Colapinto, 1979); (ii) subjective claims of therapeutic effectiveness completely unfounded and unsupported by external, objective evidence of either short- or long-term changes; (iii) impressionistic claims of effectiveness without documentation derived from the tendency to overstress the personally subjective at the expense of the externally objective. As a result, one's claims of therapeutic success are as good as another's. This antiempirical stance sees research and evaluation as distasteful enterprises in the hands of few rigid diehards (Gurman, 1983).

3) *An overly antieclectic and overparticularistic bias that encourages*: (i) a proliferation of schools and gurus, ultimately resulting in what amounts to cults and cultism, the elevation of certain individual theorists to the level of sainthood, as in the case of M. H. Erickson or Bateson (Dell, 1985; Keeney, 1983), not too different from practices found in totalitarian countries; (ii) Liddle's (1982) attack on eclecticism is a good example of this trend, a trend that ignores the often-found conclusion that most practicing therapists are eclectic (L'Abate, 1985b); (iii) the outcome of this bias results in the word of individual gurus becoming more important than evidence or data generated from careful evaluations and observations. What is shown on videotape at workshops is taken as the final criterion of successful therapeutic strategies, but no one asks what happened to the family after one year from termination of therapy.

In addition to these shortcomings, there is another feature of family systems thinking that makes it difficult to relate it to the body of psychology as a science and as a profession, and that is: its *discontinuity* from well-established and empirically tested theories and concepts in the field of psychology and sociology. This discontinuity, both conceptual and practical, makes family systems thinking questionable as to its theoretical as well as to its empirical usefulness. In fact, one would even question its practical usefulness as long as it has not been demonstrated that this thinking leads to "better" i.e., more effective and cheaper, types of interventions with families than interventions derived from more linear or empirically based theories. Consequently, systems thinking may be necessary, but it may be insufficient to understand, predict, and control behavior in the family. The emperor has no clothes but is still the emperor! Thus, one would argue that behavior in the family can be understood, predicted, and controlled more parsimoniously through concepts and approaches derived from the field of psychology than from systems thinking.

A REDUCTIONISTIC PROPOSAL

Instead of being concerned about the individual vs. system dichotomy, one would propose to specify family characteristics on the basis of individually derived concepts and notions that have been empirically tested and validated. To make up for the shortcomings listed above, a reductionistic proposal based on three different but related concepts, all derived from monadic psychology, is presented here: Development over the life span, whether of the individual, the marriage, or the family, is the major dependent variable, which is a function of two process functions: 1) ability to love and to regulate distance (Swensen, 1985b); and 2) ability to negotiate power (L'Abate, 1986). In other words, development throughout the individual, marital, and family life cycles is a multiplicative function of the ability to love and the ability to negotiate (L'Abate, 1985a).

Development as a dialectical struggle of the life span (Ault, 1980; Riegel, 1979; Riegel & Rosenwald, 1975; Sears & Feldman, 1973) finds its empirical case in various studies of dependence in children, independence or denial of dependence in some adolescents, autonomous interdependence in adulthood, and a possible return to dependence in old age.

The notion of love finds its developmental biases in the concept of closeness-distance as studied by most social psychologists (Druckman et al., 1982; Knapp, 1972; Waxer, 1978; Weitz, 1974; Wiemann & Harrison, 1983). It may vary from too close and enmeshed, as in *folie à deux*, to complete distance, as in alienation.

The third concept of power as the ability to negotiate is derived from abnormal psychology. Most of what goes on as abuse, punishment, blaming, criticisms, and put-downs represents defeats that result from negative family interactions. Victories result from positive family interactions, where being oneself with a minimum of criticism and put-downs is the norm (Lewis et al., 1976). The positive extreme is represented by direct and indirect acceptance, affirmation, praise, and encouragement (Table 1).

From these three concepts one can derive the following about functional or dysfunctional behaviors in the family:

1) Functional families tend to express their love according to a balanced modulation of distance and a clear differentiation of issues of love from issues of power. Dysfunctional families tend to confuse love with power and are able to negotiate neither their distance nor other issues.

8

TABLE 1

A Reductionistic Proposal for Behavior in the Family

State of Development Increasing Differentiation	Processural Functions	Testable Models
Childhood— Dependence	*Love*: The ability to be: Oneself	*Being*: The ability to: Care
Adolescence—Denial of dependence (i.e., Independence)	Intimate	See the good in oneself and others
	Power: The ability to:	Forgive
Adulthood— Autonomous interdependence: Personhood Partnerhood Parenthood	Influence: Negotiate: Functioning Competence Motivation	*Intimacy*: The ability to share one's hurts
Old Age—Return to dependence?		A-R-C E-R-A-Aw-C Priorities

2) In functional families love and power are modulated more through victories rather than defeats, while in dysfunctional families this ratio is reversed, love and power are negotiated more through defeat than victories.

3) Victories tend to push development toward greater autonomy and interdependence, while defeats tend to keep family member over-dependent on each other in centrifugal families, or on the outside world in centripetal families. Victorious families will tend to produce individuals who will admit to their inherent interdependence but who are also able to maintain their personal autonomy as separate but equal human beings. Defeating families, on the other hand, would tend to keep their members dependent either on each other or on outside sources, i.e., welfare agencies, criminal justice system, etc.

4) Consequently, a great deal of family dysfunctionality is produced by defeats that keep family members close and dependent on each other, while victorious families tend to produce adults who are autonomous within the context of interdependence.

The most appropriate and testable model for development, in spite of criticisms to the contrary (Hauser, 1976) is Loevinger's (1976) as elaborated more recently by Swensen (1985a). The most appropriate model for dysfunctions in distance regulation is the Pursuer-Regulator-Distancer, elaborated elsewhere (L'Abate, 1986). The most appropriate model for defeating behaviors in the family is the Drama triangle, elaborated elsewhere (L'Abate, 1986) and consisting of three parts we all play, i.e., Victim, Rescuer, and Persecutor.

Definitions of Terms

By development is meant the progressive growth that takes place as we age intellectually, emotionally, interpersonally, educationally, and occupationally over the life cycle. Functionality in development means assuming roles and responsibilities appropriate to our age and station in life. Dysfunctionality takes place developmentally when we are not able to assume those roles and those responsibilities that are required and assumed by us (Loevinger, 1976; Swensen, 1985a). By distance is meant the degree of emotional involvement as well as the amount of face-to-face contact between and among family members. Power, when not used constructively and creatively (i.e., democratically, effectively and, hence, victoriously), tends to produce defeats (L'Abate, 1985a), which include any kind of behavior that tends to lower the level of functioning of individuals in the family, i.e., critical and abusive comments, accusations and blame, put-downs, ultimatums, threats, and name-calling. By autonomous interdependence is meant the realization that all of us, in one way or another, are separate individuals in our own right who need to stand on our own two feet. However, as separate individuals we also realize that we need others to depend on us as we need to depend on the same others in a reciprocal fashion, i.e., no person is an island unto itself. To achieve this criterion we need to be able to love and to be loved in return and to negotiate instrumental issues in order to affirm ourselves and those we love. In the present proposal, ability to love will be equated with such similar concepts as: distance, closeness, emotional involvement, feelings and emotions, and the like. By power is meant any process involving functional solution of problems, decision making, and control issues. An elaboration of this proposal can be found in L'Abate (1986).

In Summary

Development = f(Ability to Love × Ability to Negotiate)
Ability to Love = f(Ability to Be × Ability to Share Hurts)
Ability to Negotiate = f(Level of Functionality/Dysfunctionality (A-R-C Model) × Level of Competence to Negotiate (E-R-A-Aw-C Model) × Willingness or Motivation to Negotiate Priorities) (L'Abate, 1986)
Distance = Degree of emotional involvement, which may vary from enmeshment to isolation as a function of the ability to love
Defeats = Abusive and demeaning behavior, leading to reduction of effectiveness and competence in negotiating power
Victories = enhancing and positive processes designed to elevate the level of competence and power sharing in the family

Briefly, the models alluded to in Table 1 stand for the following:

Styles:
    A = Apathy, Abuse, Athrophy
    R = Reactivity, Repetitiveness, Rebuttals
    C = Conductivity, Creativity, Commitment to Change
Competence:
    E = Emotionality
    R = Rationality
    A = Activity
    Aw = Awareness
    C = Context
Priorities:
    Selfhood
    Marriage
    Parenthood
    Parents/In-laws/Siblings
    Work
    Friends
    Leisure

Evidence to Support a Reductionistic Proposal

To the extent that this proposal elaborates on Parsons' (Parsons & Bales, 1955) early dichotomy of nurturance (i.e., love, in this proposal) and instrumentality (i.e., power, in this proposal), it could be considered regressive or retrogressive rather than reductionistic. To the extent that this proposal links seemingly different intrapsychic, psychological, intra-familial, and sociological thinking, it could be also considered a decided advancement and integration of various sources and convergent strands of evidence and thought.

This proposal is also in line with previous (1976) and current (1986) thinking by L'Abate. There are at least five sources of evidence that can be used to support the foregoing proposal (Table 2). Even though these different sources use different terms, there seems to be a convergence concerning the importance of two major process functions, like love and power, in the same general direction as found in this proposal. These major sources of evidence are: Gottman (1979); Leff and Vaughn (1985); Lewis, Beavers, Gossett, & Phillips (1976); McAdams (1985); and Olson and his associates (1979, 1980a, 1980b).

Previously (L'Abate, 1976), two major dimensions were postulated as relevant to an understanding of behavior in the family. They are: space, as defined by approach and avoidance, i.e., distance; and time, i.e., control, as defined by extremes in discharge and extremes in delay. A balance of approach/avoidance would produce functionality, while extremes in either approach or avoidance would produce dysfunctionality. A balance of discharge/delay would produce victorious outcomes, while extremes in discharge or delay would produce defeating outcomes. More recently (L'Abate, 1986), these two major dimensions, which could be considered as the developmental bases of more complex behaviors, have

11

TABLE 2

Summary of Some Theoretical Viewpoints
Supporting a Two-Functions Proposal
of Behavior in the Family

	Ability to Love	Ability to Negotiate
L'Abate (1976)	Approach/Avoidance	Discharge/Delay
Gottman (1979)	Validation	Contracting
Olson et al. (1979, 1980)	Cohesiveness	Adaptability
McAdams (1985)	Intimacy	Power
Leff & Vaughan (1985)	Distance	Problem Solving
L'Abate (1986)	Intimacy	Power

been replaced by the ability to love and to be intimate, and the ability to influence and to negotiate (i.e., power). The "duality of human existence" was noted by Bakan (1966), who considered two fundamental senses of self: 1) agency, as expressed by self-assertiveness and self-protection, which in this proposal would be equivalent to the ability to negotiate; and 2) communion, as expressed by the desire to be and to become one with loved ones, which in this proposal would be equivalent to the ability to love. Since these latter sources are mostly theoretical and admittedly biased, they will not be used as evidence but as backdrop to the present proposal, which is actually an elaboration and clarification of those previous proposals.

Gottman (1979), on the basis of his extensive and painstaking research with clinical and nonclinical couples, concluded that most clinical couples showed deficit in two major areas: 1) validation, and 2) contracting. Without distorting his definitions of these two terms, it seems very likely that by "validation" Gottman means a process very close to what here is called "love" or "distance." By "contracting," Gottman means exactly a process of negotiation, decision making and problem solving that is quite similar to what is called "power," "control," or simply "negotiation" here.

Leff and Vaughn (1985), in an extremely important line of research with families of individuals labeled "schizophrenic patients," found that: 1) distance, as measured by emotional involvement through indices of expressed emotions and amount of face-to-face contact; and 2) the ability to negotiate and to solve problems together were two major dimensions of family functioning. In addition, this series of studies suggests that behavior in families can be described accurately and appropriately according to linear procedures and concepts and that interventions with this type of families can be straightforward and not at all circular, as a systems view would want us to believe.

Lewis, Beavers, Gossett, and Phillips (1976), in what can be considered a classic in the field, found a variety of dimensions separating functionality and dysfunctionality in families, where they could discern "no single thread." However, their more consistent results concerned what they called two "leadership" styles: collusion and closeness. Most of the other dimensions, such as affect, self-disclosure, invasiveness, and permeability, defined a major dimension of distance; while dimensions of responsibility, power and powerlessness, and negotiation described the presence of a major, underlying dimension of decision making and problem solving.

McAdams (1985) is a personologist whose research is in the tradition of monadic and acontextual ego psychology (E. H. Erickson), using intrapsychic and subjectively internal, i.e., phenomenological variables and relying on recollections, fantasies, self-reports, and revelations. On the basis of extensive and intensive studies, he isolated two basic "intrapsychic" variables, which he felt accounted for a great deal of the variance in his results. He called these two variables "power" and "intimacy." In fact, on the basis of this research, he isolated a triad of functional images that could serve as the functional basis for the Drama Triangle which underlies family dysfunctionality in the form of Victim-Rescuer-Persecutor (L'Abate, 1976, 1986). In the area of power, McAdams found images of: master/servant, soldier/deserter, adventurer/housewife, sage, artist/moneymaker, and independent woman/weak wife. In the area of intimacy he found images of: lover/nun, caregiver/student, mentor/student, communicator, helper/clown, humanist/barbarian. In a third area, left somewhat undefined, McAdams found images of: epicure/stoic, worker/escapist, wanderer, homemaker, good citizen/bum, pawn/escapee, and victim/survivor. In other words, McAdams' work is the intrapsychic basis for and the link with the same type of interpersonal and familial processes.

Olson and his associates (1979, 1980a, 1980b) based their circumplex model of family functioning and dysfunctioning on two basic dimensions: 1) cohesiveness, and 2) adaptability. The first dimension deals with the degree of distance among family members, the second deals with the ability to give and take and negotiate a variety of instrumental issues.

In addition, this proposal is in line with and parallel to Wynne's (1984) model. He proposed five major processes to account for the development of behavior in the family: 1) attachment; 2) caregiving; 3) communication; 4) joint problem solving; and 5) intimacy. The first two processes are characterized by emotional involvement and expressed emotions, which, together with intimacy, stem from the ability to love and to maintain optimal distance. The third and fourth processes clearly deal with issues of power and the ability to negotiate disagreements.

Admittedly, this proposal has linked together seemingly disparate sources of information that use different methodologies and populations. They even use different terms and terminology. However, the similarities

13

among these terms, and more relevantly, the processes underlying these terms, are more than accidental and need serious consideration because they would serve as basis for a reductionistic, empirically based understanding of behavior in the family.

No theoretical proposal is free from possible pitfalls, as evidenced by recent controversies about issues of measurement in the assessment of family functioning (Fisher et al., 1985; Olson, 1985; Sigafoos & Reiss, 1985; Sigafoos et al., 1985). Most empirical analyses of family functioning (Bloom, 1985) or of major family therapy models (Doherty et al., 1985) support the importance of three or more crucial dimensions in family behavior. A future theoretical issue will be to focus on the adequacy of two versus more crucial dimensions. Ultimately, however, this theoretical issue will need to yield to the consistency of empirical evidence, if indeed such consistency is human, possible or desirable.

THERAPEUTIC IMPLICATIONS

A two-functions proposal to account for development in the family implies the presence of at least three stages in the process of therapy (L'Abate, 1986). The first stage would need to deal with crisis intervention and symptom removal through circular or not so circular prescriptions of activities. While the proponents of brief therapy would find this goal sufficient to help families, the present proposal would suggest that symptom removal or conflict resolution may not be sufficient. Families whose symptom has been removed or whose conflict has been reduced remain at high risk for future relapse, as the work of Leff and Vaughn (1985) clearly indicates. Therefore, they need to enter a second stage of intervention that would entail negotiation skill training (L'Abate & Milan, 1985) or many other types of preventive, educationally based programs (Giblin et al., 1985). Eventually, if the family learns to negotiate, it needs to deal with issues of intimacy and love. In fact, in addition to these three stages, a fourth stage of follow-up is necessary to assess whether positive changes have been maintained over time and spread positively to other behaviors. "Change" may be necessary in the first stage of therapy, but "growth" may be just as necessary in the next three stages (L'Abate, 1986).

This proposal is also consistent with the two major factors that account for outcome variance in family therapy: relationship and structuring skills that would parallel, respectively, the ability to show love and the ability to negotiate. Consequently, another implication of the present proposal would focus on training future family therapists to deal personally and therapeutically with issues of love and to learn how to negotiate and, in turn, to teach negotiation skills to families (L'Abate, 1986).

CONCLUSION

The critical issue here, is whether seemingly disparate concepts like love, distance, affirmation, nurturance, cohesiveness, and intimacy are all related to similar feelings expressed and shared in the family. While issues of love and being (i.e., nurturance) are not negotiable resources, issues of negotiating power (i.e., instrumentality) through Doing (information and services) and Having (possessions and money) are processed through apparently similar decision-making, problem-solving, contracting, and adaptability processes that involve the ability to give and take, bargain, and eyeball-to-eyeball, rational, step-wise, gradual confrontation. Issues of love based on feelings are inherently shared and nonnegotiable. Issues of power are based on rationality and are inherently negotiable. Before negotiation can take place, a full expression and sharing of relevant feelings may be necessary.

The major value of the present proposal lies in its parsimonious simplicity. Only two major process functions are deemed basic to the development of family behavior. If and when love (i.e., distance) is confused with power and either one cannot be shared or negotiated, respectively, members of the family tend to stay dependent on each other or on external agencies. If and when love and power are clearly separated, shared, and expressed creatively and constructively, family members will tend to reach higher levels of personal and interpersonal satisfaction, functioning as autonomous but interdependent individuals, both inside and outside the family. Freud's dictum of *Lieben und Arbeiten* can be paraphrased as *Lieben und Vermitteln*.

REFERENCES

Amerikaner, M. (1983). Living systems and counseling: Concepts, goals and strategies. *Counselor Education and Supervision, 13*, 311–319.

Ault, R. L. (Ed.). (1980). *Developmental perspectives*. Santa Monica, CA: Good Year.

Bakan, D. (1966). *The duality of human experience*. Chicago: Rand McNally.

Bloom, B. L. (1985). A factor analysis of self-report measures of family functioning. *Family Process, 24*, 225–239.

Buckley, W. (Ed.). (1968). *Modern systems approach and its enemies*. New York: Basic Books.

Churchman, C. W. (1979). *The systems approach and its enemies*. New York: Basic Books.

Colapinto, J. (1979). The relative value of empirical evidence. *Family Process, 18*, 427–441.

Dell, P. F. (1985). Understanding Bateson and Maturana: Toward a biological foundation for the social sciences. *Journal of Marital and Family Therapy, 11*, 1–20.

Doherty, W. J., Colangelo, N., Green, A. M., & Hoffmann, G. S. (1985). Emphases of the major family therapy models: A family FIRO analysis. *Journal of Marital and Family Therapy, 11*, 299–303.

Druckman, D., Rozelle, R. M., & Baxter, J. C. (1982). *Nonverbal communication: Survey, theory and research*. Beverly Hills, CA: Sage.

Fisher, L., Kokes, R. F., Ransom, D. C., Phillips, S. L., & Rudd, P. (1985). Alternative strategies for creating "relational" data. *Family Process, 25*, 213–224.

Garfield, S. L., & Bergin, A. E. (1978). *Handbook of psychotherapy and behavior change*. New York: Wiley.

Gottman, J. M. (1979). *Marital interaction*. New York: Basic Books.

Gray, W., Duhl, F. J., & Rizzo, N. D. (Eds.). (1969). *General systems theory and psychiatry*. Boston: Little, Brown.

Gurman, A. S. (1983). Family therapy research and the "new epistemology." *Journal of Marital and Family Therapy, 9*, 227–234.

Hansen, J. C., & L'Abate, L. (1982). *Approaches to family therapy*. New York: Macmillan.

Hauser, S. T. (1976). Loevinger's model and measure of ego development: A critical review. *Psychological Bulletin, 83*, 928–955.

Hoffman, L. (1981). *Foundations of family therapy*. New York: Basic Books.

Howard, G. S. (1985). The roles of values in the science of psychology. *American Psychologist, 40*, 255–265.

Keeney, B. P. (1983). *Aesthetics of change*. New York: Guilford.

Knapp, M. L. (1972). *Nonverbal communication in human interaction*. New York: Holt, Rinehart & Winston.

L'Abate, L. (1976). *Understanding and helping the individual in the family*. New York: Grune & Stratton.

L'Abate, L. (1985a). Descriptive and explanatory levels in family therapy: Distance, defeats, and dependence. In L. L'Abate (Ed.), *Handbook of family psychology and therapy*. Homewood, IL: Dorsey Press.

L'Abate, L. (1985b). A training program in family psychology: Evaluation, prevention, and family therapy. *American Journal of Family Therapy, 13*(4), 7-16.

L'Abate, L. (1986). *Systematic family therapy*. New York: Brunner/Mazel.

L'Abate, L., Ganahl, G., & Hansen, J. C. (1986). *Methods of family therapy*. Englewood Cliffs, NJ: Prentice-Hall.

L'Abate, L., & Jerkovic, G. (in press). Family systems theory as a cult: Boom or bankruptcy?

L'Abate, L., & Milan, M. (Eds.). (1985). *Handbook of social skills training and research*. New York: John Wiley.

Leff, J., & Vaughn, C. (1985). *Expressed emotion in families*. New York: Guilford Press.

Levant, R. F. (1984). *Family therapy: A comprehensive overview*. Englewood Cliffs, NJ: Prentice-Hall.

Lewis, J. M., Beavers, W. R., Gossett, J. T., & Phillips, V. A. (1976). *No single thread: Psychological health in family systems*. New York: Brunner/Mazel.

Liddle, H. A. (1982). Eclecticism in family therapy. *Family Therapy Newsletter, 13*, 1–3, 5.

Loevinger, J. (1976). *Ego development*. San Francisco: Jossey-Bass.

Marmor, J. (1983). Systems thinking in psychiatry: Some theoretical and ethical applications. *American Journal of Psychiatry, 140*, 833–838.

McAdams, D. P. (1985). *Power, intimacy, and the life story: Personological inquiries into identity*. Homewood, IL: Dorsey Press.

Olson, D. H. (1985). Commentary: Struggling with congruence across theoretical models and methods. *Family Process, 25*, 203–207.

Olson, D. H., Russell, C., Sprenckle, D. H. (1980a). Circumplex model of marital and family systems II: Empirical studies and clinical interventions. In J. P. Vincent (Ed.), *Advances in family intervention, assessment and theory* (Vol. 1). Greenwich, CT: JAI Press.

Olson, D. J., Russell, C., & Sprenkle, D. H. (1980b). Marriage and family therapy: A decade review. *Journal of Marriage and the Family, 42*, 973–993.

Olson, D. H., Sprenkle, D. H., & Russell, C. (1979). Circumplex model of marital and family systems I: Cohesion and adaptability dimensions, family types, and clinical applications. *Family Process, 18*, 3–28.

Parsons, T., & Bales, R. F. (1955). *Family: Socialization and interaction processes*. New York: Free Press.

Riegel, K. F. (1979). *Foundations of dialectical psychology*. New York: Academic Press.

Riegel, K. F., & Rosenwald, G. C. (Eds.). (1975). *Structure and transformation: Developmental and historical aspects*. New York: Wiley.

Sauber, S. R., L'Abate, L., & Weeks, G. R. (1985). *Family therapy: Basic concepts and terms*. Rockville, MD: Aspen Systems.

Schwartzman, J. (1984). Family theory and the scientific method. *Family Process, 22*, 223–236.

Sears, R. R., Feldman, S. S. (Eds.). (1973). *The seven ages of man*. Los Altos, CA: Kaufmann.

Sigafoos, A., & Reiss, D. (1985). Rejoinder: Counterperspectives on family measurement clarifying the pragmatic interpretation of research methods. *Family Process, 25*, 207–211.

Sigafoos, A., Reiss, D., Rich, J., & Douglass, E. (1985). Pragmatics in the measurement of family functioning. *Family Process, 25*, 175–203.

Swensen, C. H., Jr. (1985a). Personality development in the family. In L. L'Abate (Ed.), *Handbook of family psychology and therapy*. Homewood, IL: Dorsey Press.

Swensen, C. H., Jr. (1985b). Love in the family. In L. L'Abate (Ed.), *Handbook of family psychology and therapy*. Homewood, IL: Dorsey Press.

Tomm, K. (1984). One perspective on the Milan systemic approach: Part I. Overview of development, theory and practice. *Journal of Marital and Family Therapy, 10,* 113–125.

Waxer, P. H. (1978). *Nonverbal aspects of psychotherapy*. New York: Praeger.

Weitz, S. (Ed.). (1974). *Nonverbal communication: Readings with commentary*. New York: Oxford University Press.

Wiemann, J. M., Harrison, R. P. (Eds.). (1983). *Nonverbal interaction*. Beverly Hills, CA: Sage.

Wynne, L. C. (1984). The epigenesis of relational systems: A model for understanding family development. *Family Process, 23,* 297–318.

CHAPTER 2

FAMILY SYSTEMS THEORY AS A CULT: BOOM OR BANKRUPTCY?

Luciano L'Abate and Gregory Jurkovic

Abstract

The purpose of this paper is to consider family systems theory as cult, that is, as a set of uncritically accepted orthodox principles that have been incorporated into the profession on faith, without a shred of empirical evidence. Indeed, emphasis on this type of theorizing has produced a strong antiempirical stance that makes the subjective impression of the therapist the final authority on issues of relevance to families. The dangers of this stance are discussed, and the importance of objective evidence in addition to, not in contrast to, subjective evidence is stressed. Five characteristics of cults are discussed from the viewpoint of family systems theory and practices. To the extent that the field will abandon the characteristics of a cult, the more it will expand and succeed. The status quo of a cult, as in families, is ultimate bankruptcy.

In another paper (see chapter 1) we took family systems thinking to task for being too abstract and too distant from psychological, developmental, social, and personality theories and evidence, resulting in a set of untested and untestable propositions. This basic untestability is coupled with a widespread disdain for empirical evidence and demonstrable results.

The thesis of this paper is that the kind of loose and higher-order theorizing popularly referred to as family systems or, more recently, ecosystemic thinking (Dell, 1982, 1984, 1985; Hoffman, 1983; Keeney, 1979, 1983) may have outlived its usefulness. As Pittman (1983) noted, it is rapidly approaching the extremes of orthodoxy and cultism, a trend that has continued largely unchecked and that deserves further critical evaluation. By intensifying concerns about the viability of a great deal of current family systems thinking, we hope to spur the field to increase the operationalization and verification of its key constructs. By the same token, we hope to increase interest in alternative theories that lend themselves to sound empirical evaluation.

Historically and evolutionarily, family systems thinking has helped to integrate knowledge, representing a bold, fresh viewpoint that encompassed behavior not otherwise understood. By establishing a new paradigm and serving as an important tool in the discovery of family functions and dysfunctions, family systems thinking has assumed positions both of theory and of meta-theory. The main difference between these two positions lies in their testability. A meta-theory, by definition, is not testable; a theory is, or should be. Now that other, more empirically based (see chapter 1; Alexander & Parsons, 1982; L'Abate, 1976, 1983, 1985, 1986; Olson, Sprenkle, & Russell, 1979; Reiss, 1981) and parsimonious (Haley, 1976; Watzlawick, Weakland, & Fisch, 1976) viewpoints are available, it may be important to ask whether the prevailing meta-theory in the family field, that is, ecosystemic epistemology (Dell, 1982, 1984, 1985; Hoffman, 1983; Keeney, 1979, 1983), has not outlived its usefulness. Perhaps more reductionistic and testable theories have greater value at this juncture or at least provide a needed counterbalance and supplement to the existing meta-theory. It is interesting to note that the utility and validity of the meta-theory in Freud's theorizing also have not stood the test of conceptual and empirical scrutiny. However, his clinical theory, which is more closely tied to observational data, continues to receive serious attention (Schafer, 1976).

We argue that the context of aesthetic, dialectical discovery, which has supported the development of ecosystemic epistemology, without the context of pragmatic, demonstrable justification, is just as empty as the latter without the former (see chapter 1; L'Abate, 1986; Rychlak, 1968).

In evaluating a theory, one needs to know its limits: Where does it start? Where does it end? Which specific behaviors does it apply to? By its generality at all levels of biological, psychological, and societal behavior, family systems thinking risks becoming grandiose, claiming to encompass a broad range of behaviors from the functional to the dysfunctional. This generality without specificity may be its downfall. Although family systems theory includes a variety of theories, or more accurately models (Kniskern & Gurman, 1981; Hansen & L'Abate, 1982), it remains to be seen whether its overconcern with complexity could not be replaced by a more parsimonious set of assumptions (Bogdan, 1987; Falser, 1986; Shields, 1986). For instance, L'Abate and Colondier (see chapter 1) proposed that developmental competence at personal, marital, or familial levels could be reduced to two main sets of abilities that is, the ability to love and the ability to negotiate. Others with a behavioral bent have pointed to ways in which more specific units of family interaction and functional relationships can be operationally defined (Alexander & Parsons, 1982; Foster & Haier,

1982; Patterson, 1985).

Family systems theory, however, has cornered the theoretical and therapeutic markets, eschewing parsimonious theories in favor of molar descriptions that defy or at least are very difficult to verify empirically. It has, so to speak, achieved a virtual monopoly in the field of family theorizing, presenting itself as the only possible descriptive and explanatory framework for family behavior. It is critical that this theoretical hegemony be challenged, examined critically, and questioned earnestly and responsibly, as in some recent criticisms (Bogdan, 1987; Falser, 1986; Shields, 1986). Its unfortunate stranglehold on a whole profession needs to be brought into open debate in the light of demonstrable evidence rather than on the basis of personal biases, opinions, or aesthetic preferences.

Because of the widespread acceptance of its theoretical, clinical, and professional tenets, family systems thinking has achieved all the characteristics of a cult--orthodoxy, rigidity, and absolutistic stances. These stances have produced subcults and splintercults, where the word of the head guru is considered more important than any external and empirical evidence.

Cultic Characteristics

Of course, a great many of our arguments hinge on the definition of a cult. According to Webster's, a cult may be defined as follows:

1. a particular system of religious worship, especially with reference to its rites and ceremonies;

2. a veneration of a person, an ideal, or a thing, especially as manifested by a body of admirers;

3. a group or set bound together by devotion to or veneration of the same thing, person, ideal;

4. a group having a sacred ideology and a set of rites centered on sacred symbols;

5. a system for the cure of disease, based on the dogma, tenets, and principles of its promulgator and employing methods generally considered unorthodox and unscientific.

21

Characteristic No. 1: Rites and Ceremonies

The field is already chock-full of its own rites and ceremonies. They are called workshops, conferences, and meetings; unfortunately, they often seem to serve the general purpose of reinforcing existing practices by the presenters as well as the participants. One of the main sources of enlightenment during these meetings, in addition to sermons by the gurus, is either live or taped interviews, during which feats of magic and heroic deeds are laid in front of an enthralled audience. These rites are repeated over and over, but no one asks: What happened to the family after this session? What happened immediately, and what happened one year after termination of family therapy? It is as if questions of this kind would be offensive to the status of the presenter.

Characteristic No. 2: Guru Worship

There is ample evidence that a pantheon of saints has already been established. The words of Milton H. Erickson, Gregory Bateson, and the "old" Milano group are now considered gospel by many, not to be tampered with and certainly not to be questioned.

Characteristic No. 3: Splinter Groups and Groupies

We already have sects and subcults, that is, the Bowenians, the structuralists, the strategists, the existentialists. Each carries the banner of its guru. Most have no evidence (only the strength of their convictions) to support the greater validity or even tenability of their position over other positions. Plausibility and seductivity seem to be the required characteristics for the acceptance of a particular group--in addition, of course, to the charismatic influence of an original founder-guru.

Characteristic No. 4: Rites and Symbols

Each group considers its own ideology superior to other ideologies, a judgment that is personal, mostly emotional, and not based on external confirmation. Accordingly, each group follows its own procedures; e.g., Bowenians construct genograms, and structuralists set up enactments. In other words, each group tends to follow the principle of mutually exclusive practices, limiting its armamentarium strictly on the basis of the therapist's personal needs rather than on the specific needs of each family. Cultism leads to splinterism, orthodoxy, rigidity in thinking, a closed system precluding the feedback that might suggest a more pluralistic and openly diverse stance.

Characteristic No. 5:   Sole Insight into Sickness

Finally, each subcult seems to have the inside track on family functioning and dysfunctioning. The family therapy field has claimed that it has developed a novel and unorthodox view of psychopathology and the treatment of it. Such claims, however, have yet to be validated empirically. When data are collected, the quality of the research design, of the data analyses, and of the conclusions drawn are often severely compromised by various conceptual and methodological problems. For instance, many would-be researchers retreat to the position that the phenomena of interest to the family systems theorist defy systematic empirical study by the use of current methodologies (Keeney, 1979, 1983). To the extent that they do continue to conduct research, they consider themselves "clinical" researchers (Selvini-Palazzoli, 1986), relying on the impressionistic clinical case study method. Although clinical case studies are useful sources of hypotheses for subsequent empirical investigation, clinical research is not an acceptable substitute for experimental study.

The dangers of the clinical approach were clearly illustrated in Selvini-Palazzoli's keynote address at the 1985 Annual Conference of the American Association for Marriage and Family Therapy (1986). To her credit, she noted that the case examples reported in her (and her co-workers') widely acclaimed volume (Selvini-Palazzoli, Boscolo, Cecchin, & Prata, 1978), examples presumably supporting her approach to working with severely disturbed families, included only their successes among a significant number of failures. Anderson's (1986) critique of this work, a refreshing and much needed addition to the literature, clearly underscored the importance of differentiating the context of discovery from the context of justification. Emphasizing one at the expense of the other ignores their complementary relationship in any productive and dynamic program of research.

In a field that has taken pride in publicly exposing its methods and procedures, it is surprising that one of its venerable leaders, clinical researcher or not, failed to point out, at the very least, the bases and context of her findings, which have been accepted freely according to standards that would not be accepted for anybody else. Why are we accepting and basing therapeutic practices on presentations of videotapes and the word of an authority? Whom are we to believe? What will our students accept, even tentatively? The videotapes of charismatic leaders or the objective, well-controlled evidence of sound and responsible clinical practices? If family systems theorists find it difficult, for pragmatic or theoretical reasons, to follow conventional and current scientific practices, it is encumbent upon them to discover or to use some other set of rules of evidence, lest they become entrenched in a cultist movement of their own making. As Gurman, Kniskern, and Pinsoff (1986) noted:

> Unfortunately, the passion with which advocates of the "new epistemology" criticize the continuing use of family therapy research methods based on the "old" epistemology has been rarely translated into the development of experimental designs more consistent with ecosystemic views.... To our knowledge, there does not yet exist a single outcome study of family therapy whose design has been perceptibly influenced by such ecosystemic ideas [emphasis ours]. (p. 569)

Discussion

If the field of family therapy persists in its cultish practices, it may be headed toward theoretical, clinical, and professional bankruptcy. The past 30 years have seen the rise and fall of psychoanalysis, the rise and fall of learning and behavior theory, and, more recently, the rise and fall of the human potentials movement. After a meteoric rise, each of them, within a generation, became just another trend. Every success contains its own seeds of failure. What is responsible for the temporary success and the subsequent failure of a movement? In the case of psychoanalysis and humanism, the answer is clear: Both movements rejected empiricism and empirical evidence (the context of justification) as a way of evaluating therapeutic success. In the case of learning theory and its applied counterpart, behaviorism, the opposite was true. In its reactive and narrow stress on scientism and rigid empiricism, behavior theory rejected the importance of the context of discovery, a shortcoming that is now being corrected (Patterson, 1985).

The family therapy movement is no exception. Family therapy risks repeating the errors of earlier movements by rejecting the context of justification and accepting wholesale and uncritically the context of discovery. We need to attend to both contexts, avoiding mutually exclusive practices that emphasize one context at the expense of the other. Their complementarity has been nicely illustrated in an article by Bodgan (1987). He aptly noted that recent theorizing about ecosystemic and epistemological issues, issues that have been debated unencumbered by rules of science and scholarship (context of discovery), can be framed within the context of justification as interesting hypotheses that warrant empirical testing.

So-called family systems and ecosystemic theory could also benefit by greater specification of underlying assumptions,

24

postulates, and testable models. At this point the so-called systems approach in general, as well as most of the derivative models, comprises lists of loosely framed constructs that are not well operationalized (see chapter 1). A theory progresses from general statements (assumptions) to increasingly specific postulates and hypotheses (L'Abate, 1976, 1986). Although free-form conceptualization and philosophizing in the family field helped fill an important conceptual vacuum historically, it is now critical that the systems idea be subjected to more rigorous tests, theoretically and empirically.

Unfortunately, many training programs for family therapists place little, if any, emphasis on theory construction, research methodology, and the systematic evaluation of treatment outcome. As a result, we are producing a profession that is and will be unprepared to apply results based on empirical evidence and to critically evaluate the steady stream of new theoretical arguments and approaches that are flooding the family field. Persons who have no training in research are not in a position to be research consumers (let alone producers), and perhaps more distressingly, they may be openly opposed to considering evidence they cannot understand.

Unless the context of justification receives greater attention in our training programs, standards of accountability and objective (replicable) evidence are likely to be met with increasing suspicion, even hostility. If not for scientific reasons, then research and scholarly caution ought to be supported for pragmatic reasons to help address growing demands from employee assistance programs, insurance companies, and other consumer groups and referral sources for documentation of treatment efficacy.

It has not been our intention to diminish the importance of recent creative and often provocative theoretical speculation and philosophizing. Indeed, conducted in the spirit of discovery, these kinds of conceptual efforts typify the early stages of most theoretical movements. However, we are concerned that unless the ideas embodied in family systems and more recently ecosystemic thinking are critically evaluated and justified other than in terms of preference, cultish practices, and aesthetics, the family systems experiment is likely to break down.

Strong antiempirical undercurrents in the family therapy field have gone largely unchallenged not only in the family literature but also in many training programs in which research and the context of justification receive minimal attention. Both discovery and justification processes are needed. The healthy tension and recursive feedback between the two can help the field move forward. For example, from the perspective of empirical researchers, it is frustrating to read the continuing arguments about such key constructs as homeostasis or the claims of treatment effectiveness that are supported only by case examples-- issues that well-designed and theoretically rigorous programs of research could help evaluate.

Conclusion

Work within the contexts of discovery and justification entails different skills. It is probably rare that the same individual is strong in both, thus underscoring the need for theorists and empirical researchers to talk with and learn from each other in the development of increasingly effective and responsible approaches to treating problem behaviors. Hopefully, the substance of what family therapy is or could be, will endure.

References

Alexander, J., & Parsons, B. V. (1982) Functional family therapy. Monterey, CA: Brooks/Cole.

Anderson, C. M. (1986). The all-too-short trip from positive to negative connotation. Journal of Marital and Family Therapy, 13, 351-354.

Bogdan, J. (1987). "Epistemology" as a semantic pollutant. Journal of Marital and Family Therapy, 13, 27-35.

Dell, P. (1982). In search of truth: On the way to clinical epistemology. Family Process. 21, 407-414.

Dell, P. (1984). Why family therapy should go beyond homeostasis: A Kuhnian reply to Ariel, Caorel & Tyrano. Journal of Marital and Family Therapy, 10, 351-356.

Dell, P. (1985). Understanding Bateson and Maturana: Toward a biological foundation for the social sciences. Journal of Marital and Family Therapy, 11, 1-20.

Falser, P. R. (1986). The cybernetic metaphor: A critical examination of ecosystemic epistemology or a powerhouse of family therapy. Family Process, 25, 353-363.

Foster, S. L., & Haier, T. S. (1982). Behavioral and systems family therapies: A comparison of theoretical assumptions. American Journal of Family Therapy, 10, 13-23.

Gurman, A. S., & Knistkern, D. P. (1981). Handbook of family therapy. New York: Brunner/Mazel.

Gurman, A. S., Kniskern, D. P., & Pinsoff, W. (1986). Research on the process and outcome of marital and family therapy. In S. Garfield & A. Bergin (Eds.), Handbook of psychotherapy and behavior change (pp. 565-624). New York: Wiley.

Haley, J. (1976). Problem-solving therapy. San Francisco, CA: Jossey-Bass.

Hansen, J. C., & L'Abate, L. (1982). Approaches to family therapy. New York: Macmillan.

Hoffman, L. (1983). Foundations of family therapy. New York: Basic Books.

Keeney, B. F. (1979). Ecosystmic epistemology: An alternative paradigm for diagnosis. Family Process, 18, 117-129.

Keeney, B. F. (1983). Aesthetics of change. New York: Guilford.

L'Abate, L. (1976). Understanding and helping the individual in the family. New York: Grune & Stratton.

L'Abate, L. (1983). Family psychology: Theory, therapy and training. Washington, DC: University Press of America.

L'Abate, L. (Ed.) (1985). Handbook of family psychology and therapy. Homewood, IL: Dorsey Press.

L'Abate, L. (1986). Systematic family therapy. New York: Brunner/Mazel.

Olson, D. H., Sprenkle, D. H., & Russell, C. S. (1979). Circumplex model of marital and family systems: Cohesion and adaptability dimensions, family types, and clinical applications. Family Process, 18, 3-28.

Patterson, G. R. (1985). Beyond technology: The next stage in developing an empirical base for parent training. In L. L'Abate (Ed.), Handbook of family psychology and therapy (pp. 1344-1379). Homewood, IL: Dorsey Press.

Pittman, F. (1983). Of cults and superstars. Family Therapy Networker, 2, 28-29.

Reiss, D. (1981). The family constructions of reality. Cambridge, MA: Harvard University Press.

Rychlak, J. F. (1968). A philosophy of science for personality therapy. Boston: Houghton-Mifflin.

Schafer, R. (1976). The language of action. New Haven, CT: Yale University Press.

Selvini-Palazzoli, M. (1986). Towards a general model of psychotic family games. Journal of Marital and Family Therapy, 13, 339-349.

Selvini-Palazzoli, M., Boscolo, L., Cecchin, G., & Prata, C. (1978). Paradox and counterparadox. New York: Jason Aronson.

Shields, C. G. (1986). Critiquing the new epistemologies: Toward minimum requirements for a scientific theory of family therapy. Journal of Marital and Family Therapy, 12, 359-372.

Watzlawick P., Weakland, J., & Fisch, R. (1976). Change: Principles of problem formation and problem resolution. New York: Norton.

Chapter 3

Testing a Theory of Developmental Competence in the Family

Luciano L'Abate and Victor Wagner[*]

Abstract

This paper describes how a theory of developmental competence in the family was tested evaluatively by the use of measures of therapeutic outcome. Subjects were 138 undergraduates, who were administered a battery of six theory-derived tests twice. Results lend support to the psychometric properties of the tests in this battery and, indirectly, to the theory from which these tests were derived.

This paper presents evidence to support, in part, the validity of a theory of developmental competence in the family (L'Abate, 1976). This theory, in brief and in its latest revision (L'Abate, 1985a, 1986; L'Abate & Colondier, 1987), is made up of two assumptions about space and time. Both assumptions are based on the construct of developmental competence (L'Abate & Colondier, 1987). Developmental qualifies at least four stages of competence over the family life-cycle: from (a) dependency, to (b) denial of dependency (independence), to (c) autonomous interdependence (adulthood), and finally back to (d) dependency.

Summary of the Theory

Competence, as described by many writers (Albee, 1984; Danish and D'Augelli, 1984; Hunt, 1969; Laosa, 1984; Marlowe & Weinberg, 1985; Phillips, 1968; White, 1984; Wine & Smye, 1981), has been considered in a vacuum, monadically, without its most immediate and pervasive context, namely, the family. This theory, instead, emphasizes the critical and fundamental importance of competence within the context of the family. Competence in the family develops along two main assumptions about space and time. Space subsumes a postulate of distance (approach-avoidance). Time subsumes a postulate of control (discharge-delay). The postulate of space underlies the ability to be close to loved ones. The postulate of time underlies the ability to negotiate with them.

From each of these two postulates, in turn, are derived a variety of testable models. From the postulate of being derive two models--love and status. Love implies at least four different processes: (a) physical and emotional caring, (b) seeing the "good" and minimizing

---

[*]This paper is based on data gathered by Victor Wagner for his doctoral dissertation and reanalyzed by Dr. L'Abate.

the "bad" qualities in self and in other family members, (c) forgiving oneself and loved ones for current and past errors, and (d) intimacy, the sharing of past hurts and the fear of future hurts. Status implies the attribution of importance to self and loved ones in order to be present and available to loved ones when they hurt and to have them available to us when we hurt (L'Abate, in preparation). This sense of self-importance is crucial in determining how we act toward loved ones and how they, in turn, act toward us.

From the postulate of negotiation derive two different aspects of this process: negotiation structure and negotiation skills. Negotiation structure is made up of three component models: (a) division of authority/responsibility (authority represents who makes decisions; responsibility represents who carries those decisions out); (b) orchestration/instrumentation decisions (orchestration means infrequent, important decisions, such as moving to a new job, buying a house; instrumentation means small, routine, everyday decisions, such as what we will eat for supper, whether or not we should buy shoes for X); and (c) the negotiation of doing/having tasks (doing tasks require the use of services, e.g., household chores, and information, e.g., which TV program to watch, what literature to allow in the house; having tasks require the use of money and possessions.

Most conflicts in families derive from the inability to separate issues of being (love and status) from issues of doing and having. Fundamental to these conflicts is the inability to express constructively feelings that are related to past hurts and the possibilities of future hurts (i.e., intimacy).

Negotiation skills require a certain degree of functionality as assessed by three models: (a) style is divided into abusive-apathetic-atrophied (A), reactive-revengeful-repetitive (R), and conductive-creative-change (C) styles (the A-R-C model). The first two styles are dysfunctional; the third is functional. (b) Interpersonal competence is made up of five components: emotionality (E), rationality (R), activity (A), awareness (Aw), and context (C) (the E-R-A-Aw-C model). In this model, functionality is achieved through the balance and appropriate use of the five components. Dysfunctionality is present when one component is stressed at the expense of the other components. Motivation to negotiate is assessed by (c) priorities in the family, which consist of the functional ranking of selfhood, marriage, parenthood, parents/in-laws, siblings, work, friends, and leisure in the individual, marital, and family life cycles.

Theory Testing

This theory has been revised repeatedly since its inception. Its latest formulation (L'Abate, 1986; L'Abate & Colondier, 1987) is presented here. Further revisions will no doubt be made as the structure of the theory follows the evidence gathered to test and verify it. Because testability is considered a sine qua non (among many other requirements, of course) for any theory, it is important from the outset to indicate how this theory can be and is being tested in a variety of ways.

As summarized in Table 1, this theory is being tested through evaluation and through therapeutic intervention. It has been tested evaluatively more extensively than in any other way, through paper-and-pencil tests derived originally from the theory. For a review of the evidence to measure pre-post intervention therapy outcome gathered from a verbal (relying on the written word) and a visual (card-sorting) family evaluation battery, see L'Abate and Wagner (1985). A way to test this theory evaluatively, through processual content and content-free analyses of therapy transcripts, is still being worked out (Caiella, research in progress). The plan is to develop objective measures to score transcripts of family therapy sessions by the use of criteria derived from the models.

Table 1

Approaches to Test a Theory of
Developmental Competence in the Family
(L'Abate, 1976, 1985a)

Evaluation

Outcome   Paper-and-pencil verbal tests (Marital Evaluation Battery)

               Visual tests (Family Evaluation Battery) (L'Abate & Wagner, 1985)

Process   Content analyses of therapy transcripts and videotapes

               Content-free family interactions (Caiella, research in progress)

Intervention

Enrichment   Psychoeducational, skills-oriented, structured exercises, lessons, and programs derived from models (L'Abate, 1985b)

Therapy   Systematic homework assignments derived from theoretical models (L'Abate, 1986)

This theory can be tested interventionally through the administration of psychoeducational structured enrichment programs that have also been derived from the models of the theory (L'Abate, 1985b; L'Abate, Kearns, Richardson, & Dow, 1985; L'Abate & Weinstein, 1986; L'Abate & Young, 1987). Therapeutically, this theory can be tested through systematic homework assignments, also derived from the models (L'Abate, 1986). A beginning test of the applicability and usefulness of these homework assignments has been conducted by Lutz (1985), and further research is in progress (Johnston, Levis, & L'Abate, 1987; L'Abate, Young, Joiner, & Bond, research in progress; Levis, 1987).

This paper is limited to a description of how the paper-and-pencil tests designed to evaluate the theory were administered in order to find their psychometric properties of internal (discriminant) consistency and reliability. Note that these tests were constructed at the inception of the theory, so they tested parts of the theory as originally formulated (L'Abate, 1976), not as recently revised (L'Abate, 1985a, 1986; L'Abate & Colondier, 1987). In fact, certain aspects of the theory were revised on the basis of these and other results.

Table 2

Postulates in the Original (L'Abate, 1976) Version of a Theory of Developmental Competence in the Family and Instruments to Test It

Postulates	Instruments
Differentiation	Marital Questionnaire-Likeness scale Likeness Grid
Priorities	Marital Questionnaire-Priorities scale Priorities Inventory
Incongruence	
Blaming	Marital Questionnaire-Blaming scale What Would You Do?-Blaming scale
Placating	Marital Questionnaire-Placating scale What Would You Do?-Placating scale
Distracting	Marital Questionnaire-Distracting scale What Would You Do?-Distracting scale
Computing	Marital Questionnaire-Computing scale What Would You Do?-Computing scale

Each model was tested by two different paper-and-pencil tests. One would expect that tests measuring the same dimension would correlate with each other more highly than would the tests measuring different dimensions. In the original formulation of the theory (L'Abate, 1976) these dimensions were differentiation, priorities, and incongruence. Differentiation was made up of a continuum of likeness, with symbiosis-autism at the two extremes of a bell-shaped distribution, sameness-oppositeness next (toward the middle), and similarity-difference in the center. Congruence was represented by a dimension made up, on the negative side, of the incongruent stances suggested by Satir (1972): blaming, computing, distracting, and placating. These incongruent stances were incorporated in the A-R-C model as a brief part of the reactive style. Thus, this early version of the theory comprised six dimensions: (differentiation, priorities, incongruence in blaming, computing, distracting, and placating. Each dimension was tested by two different tests, as shown in Table 2.

Method

Subjects

The participants in this study were 138 Georgia State University undergraduates: 77 (56%) males and 61 (44%) females. Most of the subjects were white (73%), between the ages of 17 and 35 (95%); 40 (29%) were married; and 30 (21%) had children.

Tests

The Marital Evaluation Battery (MEB) comprises four paper-and-pencil instruments: the Marital Questionnaire (MQ); the Likeness Grid (LG); the Priorities Inventory (PI); and the What Would You Do? (WWYD) test. Each instrument has been designed to measure the six dimensions of personality development in the family (L'Abate, 1976). The earliest version of this theory postulated that differentiation, priorities, and congruence were key factors in evaluating the adjustment of married couples and families. The most recent revision of this theory postulates that negotiation and being are the two key factors in evaluating developmental competence in the family.

The Marital Questionnaire (MQ) is an experimental assessment device derived from the theoretical notions of L'Abate (1976) and Satir (1972). In its current form, the instrument is composed of six scales of 20 items each. Each scale is related to one of the three postulates of L'Abate's (1976) theory of personality development in the family. Hence, this questionnaire includes scales that measure the degree of likeness (used for differentiation), the ordering of priorities, and incongruence in terms of Satir's (1972) four modes—blaming, placating, computing, and distracting. The questions are true-false. The person taking the test is given 1 point on the relevant scale for indicating agreement with a statement that, from

33

a theoretical point of view, indicates a healthy attitude. A person is also given 1 point for rejecting a statement that suggests an unhealthy attitude. Participants can score from 0 to 20 on each scale. The higher the score on a particular scale, the stronger the indication that the respondent possesses psychologically healthy attitudes in that area (L'Abate, 1976).

The Likeness Grid (LG) was developed (L'Abate & Wildman, 1973) as a measure of self-differentiation; it is derived from Kelly's (1955) test of Personal Constructs. The LG consists of a list of 24 persons related in some way to the subject. For each of the 24 persons, participants rate themselves as "completely the same as," "the same as," "similar to," or "different from," "opposite from," or "completely opposite from" that person. In keeping with the theoretical notions of the continuum of likeness (L'Abate, 1976), ratings of "completely the same" (symbiosis) or "completely opposite" (autism and alienation) are considered equivalent and are scored 1. Ratings of "same" or "opposite" are likewise considered equivalent and are scored 2. Ratings of "similar" and "different" are scored 3. The ratings of the 24 items are then summed to provide a total differentiation score.

The Priorities Inventory (PI) was developed (Wagner, 1980) to assess an individual's functionality in ordering priorities inside and outside the family. The test comprises the 56 possible permutations in triads of the following categories: self, spouse, children; parents, in-laws, siblings; and work, leisure, and friends. The task is to rank the items in a given triad as to their relative importance (1, 2, or 3). The rankings for each item were summed, and the total score of rankings for each item represented its value in relationship to the ranks of the other items: the smaller the score, the higher the value of that item, for instance, self in comparison with the other priorities.

The original What Would You Do? (WWYD) test (L'Abate & Wildman, 1973) was composed of 26 multiple-choice problem situations; the subject was asked to choose the response that most closely resembled how the subject would behave in similar situations. For each situation described, there were four alternatives, each corresponding to one of Satir's (1972) four responses, developed primarily for use with adolescents and their families. In Wagner's (1980) study a revision of this test was used to reflect situations more relevant to a general adult population. The WWYD in its current form consists of 20 hypothetical situations in which the subject is asked to rate each alternative response as to the likelihood that she or he would respond in a manner similar to that described by the alternative. A composite score is obtained for each subject on each of the Satir response styles by computing the subject's ratings of the alternative responses to all 20 situations. Thus, through a comparison of a total ratings for each Satir category, the

34

subject's propensity for responding in one manner as opposed to another can be determined.

Although some evidence supports the WWYD as useful for differentiating dysfunctional styles, the evidence for the utility of this test is limited. We have only limited data, as well, on the scales of Blaming, Placating, Distracting, and Computing on the Marital Questionnaire. Clearly, more research on both instruments is necessary before a definitive statement can be made about them.

The results from studies (L'Abate & Wagner, 1985) that have attempted to verify the psychometric properties of these instruments have been inconclusive. Some studies have found strong relationships between L'Abate's constructs and instruments, and similar constructs with differing assessment techniques. The results of other studies have been less impressive because of their failure to support studies in which the same evaluation instruments were used. Further research is needed on the evaluation of the reliability and validity of these measures.

The Marital Evaluation Battery (MEB) seems to satisfy most of the criteria that Reiss (1980) and Olson (1976) cited in assessing the utility of an assessment device (one important criterion, of course, is the reliability and validity of the instrument, which is the subject of Wagner's study). The MEB provides assessment in three areas related to personality functioning in marriage and can thus be conceptualized as multidimensional, a characteristic of assessment devices that Olson, Sprenkle, and Russell (1979) stress. The MEB is derived from a theory of personality development in the family and thus satisfies Olson's criterion of limiting assessment to theory; it also avoids the pitfall of being grounded in nonsystemic thinking. Both Reiss (1980) and Olson (1976) stressed the role that a useful assessment device can play in the evaluation of therapy and in treatment planning. The multidimensionality of the MEB, as well as its foundation in a theory of personality development in marriage and the family, result in its usefulness in the development of treatment planning and in the evaluation of treatment progress.

Procedure

The six assessment instruments already described were used in the study (see Table 2). Two instruments were used to measure each of six constructs: differentiation, priorities, blaming, placating, distracting, and computing. To evaluate test-retest reliability, the subjects were administered the same battery twice within the same quarter, with an interval of at least one month between the two administrations.

The reliability of each instrument was assessed along two separate methodologies of reliability estimation: stability/test-retest reliability and internal stability/consistency reliability.

The Pearson Product-Moment Correlation Procedure was used to calculate test-retest reliability; scores on the pretest for a given instrument were correlated with scores on the posttest for that instrument. The results of the test-retest reliability calculations are shown in Table 3. All correlations are in the moderate-to-high range ($p < .01$). The values for the ts for the difference between the means of the two administrations were not significantly different, with the exception of the Distracting scale of the MQ, the LG, and the Mate Priority of the PI.

The coefficient alpha procedure for calculating internal consistency reliability, which estimates the internal consistency of a test on one particular administration, was used on the pretest data for each instrument. These reliability coefficients, all in the moderate-to-high range, indicate that each instrument evidences satisfactory internal consistency reliability with the possible exception of the Distracting scale of the MQ ($\alpha = .34$). The test-retest reliability coefficients, as well as the internal consistency reliability coefficients, indicate that, as a whole, the reliability for all the instruments being evaluated ranges from moderate to high.

The convergent and divergent (discriminant) validity of this battery was evaluated through a correlation matrix of Pearson's rs, as shown in Tables 4-6. As the matrices indicate, there were more significant ($p < .05$) correlations than one would expect of a chance level, especially between tests measuring the same dimension. For instance, the Likeness scale of the MQ was significantly correlated with the LG; the Priorities scale of the MQ was significantly and highly correlated with self (negatively), children (positively), parents (positively), siblings (negatively), friends (negatively), and leisure (negatively) from the PI. Blaming from the MQ correlated with Distracting and with 4 (of 36) variables of the PI, correlations that could be due to chance. Many of the variables in the PI correlated with each other, as one would expect; the incongruent stances from the MQ correlated with the same dimensions measured by the WWYD test, with the exception of the Computing scale, which failed to show any correlations. Unexpectedly, the PI also showed quite a few (15 of 32) significant correlations with the WWYD test, especially concerning children, friends, and leisure.

Table 3

Test-Retest Reliability ($\underline{r}$ and $\underline{t}$) and Internal Consistency (α)
for a Marital Evaluation Battery

Test	$\underline{N}$[a]	Administrations Means	SD	Means	SD	$\underline{r}$[b]	$\underline{t}$	$\underline{p}$	α
Marital Questionnaire									
Likeness	123	15.18	3.12	15.03	3.39	.75	.70	.49	.74
Priorities	130	11.78	4.94	11.94	4.40	.85	-.73	.47	.85
Incongruence									
Blaming	119	14.82	2.42	14.75	2.77	.54	.33	.74	.54
Placating	129	13.29	2.51	13.02	2.66	.62	1.36	.18	.46
Distracting	128	11.44	.60	11.11	2.40	.65	1.77	.08	.34
Computing	127	10.55	2.72	10.28	3.00	.64	1.23	.22	.56
Likeness Grid	80	55.47	7.25	56.95	6.17	.56	-2.09	.04	.79
Priorities Inventory									
Self	130	1.48	.52	1.48	.53	.81	.17	.86	.97
Mate	127	1.34	.30	1.39	.37	.75	-2.62	.01	.92
Children	129	1.51	.43	1.47	.39	.85	1.67	.10	.96
Parents	133	1.92	.38	1.93	.36	.78	-.53	.60	.92
Siblings	128	2.19	.39	2.17	.37	.76	.89	.37	.92
Work	128	2.45	.43	2.46	.43	.77	-.34	.73	.94
Friends	127	2.40	.36	2.42	.33	.74	-1.01	.31	.92
Leisure	127	2.67	.33	2.67	.36	.69	-.01	.99	.92
What Would You Do?									
Blame	126	76.52	7.73	75.88	9.30	.66	1.01	.31	.69
Placate	126	51.90	8.12	51.60	8.50	.68	.51	.61	.66
Distract	124	77.02	8.29	76.19	8.81	.66	1.30	.20	.73
Compute	123	52.19	7.43	53.11	7.46	.55	-1.45	.15	.66

[a]$\underline{N}$ is variable because of missing individual data.

[b]All probability values for these correlations exceed $\underline{p} < .01$.

Table 4

Correlation Matrix for Marital Questionnaire[a]

	Marital Questionnaire					
	Likeness	Priori- ties	Blaming	Placat- ing	Distract- ing	Com- puting
Marital Questionnaire						
Likeness	1.00	.11	.20*	.14	.20	.13
Priorities		1.00	-.20	.06	.03	.08
Incongruence						
Blaming			1.00	.19	.37**	.12
Placating				1.00	.02	.12
Distracting					1.00	-.08
Computing						1.00

*$p < .05$
**$p < .01$
[a]N is variable because of missing individual data.

Table 5

Priorities Inventory

	Grid	Self	Mate	Children	Parents	Siblings	Work	Friends	Leisure
Marital Questionnaire									
Likeness	.27*	-.08	-.01	.10	.17*	.06	.04	-.05	-.02
Priorities	.08	-.51**	-.01	.63**	.24**	-.30**	-.05	-.17*	-.20*
Incongruence									
Blaming	.16	.10	-.07	-.17*	-.16	-.06	.10	.10	.18*
Placating	.06	-.22*	.11	.10	.13	.15	.04	-.08	-.19*
Distracting	.08	-.02	-.03	-.01	-.06	.01	-.02	-.14	.12
Computing	.14	.12	.06	-.03	.08	.04	.02	-.14	.00
Likeness Grid	1.00	-.01	.06	.13	.03	-.01	.11	-.17*	.03
Priorities Inventory									
Self		1.00	-.20	-.42**	-.34**	-.39**	-.04	-.34**	-.30**
Mate			1.00	.05	-.07	-.09	-.22*	.11	-.13
Children				1.00	.10	.18*	-.02	-.26	-.36**
Parents					1.00	.49**	-.10	-.10	-.32**
Siblings						1.00	-.16	.08	-.24**
Work							1.00	-.11	-.05
Friends								1.00	.34**
Leisure									1.00

*p < .05
**p < .01

Table 6

What Would You Do?

	Blaming	Placating	Distracting	Computing
Marital Questionnaire				
Likeness	.00	.09	.15	-.09
Priorities	-.10	.25**	.06	.08
Incongruence				
Blaming	.29**	-.22*	.11	.03
Placating	-.12	.25**	-.06	.12
Distracting	.03	.04	.32**	-.13
Computing	.07	-.07	-.03	.15
Likeness Grid	.05	.06	-.02	-.09
Priorities Inventory				
Self	.18*	-.32**	-.06	-.03
Mate	.04	.10*	-.10	-.04
Children	-.24**	.22*	-.18*	.19
Parents	-.18*	.15	-.09	.08
Siblings	-.14	.13	-.10	.03
Work	-.13	.12	.09	.04
Friends	.23*	-.03	.27**	-.25**
Leisure	.30**	-.31**	.26**	-.17*
What Would You Do?				
Blame	1.00			
Placate		1.00	.07	-.25**
Distract			1.00	-.26**
Compute				1.00

Discussion

What can be said about the internal consistency of the Marital Evaluation Battery and its relationship to the theory behind it? How can a theory be separated from the instruments designed to test it? Clearly, these are not perfect or psychometrically precise tests. Their internal consistency and reliability, although not ideal, are within acceptable limits. They need further refinement and continued testing. For instance, on the basis of the correlations between measures of differentiation (the Likeness scale and the Likeness Grid) and the four measures of incongruence (Blaming, Placating, Distracting, and Computing scales) plus, of course, additional theoretical considerations (L'Abate, 1985a, 1986, L'Abate & Colondier, 1987), a third postulate of the original theory (L'Abate, 1976) was incorporated in the reactive style of negotiation, as described by the A-R-C model. Thus, the revision of the original theory is made up of two rather than three postulates: the ability to love and the ability to negotiate.

The primary question, not answered in this research, pertains to the validity of the theory in regard to marriage and family functioning. How can a theory be validated through external criteria of validity? This question was answered, in part, by Goodrich (1984), who attempted to validate the MQ with couples rather than with mostly single (and young!) undergraduates as in the present research. She administered the MQ, the PI, the Family Environment Scale (FES), and the Dyadic Adjustment Scale (DAS) to 100 married couples, all volunteers. In addition to further evidence in support of the internal consistency of the various MQ scales, Goodrich found confirmation for the concurrent validity of the MQ and the PI from the intercorrelations among the various scales. The ordering of the Priorities was correlated (in three of four analyses, $r = .38$, $p < .001$) with marital quality (as measured by the DAS) in that the wife's perception of marital quality was significantly and positively correlated ($r = .38$, $p < .01$) with the husband's priorities, and the husband's perception of marital quality was significantly correlated ($r = -.19$, $p < .03$) with the similarity between his and his wife's scores on the Priorities Inventory. Two (Blaming and Distracting) of four incongruence scales correlated significantly with marital quality both for husbands ($r = .21$, $p < .02$) and for wives ($r = .28$, $p < .003$). For both husbands and wives, similarity on the Blaming scale was significantly but negatively correlated with marital quality; for the husbands, similarity on the Priorities scale was negatively correlated with marital quality ($r = .19$, $p < .03$). In other words, the MQ written from the viewpoint of a theory of personality development in the family, showed a certain degree of relationship with at least one measure of marital quality, as did DAS, and the FES served as a moderating variable for both measures because, in general, it correlated significantly with the DAS but not with the MQ.

Owen-Smith's (1985) research added further evidence for the concurrent validity of the Likeness and Priorities scales of the MQ and of the PI, which she administered to 53 pairs of parents of 53 preschool children. She found highly positive intercorrelations among the scales of the MQ for both parents. The ordering of the PI supported the same kind of ordering found in our research, that is, the self was rated third (after mate and children), and work was rated seventh (after friends and before leisure) (see Table 3). Owen-Smith found the same ordering except for work, which in her much older sample, was rated sixth (before friends and leisure), more in line with theoretical expectations. Perhaps college students who are still economically dependent on their parents do not value work as much as older people do. These findings are also consistent with those of Fisher, Giblin, and Hoopes (1982), who found, in a

41

large sample of families, a general downgrading of the self in relation to other family priorities, contrary to what most family therapists (and at least one theoretician!) would have expected.

Conclusion

The reliability and internal consistency of the Marital Evaluation Battery are quite acceptable, and its convergent and divergent discrimination is satisfactory or at least promising. When testability has been established as a criterion for theory construction, one needs to establish the adequacy, that is, the psychometric properties (validity and reliability), of the instruments designed for theory testing. One needs to answer the question: Once a theory becomes verifiable, how adequate are the instruments that have been designed to verify it? From the results of the present study, the answer seems to be: They are sufficiently adequate to warrant changes in the theory and further research to test revisions of the theory. For instance, from a generally grandiose and much more encompassing "theory of personality development in the family," the title of this theory has now been changed to a much more modest and specific "theory of developmental competence in the family."

References

Albee, G. W. (1984). A competency model must replace the defect model. In J. M. Joffe, G. W. Albee, & L. D. Kelley (Eds.), Reading in primary prevention of psychopathology: Basic concepts. Hanover, NH: University Press of New England.

Caiella, C. (research in progress).]Tentative title:[Theory-derived analyses of therapy transcripts. Proposed doctoral dissertation, Georgia State University, Atlanta.

Danish, S. J., & D'Augelli, A. R. (1984). Promoting competence and enhancing development through life development interventions. In J. M. Joffe, G. W. Albee, & L. D. Kelly (Eds.), Readings in primary prevention of psychopathology: Basic concepts. Hanover, NH: University Press of New England.

Fisher, B. L., Giblin, P. R., & Hoopes, M. H. (1982). Healthy family functioning: What therapists say and what families want. Journal of Marital and Family Therapy, 8, 273-284.

Goodrich, M. (1984). Concurrent validation of the GSU Marital Evaluation Questionnaire. Unpublished doctoral dissertation, Georgia State University, Atlanta.

Hunt, J. McV. (1969). The challenge of incompetence and poverty: Papers on the role of early education. Urbana, IL: University of Illinois Press.

Johnston, T. B., Levis, M., & L'Abate, L. (1987). Treatment of depression in a couple with systematic homework assignment (SHWAs). Journal of Psychotherapy and the Family.

Kelly, G. (1955). The psychology of personal constructs. New York: Norton.

L'Abate, L. (1976). Understanding and helping the individual in the family. New York: Grune & Stratton.

L'Abate, L. (1985a). Descriptive and explanatory levels in family therapy: Distance, defeats, and dependence. In L. L'Abate (Ed.), Handbook of family psychology and therapy (Vol. 2, pp. 1218-1245). Homewood, IL: Dorsey Press.

L'Abate, L. (1985b). Structured enrichment (SE) with couples and families. Family Relations, 34, 169-175.

L'Abate, L. (1986). Systematic family therapy. New York: Brunner/Mazel.

L'Abate, L. (in preparation). A theory of personality development.

L'Abate, L., & Colondier, G. (1987). The emperor has no clothes! Long live the emperor! A critique of family systems thinking and a reductionistic proposal. American Journal of Family Therapy, 15(1), 19-33.

L'Abate, L., Kearns, D., Richardson, W., & Dow, W. (1985). Enrichment, structured enrichment, social skills training, and psychotherapy. In L. L'Abate & M. Milan (Eds.), Handbook of social skills training and research. New York: Wiley.

L'Abate, L., & Wagner, V. (1985). Theory-derived, family-oriented test batteries. In L. L'Abate (Ed.), Handbook of family psychology and therapy (Vol. 2, pp. 1006-10031). Homewood, IL: Dorsey Press.

L'Abate, L., & Weinstein, S. (1986). Structured enrichment programs for couples and families. New York: Brunner/Mazel.

L'Abate, L., & Wildman, R. R., Jr. (1973). Marital Evaluation Questionnaire. Atlanta: Georgia State University.

L'Abate, L., & Young, L. (1987). Casebook: Structured enrichment programs for couples and families. New York: Brunner/Mazel.

L'Abate, L., Young, L., Joiner, M., & Bond, L. (research in progress). Increasing intimacy in couples through systematic homework assignments.

Laosa, L. M. (1984). Social competence in childhood: Toward a developmental, sociocultural relativistic paradigm. In J. M. Joffee, G. W. Albee, & L. D. Kelly (Eds.), Readings in primary prevention of psychopathology: Basic concepts. Hanover, NH: University Press of New England.

Levis, M. (1987). Short-term treatment for depression using systematic homework assignments. Unpublished doctoral dissertation, Georgia State University, Atlanta.

Lutz, J. (1985). Empirical evaluation of a set of structured communication tasks with couples: Home assignments-practice versus traditional workshop format. Unpublished master's thesis, Georgia State University, Atlanta.

Marlowe, H. A. Jr., & Weinberg, R. B. (1985). Competence development: Theory and practice in special populations. Springfield, IL: Charles C. Thomas.

Olson, D. H. (1976). Bridging research, theory, and application: The triple threat in science. In D. H. Olson (Ed.), Treating relationships. Lake Mills, IA: Graphic.

Olson, D. H., Sprenkle, D., & Russell, C. (1979). Circumflex model of marital and family systems: 1. Cohesion and adaptability dimensions, family types, and clinical applications. Family Process, 18, 3-28.

Owen-Smith, P. L. (1985). Family process and self-concept in early childhood. Unpublished doctoral dissertation, Georgia State University, Atlanta.

Phillips, L. (1968). Human adaptation and its failures. New York: Academic Press.

Reiss, D. (1980). Pathways to assessing the family: Some choice points and a sample route. In C. Lewis & C. Hofling (Eds.), The family: Evaluation and treatment. New York: Brunner/Mazel.

Satir, V. (1972). Peoplemaking. Palo Alto, CA: Science and Behavior Books.

Wagner, V. (1980). An evaluation study of a theory-based marital assessment battery. Unpublished doctoral dissertation, Georgia State University, Atlanta.

White, R. W. (1984). Competence as an aspect of personal growth. In J. M. Joffe, G. W. Albee, & L. D. Kelly (Eds.), Readings in primary prevention of psychopathology: Basic concepts. Hanover, NH: University Press of New England.

Wine, J. D., & Smye, M. D. (Eds.). (1981). <u>Social competence</u>. New York: Guilford.

The author presents an Emotionality-Rationality-Activity model that integrates recent classifications of counseling and psychotherapy. The model also serves as a theoretical basis from which methods, goals, and processes during counseling, psychotherapy, and training can be derived and integrated.

CHAPTER 4

LUCIANO L'ABATE

Classification of Counseling and Therapy Theorists, Methods, Processes, and Goals: The E-R-A Model

Recent presentations by Hutchins (1979) and Frey and Raming (1979) have contributed to a more systematic understanding of how counseling and psychotherapy theorists and their processes and goals can be classified. Hutchins (1979) used a thinking, feeling, and acting trichotomy to classify theories that emphasize one of the three aspects over the other two. For instance, he classified rational-emotive, reality, Gestalt, and logotherapy as related to thinking. Nondirective, client-centered, existential, experiential, and nonrational therapies emphasize feelings, while learning, social learning, and behavior therapies emphasize acting. As interesting as this classification may be, it contains contradictions to these theories as they have been considered by most reviewers (Havens, 1973; Patterson, 1973; Schlien, 1963; Schultz, 1977), who place Gestalt and logotherapy within the humanistic approach. In theoretical assumptions and clinical emphases, these approaches focus on the irrational, the here-and-now, and the overall emotional experience, rather than rational aspects of behavior. Of course, no classification is absolute, and at this point we consider "pure" theories rather than combinations or eclectic theories.

Why are classifications important and relevant to the process of therapeutic intervention and counseling? The purpose of any classification of behavior is to increase the likelihood of an optimum match between the behavior and the method used to improve that behavior. If an individual, for instance, uses a great deal of affect and emotionality, should a counselor react "rationally" or allow it to dilute into activity? Hence, classification would allow us to test one of the questions that has plagued counseling and therapy since their inception, Which method should be used with which behavior, by whom, and at what price (L'Abate, 1969).

More recently Frey and Raming (1979) proposed another taxonomy of counseling goals and methods based on factor analysis of 15 major theorists in counseling and psychotherapy (Alexander, Berne, Dollard and Miller, Dreikurs, Ellis, Frankl, Kelly, Krumbolt, Perls, Rogers, Sullivan, Thorne, Williamson, and Wolpe). Their analysis generated seven goal clusters (transfer, awareness, symptom removal, ego functioning, inner resources, environmental control, and negative reactions) and six processes clusters (acceptance, questioning, unconscious materials, manipulate anxiety, reeducation, and support).

A very similar, eclectic model, Emotionality-Rationality-Activity (E-R-A), was developed by L'Abate and Frey (in press). A classification derived from an E-R-A model, in contrast to Hutchins's classification, is supported by the work of Havens (1973), Patterson (1973), Schlien (1963), and Schultz (1977). This model recognizes that competence in relationships consists of at least four basic components, affects (E), reasons (R) and actions (A), plus awareness, that will need closer consideration in further work. E is the structural input, R is the processing throughput, and A is the outcome output. Awareness has feedback functions for each of the three components as well as the context of each relationship. This classification reveals at least two major differences between Hutchins and the E-R-A model. First, the E-R-A model differs from Hutchins's in making emotionality the initial input of an information processing framework in which rationality is the throughput and activity the output. Secondly the model classifies family therapists and the schools mentioned by Hutchins in a different way. Logotherapy and Gestalt therapy are considered under existential and experiential schools within a Humanistic construct that also in-

LUCIANO L'ABATE *is a professor and Director of the Family Study Program in the Department of Psychology at Georgia State University, Atlanta.*

FIGURE 1

A Classification of Psychotherapy Theorists, Goals, and Processes According to an E-R-A Model (from Frey & Raming, 1979)

	Emotionality	Rationality	Activity
Theorists	Rogers Perls Frankl	Berne Ellis Alexander Kelly Sullivan	Dreikurs Wolpe Dollard & Miller
Goals	Awareness and acceptance of self in conflict and of inner resources Awareness of negative feelings	Strengthening of ego functioning Awareness of negative thoughts	Transfer of therapy Symptom removal Learning to respond and to control the environment
Processes	Acceptance Support of client's autonomy	Recognition and interpretation of the unconscious material Manipulation of client anxiety	Active initial questioning Reeducation about emotional conflicts

FIGURE 2

Classification of Intervention Methods According to the E-R-A Model (from Ulrici, L'Abate, & Wagner, 1980)

Emotionality	Rationality
Methods focus on experimental exercises that differentiate feeling states of solitude and solidarity. 1 Developing intrapersonal awareness through individual exercises of mediation fantasy trips, imaginary dialogues, here-and-now awareness. 2 Developing awareness of interpersonal relationships through interactional task of role play, sculpting, et cetera. 3 Developing bodily awareness through physical exercises of creative movement and interpersonal body contacts. 4 Teaching skills of interpersonal sensitivity and communication through lectures, readings, demonstrations, and practice exercises.	Methods focus on the development of conscious understanding that supports reality based controls. 1 Teaching new facts, concepts, and theories through lectures, readings, and discussions. 2 Relating past influences to present functioning through cognitive recreation of past events (e.g., psychoanalytic dialogues, genograms, and rational reevaluations). 3 Developing insight to differentiate feelings from actions through analysis of one's present and past relationships (e.g., working through transference, understanding defense operations, and ego controls). 4 Teaching skills of rational thinking and ego control through lectures, discussions, and practice at rational problem solving and decision making.

Activity

Behavioral	Systemic
Methods focus on the application of scientific principles to shape and control behavior 1 Solving behavioral problems through experimental analysis—quantifying behavior, determining controls, and implementing interventions. 2 Teaching and increasing desired behavior and extinguishing unappropriate behavior through techniques of: a respondent conditioning (e.g., stimulus pairing, desentization) b operant conditioning (e.g., positive reinforcement, punishment.) 3 Teaching desired behavior through social learning (e.g., modeling, films). 4 Increasing and maintaining behavior through evaluative feedback. 5 Practice application of learned behavior through role play and simulated exercises. 6 Implementing desired behavior or its approximation through behavioral tasks performed in daily context. 7 Teaching behavioral principles through lectures, models, and practice exercises.	Methods focus on adjusting dimensions of cohesion and adaptability that maintain family functioning. 1 Establishing appropriate boundaries for cohesion and autonomy through: a directives given in session (e.g., interactions, blocking others, bringing members of the social network) b behavior assignments for daily context (e.g., rituals, paradoxical exercises, age-appropriate tasks, activities to support coalitions or limit enmeshment). 2 Restructuring operations in response to situational stress or developmental change through: a assigning linear tasks to directly change operations (e.g., rescheduling, assigning family duties) b assigning paradoxical tasks that emphasize operations problems (e.g., role reversals, behavioral extremes).

cludes client-centered phenomenology. These schools focus on emotions, the here-and-now, the imminent, and the transcendent. The psycho-dynamic-psychoanalytic approach would agree with Hutchins's placement. It would also add transactional approaches that emphasize rational, cool, calm, and collected discussion and consideration of the past and present, as well as rational-emotive and reality therapies. The activity approach covers Adlerian, behavioral, and systems schools. More specifically, within Humanism (emotionality), in the phenomenological school, one would consider Snygg and Coombs, and Rogers, among recent and still living theorists. In existentialism, in addition to Frankl, one would include May. Experientialism actually can be subdivided into three trends according to Schur (1976): (a) expressivists such as Moreno, Perls, and Schultz; (b) the detachers and transcendental meditators such as Watts; and (c) the communicators such as Satir, Bandler, and Grinder.

The psychoanalytic-psychodynamic (rationality) schools have at least three subdivisions: (a) historical-orthodox (Freud, Adler, Jung, Fenichel, etc); (b) interpersonal-adaptational (Hartmann, Horney, Fromm, Meyer, Sullivan, Rado); and (c) modern-day revisionists (Erickson, Grinker, Berne, and the British object-relations school).

The activity approach contains: (a) the Adlerian; (b) the behavioral (classical-historical, drive, and reinforcement subdivisions); and (c) systems that themselves could be further subdivided into: communication-information theorists (Ruesch and Beteson, Watzlawick, Haley, etc.); transactional (Dewey & Bentley, and Spiegel who are theorists rather

48

than therapists); and general systems purists (von Bertailanffy).

How the E-R-A model would deal with the results of Frey and Raming's taxonomy is shown in Figure 1.

From the E-R-A model, Ulrici, L'Abate, and Wagner (1980) proposed a classification of counseling and psychotherapeutic techniques, as well as specific training programs for couples and families (Figure 2).

In conclusion, the purpose of this article has been to show how an E-R-A model fits in the subjective (Hutchins, 1979) and empirical (Frey & Raming, 1979) classifications previously published in the *Personnel and Guidance Journal*. The degree of fit is thus far promising. The degree of diagnostic and therapeutic applicability is still problematic, but not insurmountable. The E-R-A approach would separate thoughts and feelings, regardless of whether they are positive or negative, and, of course, could not accommodate eclectic theorists like Krumholtz, Thorne, or Williamson who consider equally most aspects of E-R-A. The only contention here would be whether rationally derived taxonomies (Hutchins's and E-R-A) are as valid as those factor-analytically derived. If the E-R-A model seems to encompass an empirical taxonomy with little problem, is the reverse of this conclusion also valid?

REFERENCES

FREY, D. H., RAMING, H. E. A taxonomy of consulting goals and methods. *Personnel and Guidance Journal*, 1979, 58, 26–33.

HAVENS, L. L. *Approaches to the mind: Movement of the psychiatric schools from sects toward science*. Boston: Little, Brown, 1973.

HUTCHINS, D. E. Systematic counseling: The T-F-A model for counselor intervention. *Personnel and Guidance Journal*, 1979, 57, 529–531.

L'ABATE, L., & FREY, J. The E-R-A model: The role of feelings in family therapy reconsidered: Implications for a classification of theories of family therapy. *Journal of Marriage and Family Therapy*, in press.

L'ABATE, L. The continuum of rehabilitation and laboratory evaluation: Behavior modification and psychotherapy. In C. M. Franks (Ed.), *Behavior therapy: Appraisal and status*, pp. 476–494. New York: McGraw-Hill, 1969.

PATTERSON, C. H. *Theories of counseling and psychotherapy*. New York: Harper & Row, 1973.

SCHLIEN, J. M. Phenomenology and personality. In J. M. Wepman & R. W. Heine (Eds.), *Concepts of personality*. Chicago: Aldine, 1963.

SCHULTZ, D. *Growth psychology: Models of the healthy personality*. New York: D. Van Nostrand, 1977.

SCHUR, E. M. *The awareness trap: Self-absorption instead of social change*. New York: Quadrangle/New York Times Book Co., 1976.

ULRICI, D.; L'ABATE, L.; & WAGNER, V. The E-R-A model: A heuristic framework for classification of social skills training programs for couples and families. *Family Relations*, (in press).

CHAPTER 5

Love, Intimacy, and Sex

Luciano L'Abate and
William C. Talmadge

Writing of such concepts as love, sex, and intimacy is asking for trouble. As psychotherapists we talk around and about these feelings, behaviors, and concepts frequently with our patients. In fact, just recently one of us asked a husband in a couple's interview, "When do you feel most loved by your wife?" He stared for what seemed to be a long time, then proudly stated, "When I hurt my back about a month ago and she rubbed Ben-Gay on it." This husband continued by saying that his wife sometimes got angry when he hurt his back. It was reframed to him that she was probably angry at times like that because she was scared and loved him. While leaving the interview, Mr. Smith commented, "This love thing sure is complicated."

Love, intimacy, and sex *are* complicated, but they are at the basis of primary, intimate, committed relationships, such as marriage, in a most profound and primitive manner. The thesis of this chapter is twofold. First, the ability to share love, negotiate power, and establish an intimate foundation are three of the necessary and sufficient conditions for a satisfactory and fulfilling marital and sexual relationship (L'Abate, 1986; L'Abate & Colondier, in press; L'Abate, submitted for publication; Talmadge & Talmadge, 1985, 1986). Second, the ability to share love, negotiate power, and establish an intimate foundation are colored, shaped, and set in motion by our early primary relationships, primarily the family of origin. This position assumes that both partners are physically healthy, fully functioning individuals.

The chapter is also based on the assumption that love and intimacy can only be *shared* and are not subject to negotiation. This does not mean that couples do not struggle with these issues, but, rather, they represent interpersonal resources which cannot be exchanged like many other interpersonal resources. Money, and its use, for example, can be negotiated in a relationship. Love and intimacy are based on feelings and must be shared—not bargained for other interpersonal resources. Sex in a relationship has multiple functions. Sex as a physical act may be negotiated or exchanged for other resources. However, sex as an act of love cannot be negotiated. It can only be given or shared. Sex manuals have unfortunately fostered the negotiation of sex because of the emphasis on technique and performance rather than love and intimacy.

SEXUALITY

Sexuality is a primary force in the life of every individual. It is a pervasive and integral force, involving physiological and psychological processes. It is an active, dynamic, and organic process with a multiplicity of interrelated and changing variables. It is a force not to be denied without heavy expense to the individual. We think of sexuality more broadly than just penises, vaginas, and intercourse. Sexuality is the process of *being* that we express through our manifestation of *being* male or female, a man or woman, masculine or feminine; it is how we think and feel about and express our gender, our sex organs, our body, our self-images, and our choices and preferences.

A sexual script forms through early developing self-image, sexual experience, culture, parental role models, and peer relationships. Our script continues to evolve over the years of our living. However, the basic foundation of the sexual script is laid in our early development through our *attachment* and bonding with our primary care providers (usually the family of origin) and all that these relationships were and were not (Bowlby, 1969, 1973; Harlow, 1958; Kaplan, 1978). The quality of the attachment in the primary years shapes our ability to love, touch, give, receive, and commit. Our contention is that the quality of attachment and affectional care sets the tone of future intimate sexual relationships (Scharff, 1982; Talmadge & Talmadge, 1985; Wallace, 1981). For instance:

Jerry was a strong, entertaining, and handsome young man who repeatedly had difficulty getting close to women. He was very capable of starting relationships; however, as these relationships moved toward more intimate forms, he would sabotage them or take flight. He sought therapy for himself after several episodes of being unable to maintain an erection with two different partners. Jerry was frustrated, angry, and ashamed. He did not understand what was happening to him. Shortly after his birth his parents divorced, his mother was institutionalized for depression, his father went broke, became destitute, and the children were divided among relatives and foster homes. Jerry was placed in a number of different foster homes, some of which were good and some bad, during the first 26 months of his life before being returned to his mother's care.

Developing an intimate sexual relationship had become a tragic problem for this man, which was related to his poor attachment foundation in his first years of life. In the continuing therapy Jerry became increasingly aware of his intense fear of abandonment. His erectile losses served him by preventing him from getting closer to these two women although both were understanding and did not make a fuss when this happened. It was Jerry who was most agitated and would distance himself from his partner. In therapy he began to find a very frightened and hurt little boy under his presenting frustration, anger, and shame. Jerry was terrified of being left as he had been so many times in his early life.

Sexual expression, especially the act of intercourse, is one of the most vulnerable interactions that a couple undertakes. The experience of lying nude with one's partner in the process of giving and receiving pleasure is a most vulnerable and dependent state. At no other ordinary time in the life of a couple are they more vulnerable. The act of intercourse, of having a portion of another person's body inside another's body cavity, is an extremely vulnerable physiological position. Because of this highly physiological openness and vulnerability, the symbolic reawakening of the unconscious processes is likely. This sexual expression in a committed relationship is a "physical expression of the primary emotional bonds and is best understood in the context of the relationships which govern it, primarily the family of origin and marriage" (Talmadge & Talmadge, 1985, p. 1107). For instance:

> Cathy and Harry were referred by her individual therapist, who thought the couple needed conjoint therapy because of their unhappiness with each other, Cathy's inorgasmia, and Harry's premature ejaculation. In the process of therapy they were given the homework assignment of genital sensate focus, which is an erotic touching exercise where both people are nude and one partner touches the erotic and exciting areas of the other partner's body. Up to this point in therapy, Harry had been very successful in controlling his ejaculation. However, in this exercise when Cathy began touching around his genitals, he ejaculated. Cathy became tearful and ran from the room. As the couple talked about this, all they understood was Cathy's deep sense of sadness.
> In their next therapy interview, the therapist asked Cathy to picture herself in that same situation and to feel that sadness. When Cathy acknowledged imagining herself there, the therapist asked her to go back in time and report the first memory that came to mind. She slowly started to weep as she reported two incidents. The first was when she was about eight years old and her mother had awakened her in the middle of the night pretending as though it were the next morning and time for school. When Cathy got to the breakfast table, Mom said, "Surprise, I fooled you," at which point Cathy learned it was about 2:00 or 3:00 A.M. The second memory was of a Christmas morning. Cathy and her brother hurried to the living room where Santa Claus was to have left their presents, but nothing was there. The kids were very disappointed. Soon they aroused Mom to explain what had happened, to which she laughingly replied that today was really the day before Christmas. However, shortly thereafter she joked with the kids that she had fooled them as she presented them with hidden presents in another room. Through the sexual exercise, Cathy's unconscious was symbolically triggered in exposing the deep sadness and hurt she had felt in growing up with a sadistic mother.

The sexual interaction of a couple who love one another is one of the most intimate and exciting forms of relating in which they engage. The love drives them to closeness, both emotionally and physically. This desire for closeness is satisfied emotionally through each individual's understanding of her/his self and the sharing of the self with the loved one, while the drive for closeness physically is satisfied through touch, affection, and sexual intercourse (Lowen, 1965). At the same time it is understood that couples do not live in a vacuum of love and intimacy. All the other interactions, roles, and stresses of life impact on the couple's love life. However, it is our belief that those couples who love one another, profess their love, and work at it are among the happiest in their sexual relating. We believe for the marital sexual relationship to fully develop it must be bound in love, intimacy, and negotiated power.

LOVE AND INTIMACY

Issues of love (i.e., nurturance in Parsons' view, Parsons & Bales, 1955) need to be separated sharply from issues of power (i.e., instrumentality in Parsons' view). Love and being are not negotiable resources (except when sex is for sale professionally . . .). Information and services (i.e., doing) or money and possessions (i.e., having) are all negotiable resources (L'Abate, 1986). Love, on the other hand, is not and should not be negotiable because it would be confused, fused, and diffused with issues of power. Love is based on feelings, and feelings can be shared but not negotiated. Power is negotiable, love is not.

Love as a researchable and legitimate area of study has only recently reached its peak (Branden, 1980; Coutts, 1973; Curtin, 1973; Fogarty, 1985; Fromm, 1956; Grant, 1976; Haughton, 1970; Peterson & Payne, 1975; Pope et al., 1980; Swensen, 1985), producing as many definitions as there are sources.

Initially it is the love for one another that draws individuals together in coupling relationships. In the early phase of a relationship this is characterized more as passion, lust, and attraction. However, if the relationship is to continue, a deeper caring must develop. From this deeper sense of caring the couple begins their journey of intimacy. A healthy sexual relationship grows from this intimate connection based on a love for one another. Love in an ongoing sexual relationship requires commitment and discipline. This love is an active, expressed concern for the life, growth, and well-being of one's partner. It is grounded in the knowledge of oneself (the being) and his/her partner (thou). This deeper sense of caring is based on the valuing, understanding, and expressing of self to the loved one. The valuing, understanding, and expressing of self are the primary components of being. We think of the issues of being and intimacy as two of the basic aspects of love. The following case example illustrates the issues of being, discipline, and commitment involved in love.

Mike was in his late forties when he came to therapy with his wife because of their constant arguing and his persistent premature ejaculations. However, both professed to the therapist to love each óther dearly. The couple had been married for three years. This was his wife's second marriage and his first. The couple lived with her two children in her home which she owned prior to their marriage, and he paid a modest amount each month for the maintenance of the house. Mike's ideas of loving meant that you cared for that person. However, he had experienced very little care in his growing up with a mother who had been diagnosed as "depressed," "paranoid," "hysterical," and "demented" by those physicians and institutions by whom she was treated.

In Mike's therapy group in his third year of psychotherapy he brought the following problem. When his wife had returned from a tour of Europe she brought him a gift, a beautifully engraved gold wedding ring. Until this point Mike had not worn a wedding ring. When given the gift, he graciously thanked his wife but had not worn the ring. He was in a crisis because he did not know what to do about the ring, although he professed to love his wife dearly. In the group's exploration of this problem, the group confronted Mike with his refusal to symbolically profess his love and commitment to his wife through the wearing of his ring, his unwillingness to purchase a house of their own, and his stashing money in his bank account of which she had no knowledge. Mike had been confronted with his lack of discipline and commitment in his love of his wife. During the next year and a half Mike started wearing his wedding ring, bought a house with his wife, and opened joint bank accounts. Recently Mike told his group that while visiting the country home of a friend, he and his wife were walking near the stables when suddenly horses charged them as the horses were racing back to the barn. Mike jumped out of harm's way. Immediately, he began to question himself because he had done nothing to assure his wife's safety. He was filled with shame and guilt. In discussing this he examined his conflict between the wants of his self and his love of his wife.

Issues of Being

Being is a difficult concept to understand, in spite of various attempts by humanistic writers to define it (May, 1983). It becomes clearer when we are able to separate resources into three different and nonoverlapping channels (L'Abate, submitted for publication). Money and possessions are considered as parts of having. Services and information (i.e., activities) are parts of doing. Love and status are parts of being. This latter concept, then, includes love of self and others as well as a sense of self-importance, understanding of self, and a willingness to express what is known about self to the loved one. Hence, a sense of self-valuing, -understanding, and -expressing is necessary but not sufficient to be able to love and to be loved, i.e., to share love.

What is love and how is it demonstrated, expressed, and shared? Love as a developmental process consists of at least three elements: (a) two behavioral components: received care and caring; (b) two cognitive components: seeing the good and forgiveness; and (c) an emotional component, i.e., intimacy.

Received care means it is enormously difficult, if not impossible, to give care if one has not received care. It is based in the primary caretaker's tasks of feeding, protecting, sheltering, and guiding (Harlow, 1958; Bowlby, 1969; Suomi, 1977).

Caring is the concrete, behavioral expression of love according to definite physical activities, ranging from cooking and earning a paycheck to carrying a bedpan and cleaning up a diaper. We perform services for those we love and expect them to serve us when we are incapacitated. In the sex act, caring is shown by doing and performing those activities that are pleasurable to us and to our partner.

Seeing the good is a cognitive process that represents our ability to see positive qualities in ourselves before we see them in those we love. These qualities may be physical, characterological, temperamental, etc. One of the prerequisite qualities for a "good" sex life consists of seeing oneself as a sexual human being who deserves to give and to receive pleasure. Seeing the sexual good in oneself implies a parallel process of seeing oneself as competent and important (Ford, 1985; Marlowe, 1985). Seeing the good in one's partner implies also listening and learning from him so that feedback is not taken or given as criticism. In Fromm (1956) this quality is described as respect. However, true respect develops from self-respect. In sexual interaction with the loved one this respect means desiring to please the other and oneself, inquiring and stating what is enjoyed. This feedback is crucial in negotiating pleasurable sexual activities, when, more often than not, feedback is given within a context of fears and anxieties about sex, sometimes producing conflict and distress.

Forgiveness is a second cognitive process basic to personal and marital well-being (L'Abate, 1986; L'Abate, submitted for publication) that has been neglected by most individual, marital, and family therapists. Yet, this process seems a *sine qua non* condition for seeing the good. How can we see the good in ourselves and others if we do not forgive our errors, i.e., our trespasses and those of the persons we love? Can we give up our demands for performance or perfection in ourselves? If we cannot do it for ourselves, how can we do it for those we love? Forgiveness becomes a very active issue with couples in which one of the partners has had an affair that is recognized by the couple. The "betrayed" partner can make the other partner pay for the rest of the marriage if forgiveness is not acknowledged.

Issues of Intimacy

In addition to love, intimacy has been found increasingly to be a crucial variable in marriage and family life (L'Abate, 1986; Derlega, 1984; Patton & Waring, 1984; Sloan & L'Abate, 1985). However, intimacy, like love, has as many definitions as there are authors who write about it. Two components are critical in intimacy, according to Douvan (1977): the ability and cooperation to be dependent and the ability to express, withstand, understand, and resolve the conflict and hostility that occur in intimate relationships. Others have discussed intimacy as a composite of identity, expressiveness, affection, autonomy, cohesion, compatibility, conflict resolution, and sexuality (Waring & Reddon, 1983). L'Abate (1977, 1986) concretely discusses intimacy as the sharing of hurt and fear of being hurt. Intimacy in marriage means that each partner brings and participates with ego strength, power, interdependency, vulnerability, touch, trust, mutuality, an understanding of self, and a sharing of the self as known. As is the case with most of us, the self is wanting, vulnerable, fallible, and needy. In order for intimacy to progress we must make room for the regression of the childlike and often scared needy selves (Dicks, 1967).

Hatfield (1984) has listed some of the reasons why intimacy is a fearful condition, a position already considered by L'Abate and Samples (1983): (a) fear of exposure; (b) fear of abandonment; (c) fear of angry attacks; (d) fear of loss of control; (e) fear of one's own destructive impulses; (f) fear of losing one's individuality or of being engulfed. Many of these fears can be subsumed under the rubric of hurts related to our fallibility, vulnerability, and neediness (L'Abate, 1986). We think of all of this needing to be integrated within the relationship. This integration process forms the intimate foundation in the journey of marriage and therefore must continue to be established, evolved, and developed in order for the sexual relationship to be fulfilling and growthful.

Thus, we often perceive sexual problems as indicative of intimacy difficulties. The lack of intimate, expressed emotional feeling, affection, interdependence, and vulnerability supports the lack of sexual contact. The intimacy in the life of a couple is one of the major determining factors in a satisfactory and pleasurable sex life. Only disturbed couples are able to fulfill each other sexually without intimacy. For most couples satisfactory and enjoyable sexual expression is not an option without intimacy. True orgastic pleasure reaches its heights in continually evolving intimate marriages. In the intimate marriages sex may take place for the pure fun of sex and/or the expression of love. However, this position would go a long way in explaining why most partners who feel unloved often do not want to have sex for the sake of sex alone. How can we share the high orgastic pleasure if we cannot share the lows of hurt and fears of being hurt? In fact, sex as an act, i.e., performance—doing—can be had relatively easily. It is much more difficult to share sex within the context of a loving and intimate relationship. In fact, behaviorally oriented therapists who would emphasize sex as an act without consideration of its emotional aspects as an act of love may well miss the boat! Sex as an expression of love is a sharing of feelings, sensations, and experiences related to past and present anxieties, hurts, fears, and frustrations. If and when such a sharing does not take place, sexual performance may be impaired.

We are maintaining, therefore, that sex as an activity, i.e., performance, is negotiable provided attendant feelings to the activity in terms of past experiences are shared beforehand. An example of this process could be found in the following vignette:

> A college professor and his wife plagued by severe depression with frequent hospitalizations, after sessions where they learned to work positively with their depressions (L'Abate, 1986), completed successfully the sharing of hurt exercise (contained in L'Abate, 1986) where they were able to share their past hurts together. After leaving this session, entirely on their own and without any prompting from the therapists, they called their children to check on whether they were all right, telling them that they would be away for the rest of the day but would get home by six o'clock. They checked in a nearby motel and "consummated the honeymoon" that 12 years earlier had been a dismal failure sexually.

ABILITY TO NEGOTIATE POWER

Only recently have we become aware of the importance of the ability to negotiate as the necessary ingredient of satisfactory sexual, marital, and family relationships (L'Abate, 1986; L'Abate & Colondier, in press). In fact, this important and fundamental ability is not mentioned in most texts of family, marital, and sexual therapy. We are aware that if and when this ability is missing or is incomplete, it is practically impossible to hope that a marriage or a relationship will "make it," i.e., be a mutually satisfying relationship. It may "make it" miserably, and often misery loves company. Staying together in a marriage does not necessarily mean that partners love each other or can negotiate issues! Be that as it may, the negotiation of power implies negotiation either of material resources, i.e., having (money and/or possessions), or of services and/or information, i.e., doing. Conflicts over issues of having and doing, more often than not, derive from our inability to share issues of *being* intimate and important together without demands for performance or perfection, as discussed above.

Negotiation is a difficult ability to learn because most of our models (i.e., parents, siblings, in-laws, and relatives) most of the time have failed to show us how to do it. Hence, the ability to negotiate is just as difficult to learn as the ability to love for exactly the same reason. All of us, in one way or another, mostly trial and error, learn eventually. The cost, however, is high and many of us do not make it. By negotiation here is meant a process of bargaining, problem solving, and decision making that follows invariable se-

58

quences of: (a) defining the issues, (b) proposing possible solutions (i.e., courses of action) with their rewards and costs; (c) implementing an agreed-upon course of action; (d) evaluating its outcome; and (e) deciding whether to keep that course of action or change it for a fallback or alternative solution.

Power consists of authority, i.e., who makes the decision, and responsibility, i.e., who carries out the task of implementing a course of action. Both authority and responsibility can be shared and negotiated in a balanced and equitable fashion to the satisfaction of both partners, or there can be an imbalanced and, very likely, an unsatisfactory relationship where one partner's status or sense of self-importance is achieved at the expense of the partner with lower status. Under these conditions not only is negotiation impossible, but, as discussed by Stock (1985), intimacy is also impossible, since it can be achieved mainly between partners who regard each other as *equals*.

The ability to negotiate increases multiplicatively under at least three conditions: (a) the level of functionality of the marriage, that is, the higher the level, the better the chances of successful negotiation and outcome; (b) the level of competence of both partners, that is, the higher the level of competence, the better the chances of successful negotiation; and (c) the presence and quality of motivation to negotiate, i.e., obviously one needs to want to negotiate, in addition to a satisfactory level of functionality and a certain degree of competence. These three separate but interactive conditions can be summarized under the equation that negotiation potential (NP) = level of functionality $\times$ skill $\times$ will.

L'Abate (1986) has proposed three different models to specify each of those three conditions. Level of functionality is defined by the A-R-C model that ranges from clearly dysfunctional abusive, apathetic, and atrophied (A) to somewhat more functional reactively repetitive relationships (R). The highest level of functionality is achieved under the condition of conductivity (C), where partners are in charge of themselves and are committed to creative change for the better. In addition to evidence reviewed by L'Abate (1986), a recent review by Ford (1985) cites strong supporting evidence for the existence of these three degrees of functionality.

Competence (skill) can be assessed through the E-R-A-Aw-C model, which makes successful intimate (close and prolonged) relationships, and, of course, negotiations, a function of assets in emotionality (E), rationality (R), activities (A), awareness (Aw), and context (C). As stated earlier, most of our inability to negotiate derives from our inability to share our hurts and our fears of being hurt, a process that starts from how we are in touch with our feelings, i.e., emotionality. Feelings determine how close or how far we are from each other. Hence, E deals with distance, and R determines how we modulate, modify, and moderate that distance through our activities (A). Awareness is seen as feedback originating *after* activities have taken place. On the basis of our evaluation of the outcome and the context (C) we can return circularly back to E and repeat the process. Inability to access E and to use it creatively leads to exaggerations in R (i.e., obsessions) or in A (i.e., impulsive or repetitive addictions) or in both R and A. Hence, this model makes emotionality the cornerstone of interpersonal competence. In addition to the evidence reviewed by L'Abate (1986), Marlowe (1985) has provided a review of the empirical literature that tends to support parts, if not all, of this model.

Motivation (will) to negotiate, the third condition necessary for successful negotiation, has been considered by L'Abate (1986) in terms of priorities, that is, the amount of energy expended in space and time to deal with (a) oneself, (b) marriage, (c) children, (d) parents/in-laws/siblings, (e) work, friends, and (f) leisure (Marks, 1977). In addition to intrafamily priorities, one needs to deal with one's attachments, beliefs, and commitments (the A-B-C model), and the use of resources, such as having, doing, and being, as mentioned at the outset of this chapter. When these priorities are ill defined, mixed up, and vague, it becomes very difficult to "know oneself" and to be clear about what is more or less important or relevant. Stereotypically, we men identify and equate ourselves erroneously with our workselves, that is: we men acquire an occupational definition of self according to our jobs, leaving the women the definition of selves as mothers. Either way, the self is given up either for the job, the children, or the marriage ("I want to make you happy"). How can the bridge of marriage survive when the pillars of the self are inadequate?

Lasch (1984) has condensed well the major qualities that make for the autonomous interdependence that is basic to a satisfactory marital and sexual relationship:

> The achievement of selfhood, which our culture makes so difficult, may be defined as the acknowledgment of our separation from the original source of life, combined with a continuing struggle to recapture a sense of primal union by means of activity that gives us a provisional understanding and mastery of the world without denying our limitations and dependency. Selfhood is the painful awareness of the tension between our unlimited aspirations and our limited understanding, between our original intimations of immortality and our fallen state, between oneness and separation. (p. 20)

CONCLUSION

The ability to reach orgasm is a relatively easy goal. To achieve orgasm with someone who loves us and whom we love is a very difficult task because in order to reach the peak of ecstasy, we also need to share the valleys of despair and hurt. Sex as a physical act is negotiable. Sex as an act of love-being and intimacy can only be shared.

60

REFERENCES

Bowlby, J. (1969). *Attachment*. New York: Basic Books.

Branden, N. (1980). *The psychology of romantic love*. Los Angeles: J. P. Tarcher.

Coutts, R. L. (1973). *Love and intimacy: A psychological approach*. San Ramon, CA: Consensus.

Curtin, M. E. (Ed.). (1973). *Symposium on love*. New York: Behavioral Publications.

Derlega, V. J. (Ed.). (1984). *Communication, intimacy, and close relationships*. Orlando, FL: Academic Press.

Dicks, H. V. (1967). *Marital tensions*. New York: Basic Books.

Douvan, E. (1977). Interpersonal relationships; Some questions and observations. In G. Levinger & H. Raush (Eds.), *Close relationships; Perspective on the meaning of intimacy*. Amherst: University of Massachusetts Press.

Fogarty, T. F. (1985). The role of romantic love in marriage. In D. C. Goldberg (Ed.), *Contemporary marriage: Special issues in couples therapy*. Homewood, IL: Dorsey Press.

Ford, M. D. (1985). The concept of competence: Themes and variations. In H. A. Marlowe, Jr., & R. B. Weinberg (Eds.), *Competence development: Theory ana practice in special populations*. Springfield, IL: Charles C Thomas.

Fromm, E. (1956). *The art of loving*. New York: Harper & Row.

Grant, V. W. (1976). *Falling in love: The psychology of the romantic emotion*. New York: Springer.

Harlow, H. F. (1958). The nature of love. *American Psychologist, 13*, 673-685.

Hatfield, E. (1984). The dangers of intimacy. In V. J. Derlega (Ed.), *Communication, intimacy, and close relationships*. Orlando, FL: Academic Press.

Haughton, R. (1970). *Love*. Baltimore, MD: Penguin Books.

Kaplan, L. J. (1978). *Oneness and separateness: From infant to individual*. New York: Simon & Schuster.

L'Abate, L. (1977). Intimacy is sharing hurt feelings: A reply to David Mace. *Journal of Marriage and Family Counseling, 3*, 13-16.

L'Abate, L. (1986). *Systematic family therapy*. New York: Brunner/Mazel.

L'Abate, L., & Colondier, G. (in press). The emperor has no clothes. Long live the emperor!: A critique of family systems thinking and a reductionistic proposal. *American Journal of Family Therapy, 14*.

L'Abate, L. (Submitted for publication). What is being? Notes toward a clarification of the process.

L'Abate, L., & Samples, G. (1983). Intimacy letters as invariable prescription for closeness-avoidant couples. *Family Therapy, 10*, 37-45.

Lasch, C. (1984). *The minimal self: Psychic survival in troubled times*. New York: W. W. Norton.

Lowen, A. (1965). *Love and orgasm*. New York: Macmillan.

Marks, S. R. (1977). Multiple roles and role strain: Some notes on human energy, time and commitment. *American Sociological Review, 42*, 921-936.

Marlowe, H. A., Jr. (1985). Competence: A social intelligence perspective. In H. A. Marlowe, Jr., & R. B. Weinberg (Eds.), *Competence development: Theory and practice in special populations*. Springfield, IL: Charles C Thomas.

May, R. (1983). *The discovery of being: Writings in existential psychology*. New York: W. W. Norton.

Parsons, T., & Bales, R. F. (1955). *Family: Socialization and interaction processes.* New York: Free Press.

Patton, D., & Waring, E. M. (1984). The quality and quantity of marital intimacy in the marriages of psychiatric patients. *Journal of Sex and Marital Therapy, 10,* 201-206.

Peterson, J. A., & Payne, B. (1975). *Love in the later years.* New York: Association Press.

Pope, K. S., et al. (1980). *On love and loving: Psychological perspectives on the nature and experience of romantic love.* San Francisco, CA: Jossey-Bass.

Scharff, D. E. (1982). *The sexual relationship: An object relations view of sex and the family.* Boston: Routledge & Kegan Paul.

Shapiro, D. (1981). *Autonomy and rigid character.* New York: Basic Books.

Sloan, S. Z., & L'Abate, L. (1985). Intimacy. In L. L'Abate (Ed.), *Handbook of family psychology and therapy.* Homewood, IL: Dorsey Press.

Stock, W. (1985). The influence of gender on power dynamics in relationships. In D. C. Goldberg (Ed.), *Contemporary marriage: Special issues in couples therapy.* Homewood, IL: Dorsey Press.

Suomi, S. J. (1977). Neglect and abuse of infants by rhesus monkey mothers. *Voices, 12*(14), 5-8.

Swensen, C. H., Jr. (1985). Love in the family. In L. L'Abate (Ed.), *Handbook of family psychology and therapy,* Homewood, IL: Dorsey Press.

Talmadge, L. D., & Talmadge, W. C. (1986). Relational sexuality: An understanding of low sexual desire. *Journal of Sex and Marital Therapy, 12,* 3-21.

Talmadge, W. C., & Talmadge, L. D. (1985). A transactional perspective on the treatment of sexual dysfunctions. In L. L'Abate (Ed.), *Handbook of family psychology and therapy.* Homewood, IL: Dorsey Press.

Wallace, D. H. (1981). Affectional climate in the family of origin and the experience of subsequent sexual-affectional behaviors. *Journal of Sex and Marital Therapy, 7*(4), 196-306.

Waring, E. M., & Reddon, J. R. (1983). The measurement of intimacy in marriage: The Waring Intimacy Questionnaire. *Journal of Clinical Psychology, 39*(1), 53-57.

SECTION II.　THERAPY

Chapter 6

Advances in Family Therapy:
An Outline

Luciano L'Abate

I. Family therapy's most cherished theoretical basis: family systems theory-ecosystemic epistemology

    A. Basic concepts and tenets

        1. the family as a system of interacting subsystems

        2. homeostasis, feedback, regulation, hierarchy, etc.

        3. Von Bertalanffy, Bateson, Wiener, Dewey & Bentley, etc.

    B. Historically and evolutionarily an important contribution that

        1. filled a gap left by psychology's lack of interest in the family and found the sociological literature too research oriented and relevant to the family qua family, without members.

        2. has been a useful metaphor (and remains one!) until we could find more precise <u>descriptions and explanations of how families work or fail to work</u>

        3. ceased to be useful when it became a cult and an uncritically accepted set of tenets reaching the level of cultism and unquestioned worship of some of its major proponents (gurus).

    C. Increasing criticism of family systems theory

        1. high level of abstraction

        2. distant and separate from available and relevant empirical literature in psychology, especially child development

        3. unverifiable, producing an anti-empirical stance in marital family therapy

        4. attention to process without content

II. Empirically based, content-oriented models of family functioning and dysfunctioning: a parsimonious theory--competent development is a function of the ability to love (space) and the ability to negotiate (time).

A. Development is a function of space (approach-avoidance) and time (discharge-delay)

    1. stages in development

        a. dependency (childhood)
        b. denial of dependency (adolescence)
        c. interdependence (adulthood)
        d. return to dependency

    2. stages of adulthood

        a. personhood
        b. partnership
        c. parenthood

    3. development of competence according to the interaction of

        a. settings (family, work, leisure) x
        b. competencies (Doing, Having, and Being)

B. Ability to negotiate

    1. the structure of negotiation

        a. authority-responsibility
        b. orchestration-instrumentation
        c. competencies to be negotiated--issues of Doing and Having

    2. skills necessary to negotiate

        a. A-R-C model
        b. E-R-A-Aw-C model
        c. Priorities (horizontal through competencies, vertical through settings)

C. Ability to love

    1. caring
    2. seeing the good
    3. forgiveness
    4. intimacy

III. Stages of family therapy and the practice of programmed family therapy

A. Stage 1: stress, crisis conflict, and symptom reduction with trust building

   1. written homework assignments (requirements: appointments and writing)

      a. description
      b. multiple positive reframings
      c. prescription of the behavior

   2. resistant patterns

      a. arguing and/or fighting
      b. sibling rivalry
      c. temper tantrums
      d. depression (drama triangle, distance regulation, multiple reframings, prescription, relapse prediction, appointments in writing)

B. Stage 2: negotiation

   1. homework assignments (I-statements, A-R-C, E-R-A-Aw-C, priorities, applications)

   2. structured enrichment programs for couples and families

C. Stage 3: termination and intimacy

   1. homework assignments
   2. structured enrichment

D. Stage 4: follow-up

IV. Discussion

A. The need for verifiable methods in theory construction and clinical practice

B. The personal need to combine

   1. theory with practice
   2. practice with research
   3. therapy with prevention

C. The need for standard operating procedures in the hands of subprofessional intermediaries: the laboratory method in clinical psychology

   1. in the evaluation of individuals, couples, and families

2. in therapy with individuals, couples, and families

V. Conclusions

    A. It is better to be verifiable and wrong than to be unverifiable and right.

    B. There are too many families who need help to use competitive or mutually antagonistic practices.

    C. The worst status for the field of family therapy, as for dysfunctional families, is the <u>status quo</u>.

Chapter 7

Paradoxical Therapeutic Strategies:
Current Practices and Evidence

Luciano L'Abate and Michael Levis

Paradoxical strategies in psychotherapy have received a great deal of attention in the last decade (Seltzer, 1986; Weeks & L'Abate, 1982). These strategies consist of a series of steps designed to reframe the symptomatic behavior positively in order to prescribe it to the client or asking the client not to change because change could be dangerous. The purpose of this introduction is to review their status and perhaps prognosticate about their future. Although it is clear that no specific process or school of thought can be considered exclusively paradoxical, it is also clear that paradoxical strategies have been incorporated into most therapeutic schools, cutting across established theoretical and therapeutic boundaries (L'Abate, Ganahl, & Hansen, 1986; Seltzer, 1986). These strategies have reached the level of a specific method, which is a sequence of replicable steps. They have left behind their vague status as techniques, which, in contrast to method, represent the idiosyncratic style of the individual therapist in using a particular method. Style therefore remains a chain of unique and nonrepeatable events.

As Seltzer (1986) clarified in a comprehensive and detailed review of paradoxical therapeutic techniques, no therapy can be considered strictly "paradoxical." It would be virtually impossible to follow a consistently therapeutic course of action that consists strictly of paradoxical prescriptions, messages, and injunctions. By the same token, most therapeutic schools acknowledge the need for paradoxical strategies, defined as the active use of indirect and circular interventions in addition to traditionally direct and linear approaches. By linear, we mean a gradual, straightforward, step-by-step sequence toward a stated goal. By circular, or paradoxical, we mean a single context-oriented, usually indirect and unexpected intervention that typically represents a jump that circumvents most of the steps in a linear intervention. Paradoxical strategies have thus added to the traditional therapeutic armamentarium but were never meant to displace it. L'Abate (1986) has found these strategies useful in the first stages of therapy, to deal with initial resistances toward change and in chronically rigid family patterns. However, these strategies lose their usefulness in the secondary and tertiary stages of therapy, after the effectiveness and competence of the therapist have been established and the client needs to learn new skills that go beyond the initial reason for referral.

A basic issue here is whether a therapist needs to subscribe to a paradoxical view of human nature in order to use paradoxical strategies effectively. Furthermore, what theoretical framework does one need to encourage and support the use of such strategies? As

Seltzer (1986) has amply demonstrated, most therapeutic schools accept the possibility of using these strategies, rationalizing, of course, different terminologies. Therefore, it really does not matter whether one subscribes to a paradoxical view of human nature, provided one can deliver these strategies effectively and responsibly, in a manner that is consistent with one's theoretical assumptions.

One needs to acknowledge the degree to which these strategies have threatened established, monadic views of behavior as linearly and internally caused, as in the stimulus-response paradigm, rather than in multidetermined (equipotential) and equifinal, contextually related transactions (Seltzer, 1986). By the same token, one could argue that many marital and family relationships show repetitive patterns that echo learned patterns from families of origin, which are beyond the conscious awareness of the individuals involved. Another threat to established therapeutic schools comes from the sheer ability to obtain change in behaviors that may have been deemed impossible to change. These strategies force one to rethink favored theoretical assumptions and therapeutic approaches and learn new habits of thinking and intervening that have not been part of the training and experience of most therapists.

Basic Concepts Behind Paradoxical Interventions

Seltzer (1986) concluded that "A paradoxical strategy refers to a therapist directive or attitude that is perceived by the client, at least initially, as contrary to therapeutic goals, but which is yet rationally understandable and specifically devised by the therapist to achieve these goals" (p. 10). A family comes in for help with a worldview that finds metaphorical expression in the symptom(s) or in the symptomatic (possibly scapegoated) identified patient (IP). This view is based on and made up of, among others, a sense of helplessness ("Everything we have tried has failed—we don't know what to do"), rigid digitality (either/or), acontextualism, powerlessness, negativity. This view is now contradicted in part by the therapist, by two directives: "Stay the same" and/or a positive reason for or explanation of the symptom as "good" for the family (keeping the family together, showing protectiveness, caring, sacrifice). The IP, instead of being viewed as either the victim or the persecutor of the family, is now described as the savior, the rescuer, the hero or heroine. In one way or another, the negative reason for referral is turned into a positive one, and the originally symptomatic behavior is not only accepted but encouraged. This view is then bolstered by prescriptions for continuing the symptomatic behavior and accepting the disturbing behavior with a minimal expenditure of energy. For example, the following might be suggested: This family needs to continue behaving as it has in the past, focusing on the symptom with a new, positive perspective! The symptom is good for the family! It is no longer an enemy! It is a friend (Weeks & L'Abate, 1982)! What would happen to the family without it? It might fall apart. It might change (God forbid!). It might even get better, but at what cost?

70

Rationales, either conceptual or practical, for paradoxical strategies are as numerous as the authors who have written about them (Bogdan, 1982; Cade, 1985, Cronen, Johnson, & Lannamann, 1982; Deissler, 1985; deShazer & Nunnally, 1985; Frankl, 1985; Jordan, 1985; L'Abate, 1985; Seltzer, 1986; Tennen, Eron, & Rohrbaugh, 1985; Weeks & L'Abate, 1982). Because we have no specific, empirical evidence to support one theory over another, this conceptual background leaves much to be desired. In this veritable Tower of Babel, time and research will eventually weed out the irrelevant and trivial from the relevant and important. At this time, readers can have their pick, adopting any plausible rationale for supporting the use of paradoxical strategies, as long as they are comfortable in using them creatively and responsibly and as long as they obtain results!

Basic Paradoxical Strategies

As a method, paradoxical strategies usually follow four main steps, preceded, however, by a preamble and followed by prescriptions of relapse: (a) positive reframing of the referral symptom; with a (b) prescription of this behavior; (c) in a ritualistic fashion, which includes (d) the whole family or the relevant social context (L'Abate et al., 1986; Lankton & Lankton, 1985; Seltzer, 1986; Weeks & L'Abate, 1982). The following steps, although derived from work with families, can be applied to individuals and to couples.

Preamble

A paradoxical prescription usually needs to be introduced by at least two comments. One will predict doom and gloom ("Things are going to get worse before they get better if we are going to do any good"); the other introduces positive reframing, which will not allow the family to disqualify either the therapist or the prescription. For example: "I know this is going to sound crazy to you, but at the present I really do not know what to do with you. I am kind of overwhelmed by all of this. Very likely this is not going to work, but let's try it. If this does not work, we will try something else." Or, "Please bear with me—I know you will think this is stupid, but it's probably not going to work anyway."

Positive Reframing

At least two different sets of positive reframings can be made about seeking professional help. The first set has to do with asking for help in general: "Only strong families ask for help—weak ones don't"; "You asked for help because you care about each other—is that right?" Usually this set of initial reframings does not and does not need to lead to any specific out-of-the-office prescription. At the most the reframings provide family members with an opportunity to express their love for each other verbally and nonverbally right there and then, an expression that is usually forgotten in times of crisis and hardship (L'Abate, 1985). The reframing is the least used and discussed in the literature on therapeutic paradox, but in the more than 20 years that it has been used by L'Abate, it has never failed to produce a much more positive response in the family and to reduce resistance to a considerable degree, making the next set of positive reframings easier to deliver.

The second set of reframings is what most of the literature has concentrated upon. That is the positive reinterpretation of the referral symptom in a new framework, one that the family has failed to consider: "Johnny must have put a great deal of effort in bringing you all together"; "Ann should be congratulated for assuming the role of patient. As long as she is 'sick' [misbehaving, robbing banks], you are going to be together as a family and you won't need to change, because all of you will have selflessly concentrated on her and let go of yourselves." These reframings bring about what the family probably expects and needs, a positive affirmation of the entire family that will provide some hope of relief.

Prescription

Prescriptions may be directed toward different aspects of the symptom (L'Abate et al., 1986). Basically, however, from the positive reframings described, one can derive two different sorts of prescriptions. The first consists essentially of asking the family to do exactly what they have been doing, staying the same ("Do not change a thing!"), because doing something new would be dangerous for the welfare of the whole family: "If you did something new, different, and positive, this family might fall apart"; or "Each of you may become independent of each other and leave"; or "As long as you stay the same, you can be reassured that you will be dependent on each other." One may put some teeth into this general prescription by specifying in greater detail the assignment of repetitive patterns in the family. Consequently, specific times (frequencies and durations) and places may be assigned for carrying out the prescription: "Be sure to have a fight at least three times next week on Monday, Wednesday, and Friday, at 9 o'clock in the dining room."

The second type of prescription requires the family to do something new, different, and positive, such as listening to a letter addressed to the IP, a letter that contains the positive reinterpretation of the symptom and requests that the symptomatic behavior be repeated on command, sometimes specifying times, places, and frequencies of the behavior, leading, therefore, to a ritualization of the symptom. The following example of positive reframings has been used in relationship to depression (Jessee & L'Abate, 1985; L'Abate, 1986). When depression is admitted, the therapist can respond, for example: "I am glad to hear that you are depressed; usually, only people who care and who are responsible get depressed"; or "Depression could become a friend rather than an enemy"; or "Which would you like to do: Would you prefer that the depression control you and your family, or would you like to control the depression?" From these reframings it would follow that depression is a favorable condition provided one learns to control it. L'Abate (1986) has developed a series of systematic written homework assignments that are now being studied in comparison to similar assignments based on Beck's cognitive approach to depression (Levis, 1987).

L'Abate (1985) has contended that a great many so-called paradoxical strategies allow the therapist to gain and keep control, yielding this control to the family once the depressed person has learned to control the symptom. Control is achieved by starting rather than trying to stop the symptom, repeating the procedures frequently enough to achieve a sense of the mastery and of power that has been lost in the struggle for control and that is exemplified by the development of the symptom itself. The prescription, of course, is a way to accept, enlarge, and amplify the symptom rather than fight it head-on, trying to change it without seeming to change it.

Ritualization

L'Abate (1985) has maintained that to help families establish or reestablish a sense of control, the symptomatic behavior needs to be prescribed for definite, prearranged times (e.g., Mondays, Wednesdays, and Fridays) for definite periods of time (e.g., 1 hour, 30 minutes, or 15 minutes). It is important also to keep a running, written account of what goes on during these periods ("You need to get depressed at least three times a week for at least a half-hour each time. Get yourself a notebook. During that half-hour allow yourself to become as depressed as possible and write down everything that comes into your mind while you are depressed").

A written message that would take only a few minutes for the parents to deliver to the IP child may need to be delivered once or twice a week, at a specified, prearranged time, such as after the evening meal on Friday. Temper tantrums or episodes of sibling rivalry may be scheduled when the father is at home and they can take place in a safe environment, with both parents taking notes on how long the tantrum or episodes of sibling rivalry last, the occasion for the tantrum, what the child(ren) say during this forced behavior, the outcome. Ritualization (and predictability), then, becomes the sine qua non for learning control and mastery ("If you are doing something, you may as well do it well"; "You need to practice your tantrums [sibling rivalry] so that you will become the best tantrum thrower [best rivals] in the world").

Involvement of the Whole Family

It may be important, though probably not imperative, to include in the ritualization as many people as are involved with the symptom, especially the so-called well siblings or the normal, asymptomatic spouse. In marital depression, for instance, it may be important for the asymptomatic spouse to **remind** the symptom bearer to do the assigned homework. In families, the so-called well sibling(s) may be enlisted as "spies" (they usually fulfill this function anyway) to **remind** the parents about what they need to do (read a written message, start the temper tantrum) concerning the IP sibling, "who really makes you look good." In sibling rivalry, for instance, the parents would prescribe rivalry to the siblings who are involved in it ("They love each other so much that they need to keep in continuous communication with each other"). Instead of the symptomatic behavior taking place "spontaneously," the family is asked to begin to take responsibility for it.

Prescription of Relapse

If the symptomatic behavior fails to appear, the therapist should express surprise, chagrin, even disappointment. Under no circumstances should the therapist praise the family for this "failure." Things did not go as the therapist wanted! The therapist needs to question whether this failure was not indeed a "freak" occurrence ("flight into health") or whether there is hope that the symptom will reappear ("Remember that there may be something useful in the symptom if it failed to reappear"; "What would you do without it?"). Therefore, it would help if the family made a concerted effort to make this behavior come back, with specific instructions (parroting whatever was done in the past) on how the behavior can be made to appear again ("I am really worried that otherwise things will get worse").

This sequence of steps as a whole is invariant. Of course, there are exceptions to the rule, depending on the symptom, family composition, stage of life cycle. One can deliver the prescription in writing (L'Abate et al., 1986) to avoid distortions, repressions, and deletions. This is an important practice, especially when a message needs to be delivered from one part of the family (e.g., the parents) to another part of the family (e.g., the children).

What makes paradoxical strategies different from linear ones is either an injunction to **stay the same** ("I would not change a thing for the next week [month] if I were you"), or to accept, even exaggerate, the symptom. Although linear procedures are frontal attacks on the symptom, paradoxical strategies aim at joining the symptom rather than fighting it. Three possibilities are available to therapists: (a) the symptom gets worse, (b) the symptom gets better, or (c) the symptom remains the same. Linear procedures are oriented toward making the symptom "better" through patient, gradual, planned sequences of steps, much like the procedures followed in the physical sciences and medicine. If the symptom does not get better through this approach, then paradoxical strategies fill a vacuum in the armamentarium of the therapist. They allow at least two other possibilities: making the symptom better by making it worse or making it better by keeping it the same. In this way a therapist can use therapeutic shortcuts, which, however, take as much skill and sensitivity as any traditional linear sequence.

This approach suggests that a responsible and caring therapist needs to be careful in assessing how a family will react and cooperate. It is usually much safer to institute linear procedures first. If these procedures fail, paradoxical strategies can be brought to the rescue. Here is where the therapist's skills come into play: When should one decide to go which way? Is the therapist justified in instituting paradoxical strategies right off the bat? Is a careful diagnosis and evaluation necessary before doing anything? What are the characteristics of the symptoms, individuals, couples, and families that will respond to which type of approach? Naturally, these are the questions that any responsible therapist needs to ask and for which there are still few answers. The individual judgment of the therapist is the decisive factor here. How many risks is she or he willing to take? How comfortable is he or she in working with what kind of approach? A great many of these questions can be answered by instituting prescriptions of one kind or another right from the beginning of therapy, even if the first three sessions are labeled "evaluation" (as L'Abate does): "You need to evaluate us, to see whether you are comfortable here and whether you think we can help." Homework assignments can vary--the administration of questionnaires, forms requiring consensus from the family members, rating scales, even the assignment of a similar task to see whether the family can and will follow instructions. If the family is too upset to even get together at home and work on this type of assignment, it usually indicates that the family will need more powerful interventions, such as paradoxical strategies, to break down rigidly established patterns.

These strategies greatly increase the range of treatment approaches available to therapists. They offer new, creative ways of dealing with symptoms, upsets, and crises, which were not available a generation ago. They are not, however, a panacea.

Illustrations and Applications

The literature on paradoxical strategies is chock-full of reports of magic and miraculous outcomes (Weeks & L'Abate, 1982). There is an embarrassment of riches in single-case, impressionistic clinical reports. In one case study, Bergman (1983) reported how ferocious parental criticism of children in two "fused" families was prescribed, with long-term positive outcome **as far as the specific behavior was concerned**. The parents did stop the criticism, to the delight of their children. However, the parents were still left to deal with their own depression. Changes took place in specific individuals and their interrelationships, but there were still lots of loose ends hanging on the patients (which Bergman did not deal with). This exemplifies one of the many reasons why L'Abate (1986) believes that paradoxical strategies may be useful in the beginning of therapy, for the short haul, but inadequate for long-term change.

Proponents of these strategies have claimed to cure everything from phobias, insomnia, encopresis, nail biting, bed-wetting, and temper tantrums, to sibling rivalry, marital depression, marital fighting, and more. In this section we will present examples of particularly creative uses of paradox as employed by clinicians from different theoretical backgrounds. As will become obvious, these psychodynamic-existential, behavioral, and strategic therapists have successfully integrated paradoxical strategies into their clinical work.

Frankl (1985), for example, described the case of a 35-year-old married female who was a patient at a polyclinic where Frankl had been invited to present a lecture. The patient had a 3-year history of severe hand-washing compulsion. She would wash her hands more than 100 times a day. She would not leave her house for fear of exposure to bacteria and prohibited her husband from touching their children for fear that he would infect them. The patient was institutionalized because of several suicide attempts and wanted a divorce because she felt she had made her family unhappy.

In addition to her obsessions and compulsions about cleanliness, the patient apparently was also afraid that she might become psychotic. Before the lecture audience, Frankl asked the patient if she had a "tendency to check the door many times" or to "check several times whether the gas valve is really closed." The patient readily admitted to such behaviors. Frankl proceeded to tell her that she had an unusual "anakistic" character disorder. Luckily, he told her, this disorder signified that she was completely immune to ever developing a psychosis.

Upon hearing this positive reframing of her symptoms, the patient seemed much relieved. Frankl went on to suggest, "You need not fight your obsessions. You may as well joke about them." The patient was invited to follow Frankl in stooping down and rubbing hands along the lecture floor. Frankl declared, "Instead of fearing infection, let's invite it!"

Within 5 days "90% of the symptoms" were alleviated. In a matter of weeks the 3-year problem was reportedly fully resolved. The patient's washing compulsions and obsessions stopped, and she was able to return to a normal routine. Frankl described his procedure as an example of paradoxical intention: "to do or wish for that whereof [the patient] is afraid" (p. 105).

Another example of dealing successfully with the symptom but failing to deal with its context is illustrated by L'Abate's experience with a polarized couple. The husband, a professional man, defined himself unerringly and rigidly as "good"; his wife grudgingly accepted the role of the "bad person," "bad partner," "bad mother." He would accede to all the material wishes of his children, never saying no to them, and cast his wife in the role of limit-setter and naysayer. It followed from this clear-cut definition and powerful polarization of long standing (more than 20 years of a miserable marriage) that he did not need any professional help but that his wife, of course, did. Individual therapy with her did little to improve the situation. One of their two daughters became pregnant out of wedlock as a teenager and aborted the child.

The mother felt that both daughters in their adolescence hated her for setting limits and refusing to fulfill extravagant requests for money, clothes, and cars. She felt that their third child, a son of elementary school age, was very close to her and could perhaps escape the deleterious effects of the polarization in the marriage. Individual therapy was discontinued once she became aware that, in some ways, she was in a dependency trap partly of her own making. No suggestion, advice, or recommendations helped her in getting out of this painful relationship. She would manage to fail in carrying out any instruction; her depression was rampant and reduced considerably her level of functionality.

Six years later, when her two daughters, now adult, had left home, she asked for help again, trying also to get her husband into treatment. After an initial visit designed to convince the therapist of his great, inherent "goodness," which did not require help but admiration, he refused treatment because he "did not need it." After a while, he refused to pay the therapy bills for his wife, making it difficult if not impossible for her to continue private treatment.

Shortly after treatment was terminated, she telephoned, very agitated. Her husband had given their son, now in puberty, a dirt-bike; after a couple of years of running in the backyard, the bike was old and run-down. The son wanted to trade it for a full-sized motorcycle. The father was willing, in spite of the fact that it was illegal for a 12-year-old to drive it, even in the driveway or backyard of their home. She was frantic. She not only was worried about the safety of her son's life, but she felt that by opposing this transaction she would alienate her son even further. By this time the son's love had been "bought" by the father, with gifts such as the dirt-bike and other items clearly unsuitable for a child his age.

This was a critical situation. If the father bought the motorcycle for the son, she would be even further alienated from the son. She was, of course, already alienated from the husband and slept in a separate bedroom. She was told that if she wanted to correct the situation, she would have to follow the therapist's instructions to the letter. She agreed to do so. She was instructed to call her son and have him bring her the catalog he had been using for selecting the motorcycle he wanted. Because of his size, he had set his sights on one of small size (to begin with!). She was to suggest that perhaps this size was too small--after all, he was a growing boy! Would he not like a much bigger motorcycle? Furthermore, what about all the other options? Why not add an extra mirror, and so on? Of course, this suggestion was prefaced by the acknowledgment that it would sound "crazy" to her and that it might not work. It was a last-ditch effort to see whether she would play a much more benign role than she had been playing in the past. It did sound crazy to her, and she could not understand the rationale for it, even though the rationale had been explained in all the previous therapy sessions (approximately 15) in terms of polarization in the marriage and dependency in her. However, she was desperate enough to be willing to try anything, even something "crazy."

She called next, having implemented the suggestion to the letter (and well!), on a Saturday morning, crying. Her husband and child had just left the house to trade in the dirt-bike for the desired motorcycle. She described how her son, after she asked whether indeed he would not want a bigger size machine with additional options, looked at her, speechless, turned abruptly and ran out of the room, screaming to his father at the top of his lungs: "Dad, Dad, she wants me to buy a bigger cycle!"

It looked as if the suggestion had not worked at all. The only thing to do was to commiserate with each other about a botched-up attempt. We had really failed and let her down. She asked for another therapist in a public mental health clinic nearer to her home, one whose fees she could afford out of her pocket money. She was given the names of three public mental health clinics close to her part of town. Goodbyes were said, with best wishes for good luck. She called back in the afternoon to report that her husband and son had come back from their trade-in expedition, both in a very bad mood, without a new trade-in and with just the old dirt-bike. Her husband refused to say anything to her and went directly to his office; her son tearfully reported to her, "Dad changed his mind on the way there and did not want to buy a motorcycle anymore!"

A few weeks after this episode, the husband left home, departing with a younger woman on his staff. The battle had been won, but it upset the applecart of the marriage. The husband could no longer play the "good" guy. The wife had upstaged and preempted him and could no longer play the role of the "bad gal!"

A more systematic attempt to deliver paradoxical injunctions or prescription is through written letters, a practice described in detail in L'Abate et al. (1986). They described a variety of letters designed to deal with a variety of oppositional, resistant, and rigid family patterns. One of the most illustrative of a paradoxical approach is the one that L'Abate and Samples (L'Abate et al., 1986, p. 133) have used with couples who show a strong avoidance of intimacy by failing to follow therapeutic directives (such as meeting once a week at established times and durations "to fight") missing appointments but rescheduling them after a big fight. These couples do not seem to get better; in fact, they seem to get worse after 6 months to 1 year of therapy. The following is a sample of an intimacy letter given to couples of this type:

Dear Helen and Bob,

After working with you for so long, I am fairly convinced that you need to defeat each other to avoid getting close. Emotional closeness can be a very scary and dangerous condition, and I can understand how it affects you in that way. For some people, intimacy means loss of control, loss of mind, loss of self, loss of strength, and in some cases, loss of life.

Therefore, I have no recourse but to recommend that you keep defeating each other as much as you can so that defeats will allow a certain amount of distance between you two. This distance will protect you, to some extent, from the risk of getting hurt. If you are not willing to risk hurt, you can also protect each other from the threat of closeness. This distance may be necessary for each of you at this time, to deal with your own depression and the depression in the marriage.

Your current relationship may not be very comfortable, but it is the only close relationship you have allowed each other to experience. At this moment, it would be premature and ill-advised for you to try to get too close. It may indeed be dangerous.

In conclusion, I suggest that you keep up the good work, fight without appointments, keep on defeating each other, as you have done well in the past, and try not to change how you behave with each other, lest you get dangerously close.

The most immediate outcome of this type of letter is that it helps delineate the motivation to stay in the marriage, sometimes by bringing up hidden agendas (i.e., an ongoing affair) or precipitating a decisive move by one partner (i.e., calling a lawyer for separation, getting a job, getting fired from a job). Most couples come back in a much more reflective and less belligerent mood, asking questions about what it means to be close, becoming aware that closeness is a totally alien experience to them as individuals and as a couple. This increased reflection allows more constructive discussion and an admission of depressive patterns and the inability to share past and present hurts (L'Abate, 1986).

Another way to deal with extremely polarized, stressed couples who fight a great deal is to assign their fighting (i.e., "arguments") at appointed times and for specified durations (Mondays, Wednesdays, and Fridays, or on weekends at 8 p.m., and only for 1 hour), and to write down what happens during the argument. Six "suicidal" patterns are described in detail and given to them in writing to remind them to follow the instructions to the letter!

Please Note: If you want to argue or fight really, really dirty to ensure that both of you will lose, disregard these guidelines. You may also follow part of these guidelines and ignore other parts or withdraw completely and avoid confrontation. In this way you will ensure that your arguments will go on. If you are interested in making sure that both you and your partner fail at arguments, as well as in other parts of your life, you may not only ignore these guidelines but also find something wrong with the author (he also is no darned good!).

1. Be sure to set an appointment date for the fight or argument at least 24 hours in advance. It will be most helpful if you can agree (although it may be impossible) to argue on a regular schedule, such as at a specific time on Mondays, Wednesdays, and Fridays, or only on weekends.

2. Just before the fight is to start, set a timer or an alarm clock for 1 hour. STOP the argument as soon as the alarm rings. If your argument is not finished, schedule the time for another argument at least 24 hours in advance, then separate and go as far away from each other in the house as your house (and your partner) will allow. When you meet for a second argument, before the argument starts, make sure you set the timer for 1 hour.

3. During or after the argument, make detailed written notes of what happened. Tape-record the argument if you can; listen to it afterward, taking notes to comment on what you think or feel was going on during the argument.

4. Follow as much as you can the following six suicidal patterns that typify most couples in trouble. If you follow a suicidal pattern not contained in these instructions, please make abundant notes of this new pattern, describe it in detail, and bring it up the next time we meet. Remember, in arguing, try to follow these SIX SUICIDAL PATTERNS as closely as you can:

(a) In arguing, use "you" statements exclusively, accusing, blaming, and name-calling each other as much as you can. For instance, use "You never" and "You always" statements as much as possible. Do not use either "I" or "we" statements under any conditions.

(b)   Keep bringing up the past in as much negative detail as possible. Keep remembering dates, places, situations, and occasions where you were hurt deeply. Keep on hurting each other by reliving as much as possible all of the painful experiences in this relationship that have obviously been the fault of your partner. See if each of you can top the other in remembering as many painful details as possible. Do not forget (let alone forgive!) a single past hurt!

(c)   Read each other's minds. Try to tell each other what the other one thinks or feels. Disclose to each other all the evil intentions each of you knows about the other. Bring up all the nasty and dirty thoughts or feelings that your partner is guilty of thinking and feeling, let alone doing.

(d)   Use emotional blackmail and bribery, for instance, "If you do not do what I want, I will leave you"; "If you do not give me what I want, I will call the lawyer"; "Either you quit drinking [gambling], or I will take the children away."

(e)   As part of d, give each other ultimatums. Threaten each other with the worst possible consequences that can follow from your partner's behavior. Specify dates and circumstances of your ultimatum.

(f)   Make as many excuses as you can to justify your own behavior, especially by using your partner's behavior as an excuse: "I did such and such because you did such and such." Do not allow your partner to make any excuses for his or her behavior. Follow the principle that it is perfectly acceptable to behave miserably as long as your partner behaves miserably too!

HAVE A GOOD ARGUMENT!

The most immediate result of this assignment, of course, is the realization that under these conditions no creative or constructive negotiation is possible. The couple, then, needs to decide whether they want to continue arguing ("Do you want the fighting to control you and the marriage, or do you want to control the fighting?"). Once a constructive agreement is reached, these couples may be assigned a series of written homework assignments dealing with depression, or if depression does not seem present, a series of written homework assignments to learn negotiation skills. If they complete this series successfully, they are given a series of written homework assignments dealing with intimacy (L'Abate, 1986).*

Madanes (1981) described a paradoxical treatment of a depressed, 60-year-old married male. The man complained of a 5-year history of depression, of feeling ineffectual, and of neglecting his business. He described his wife as a therapist who had tried to offer support and advice but had failed to help him with his problem.

In supervising this case, Madanes first arranged to reframe the patient's depression as "irresponsibility." Rather than supporting him, his wife was instructed to call her husband every day at work to check up on his business activities. The patient reacted to this "supervision" and began to take control of his work life.

In addition, over a series of several session, Madanes instructed the patient to "pretend" to be depressed, irresponsible, and inadequate at various times during the week. This creative variant of symptom prescription ("Is he really depressed, or is he simply pretending to be?") resulted in a further increase in the husband's "responsible" behaviors, an increased sense of control, and a decrease in levels of depression.

This treatment lasted for seven sessions. According to self-report, the patient improved dramatically and maintained gains at 4- and 8-month follow-ups. Madanes attributed the success of the intervention to an alteration of the power imbalance between the depressed man and his wife. By reframing the problem and by prescribing "pretend" symptomatic behavior, Madanes conceptualized that a significant change had taken place in the repetitive marital interactions that seemed to maintain the depressive symptomatology.

The preceding illustrations of paradoxical maneuvers are rather representative in that they offer rich descriptions of patients' presenting problems and of the types of procedures developed to resolve them. Unfortunately, they are also lacking in the kinds of experimental controls that provide clear evidence that (a) the patient has indeed changed and (b) the paradoxical procedure was solely responsible for this change.

In contrast to this tradition, the following case illustrates the combined use of greater experimental rigor and the creative, flexible interventions that are characteristic of the growing behavioral literature on paradoxical approaches.

Milan and Kolko (1982) reported the difficulties of a 33-year-old female who requested treatment for anxiety about her self-

---

*A series of written modules for the definition, positive reframing, and prescription of arguments, sibling rivalry, and temper tantrums is available on request from Dr. L'Abate.

perceived high incidence of "malodorous flatulence" (p. 168). The patient described having suffered from this condition for approximately 10 years. A series of consultation with internists and dynamic psychotherapists resulted in no improvement in her ruminations. These problems tended to interfere with her social and work-related activities, as the patient often assumed that others were reacting to her possible malodorous flatulence.

To get baseline data the clinicians initially asked the patient to self-record the intensity of every gaseous emission. However, the patient reported that this record keeping interfered with her daily activities. Thus, instead, she was requested to pause after every hour and estimate the perceived frequency and intensity of the emissions that had occurred during the preceding hour. This resulted in an average perceived "flatus score," which was calculated weekly.

After 4 weeks on baseline, an attempt was made to treat the problem by challenging the patient's "misconceptions" concerning the frequency and intensity of her self-recorded emissions. The clinicians had a colleague chemically analyze the patient's undergarments. Despite the technician's negative findings of any evidence of chemical by-products associated with flatulence, the patient continued to ruminate consistently about her supposed "condition."

Finally, the clinicians opted for a paradoxical intervention. The patient was asked to "focus on each gaseous urge and sensation and when each occurred, to force flatulence in order to expel her flatulence thoroughly and completely." The rationale was that eliminating gaseous content completely would clear her system of the bacteria that had maintained and worsened her problem with flatulence.

Following this procedure, there was an immediate and sustained reduction in perceived flatus scores. The patient reported that she had tried to expel flatus but that she had had difficulty doing so. The episodes and ruminations were significantly reduced, and 1-year follow-up showed maintenance of gains.

This example illustrates the flexible use of paradox in the treatment of unusual presenting problems. Although the procedure worked, the authors acknowledged that the "principles underlying the effects of paradoxical procedures have yet to be fully explicated" (p. 170). Theories and illustrations of paradox abound, but experimental verification of the precise mechanics of change is sorely lacking.

Current Evidence to Support Paradoxical Interventions

This section is not an exhaustive survey of the empirical literature, because most of it has been reviewed in the publications already cited. In fact, we have avoided the repetition of previously cited studies and focused on studies that have not been reviewed elsewhere (Seltzer, 1986; Shoham-Salomon & Rosenthal, 1987; Weeks

& L'Abate, 1982). The Delphi study, by Watson (1985), concerning the definition of paradoxical strategies by leading exponents of this approach found, as noted in the introduction to this chapter, a tremendous variety of definitions but practically no consensus on how to intervene paradoxically. These results were supported by lengthy interviews (Bopp, 1985), with four prominent therapists (Carl Rogers, Robert Langs, Arnold Lazarus, Ivan Boszormenyi-Nagy).

For an in-depth review of the different perspectives about how paradoxical strategies change behavior, see Seltzer (1985), the standard, milestone text on which to base research. According to the evidence reviewed by Ascher, Bowers, and Schotte (1985) and by Katz (1984) concerning insomnia and other monosymptomatic, supposedly acontextual problems (e.g., phobias, fears, and habit disorders) that do not otherwise seriously affect other areas of functioning, paradoxical strategies, especially with very resistant cases, may indeed be the treatment of choice.

Fortunately for this field, empirical evidence has been slow but sure in accumulating. Most of this evidence seems to show some positive, short-term outcomes. A meta-analysis of 12 relevant studies by Shoham-Salomon & Rosenthal (1987) found that this type of intervention was effective, but no more effective than traditional linear interventions. However, 1 month after termination, "paradoxical interventions showed relatively greater effectiveness than other treatments." This analysis suggested the advantages that derive from positive reframing but raised "serious doubts" about the effectiveness of symptom prescription that does not follow a positive connotation. In other words, families need some kind of rationale that will explain the prescription of the symptom so that they can accept it uncritically. This conclusion has been supported by the study of Wilcoxon and Fenell (1986), who used both linear and circular letters, repeating in part the methodology, developed by L'Abate, Wagner, and Weeks (quoted in Seltzer, 1986, and in Weeks & L'Abate, 1982), to lure the nonattending spouse into marital therapy. These letters, given to the attending spouses, warned about the possible dangers when just one spouse stays in therapy. Of the nonattending spouses who received the linear letters, 33 of 48 agreed to accompany the spouse in therapy; of the 48 nonattending spouses who received the paradoxical letters, only 18 agreed to attend, a statistically significant difference. Unfortunately, in this study as well as in the L'Abate et al. study, it was found to be very difficult to differentiate between linear and circular content in the letters. Most of the reframing by Wilcoxon and Fenell referred to the "hazards" of not being in therapy rather than praising the nonattending spouse for protecting the status quo in the marriage by not coming into therapy, as a truly (if there is such a thing!) paradoxical strategy would have it.

In a further attempt to assess the effectiveness of positive reframing and symptom prescription (L'Abate, 1986; Weeks & L'Abate,

84

1982) Levis (1987) compared the effectiveness of written paradoxical and cognitive (following Beck) systematic homework assignments in the treatment of moderate to severe depression. Initial results failed to demonstrate improvement in response to the paradoxical assignments, but some subjects who received the cognitive-based assignments showed marked initial improvements in levels of depression.

Obviously, one goal of paradoxical assignments is to evoke "defiance-based" behavior. Perhaps the paradoxical assignments failed to stimulate the depressed clients to respond with rebellious behavior. It may be that such clients need more tailor-made assignments.

These and similar research efforts (Ascher et al., 1985) will, we hope, clarify the procedures that are necessary and sufficient for the successful application of paradoxical strategies.

Conclusion

Paradoxical strategies in psychotherapy have allowed therapists of different theoretical persuasions to expand and extend their therapeutic interventions to deal with cases, symptoms, or relationships that a generation ago we might have been leery of approaching or might have approached with a sense of hopelessness and failure. These strategies, if they had not achieved any other outcome, have sparked debate and increased interest, hope, and even enthusiasm in the whole therapeutic enterprise. They may not be any more successful or effective than any other linear approach, but they seem to have helped quite a few therapists cope with seemingly hopeless situations. There is no question that further empirical evidence, especially concerning the long-term effectiveness of these interventions, needs to be accumulated. As with most if not all therapeutic techniques, these strategies have given some therapists an increased sense of mastery and of success. In the cold atmosphere of the laboratory this increased sense of mastery may not account for much, but in the loaded emotional atmosphere of the therapy office, it certainly does help to recognize that one can fall back on these strategies when everything else seems to fail. They may be an escape hatch and a back door to boot, but they come in handy, particularly when the therapist's creative efforts have been met by resistance and even failure.

References

Ascher, L. M., Bowers, M. R., & Schotte, D. E. (1985). A review of data from controlled case studies and experiments evaluating the clinical efficacy of paradoxical intervention. In G. R. Weeks (Ed.), Promoting change through paradoxical therapy (pp. 216-250). Homewood, IL: Dow Jones-Irwin.

Bergman, J. S. (1983). Prescribing family criticism as a paradoxical intervention. Family Process, 22, 517-522.

Bogdan, J. L. (1982). Paradoxical communication as interpersonal influence. Family Process, 21, 443-452.

Bopp, M. J. (1985). Contradiction and its resolution among psychotherapies: Results of a preliminary investigation. In G. R. Weeks (Ed.), Promoting change through paradoxical therapy (pp. 271-301). Homewood, IL: Dow Jones-Irwin.

Cade, B. W. (1985). Unpredictability and change: A holographic metaphor. In G. R. Weeks (Ed.), Promoting change through paradoxical therapy (pp. 28-59). Homewood, IL: Dow Jones-Irwin.

Cronen, V. E., Johnson, K. M., & Lannamann, J. W. (1982). Paradoxes, double-binds and reflexive loops: An alternative theoretical perspective. Family Process, 21, 91-112.

Deissler, K. G. (1985). Beyond paradox and counterparadox. In G. R. Weeks (Ed.), Promoting change through paradoxical therapy (pp. 60-98). Homewood, IL: Dow Jones-Irwin.

deShazer, S., & Nunnally, E. (1985). The mysterious affair of paradoxes and loops. In G. R. Weeks (Ed.), Promoting change through paradoxical therapy (pp. 252-270). Homewood, IL: Dow Jones-Irwin.

Frankl, V. E. (1985). Paradoxical intention. In G. R. Weeks (Ed.), Promoting change through paradoxical therapy (pp. 99-110). Homewood, Il: Dow Jones-Irwin.

Jessee, E. H., & L'Abate, L. (1985). Paradoxical treatment of depression in married couples. In L. L'Abate (Ed.), Handbook of family psychology and therapy (Vol. 1, pp. 1128-1151). Homewood, Il: Dorsey Press.

Jordan, J. R. (1985). Paradox and polarity: The Tao of family therapy. Family Process, 24, 165-174.

Katz, J. (1984). Symptom prescription: A review of the clinical outcome literature. Clinical Psychology Review, 4, 703-717.

L'Abate, L. (1985). Paradoxical techniques: One level of abstraction in family therapy. In G. R. Weeks (Ed.), Promoting change through paradoxical therapy (pp. 111-133). Homewood, IL: Dow Jones-Irwin.

L'Abate, L. (1986). Systematic family therapy. New York: Brunner/Mazel.

L'Abate, L., Ganahl, G., & Hansen, J. C. (1986). Methods of family therapy. Englewood Cliffs, NJ: Prentice-Hall.

Lankton, S. R., & Lankton, C. H. (1985). Ericksonian styles of paradoxical treatment. In G. R. Weeks (Ed.), Promoting change through paradoxical therapy (pp. 134-186). Homewood, IL: Dow Jones-Irwin.

Levis, M. (1987). Short-term treatment for depression using systematic homework assignments. Unpublished doctoral dissertation, Georgia State University, Atlanta.

Madanes, C. (1981). Strategic family therapy. San Francisco, CA: Jossey-Bass.

Milan, M., & Kolko, D. (1982). Paradoxical intention in the treatment of obsessional flatulence ruminations. Journal of Behavior Therapy and Experimental Psychiatry, 13, 167-172.

Seltzer, L. F. (1986). Paradoxical strategies in psychotherapy: A comprehensive overview and guidebook. New York: Wiley.

Shoham-Salomon, V., & Rosenthal, R. (1987). Paradoxical interventions: A meta-analysis. Journal of Consulting and Clinical Psychology, 55, 22-28.

Tennen, H., Eron, J. B., & Rohrbaugh, M. (1985). Paradox in content. In G. R. Weeks (Ed.), Promoting change through paradoxical therapy (pp. 187-214). Homewood, IL: Dow Jones-Irwin.

Watson, C. (1985). A Delphi study of paradox in therapy. In G. R. Weeks (Ed.), Promoting change through paradoxical therapy (pp. 2-25). Homewood, IL: Dow Jones-Irwin.

Weeks, G. R., & L'Abate, L. (1982). Paradoxical psychotherapy: Practice with individuals, couples, and families. New York: Brunner/Mazel.

Wilcoxon, S. A., & Fenell, D. L. (1986). Linear and paradoxical letters to the non-attending spouse: A comparison of engagement rates. Journal of Marital and Family Therapy, 12, 191-193.

CHAPTER 8

INTIMACY LETTERS—INVARIABLE PRESCRIPTION FOR CLOSENESS-AVOIDANT COUPLES

Luciano L'Abate, Ph.D. and Gregory T. Samples

ABSTRACT

The rationale and background for the use of intimacy letters with closeness-avoidant couples is explained. Five illustrative case studies are given to illustrate the use of these letters.

Letters have entered the armamentarium of therapists and have become another useful tool since the work of Selvini-Palazoli, Boscolo, Cecchin, and Prata (1978) and L'Abate (1977). A study by Weeks, Wagner, and L'Abate (1980) has shown that letters can produce significant changes in couples' self-reports. On the other hand, we are becoming increasingly aware of the importance of intimacy and close family relationships. The work of Waring and his associates (Waring, McElrath, Mitchell & Derry, 1981) does support the importance of this factor in the etiology of psychogenic and psychosomatic symptoms within the context of marital relationships. Jessee and L'Abate (submitted for publication) have argued that intimacy can serve as an antidote for marital depression. They have argued that marital depression arises from marital interactions that avoid any intimate reconciliation and sharing of hurt feelings and fears of being hurt (L'Abate, 1977; L'Abate, Weeks & Weeks, 1979). While most of the previous papers cited here, have laid the theoretical and conceptual groundwork for this thesis, the purpose of this paper is to describe the use of one letter we have used with couples who show the following characteristics of intimacy-avoidance:

1. *No visible progress in the course of long-term treatment.* Often these couples come in only during a crisis period but fail to carry through and remain in treatment after the crisis has subsided. Under these conditions the therapist can only apply short-term bandaids because s/he is limited in how and where to intervene—usually because of the short temporal perspective to treatment that many of these couples hold. Thus, treatment can be characterized by the metaphor of the roller coaster/see-saw marriage found in many of these couples.

2. *Continuation of self-other defeating patterns that eventually defeat the therapist and lead to therapeutic impasse.* Defeat is necessary for understanding the nature of the redundantly frustrating interactions that characterize the marriage. To admit defeat alone, as some therapists may do with these couples, is not enough. The defeat needs to be positively reframed as a necessary aspect of the interaction that helps the couple remain the same and continue avoiding intimacy.

3. *Inability to share with each other their deep personal feelings of hurt and fear of being hurt.* Some of these characteristics already have been described in part by L'Abate & L'Abate (1981). As the work of Waring and his associates (1981) has shown, intimacy and the negotiation of intimacy is a basic marital task that needs to be dealt with if further psychopathological consequences are to be avoided.

On the basis of these and other considerations (Jessee & L'Abate, SFP) two different strategies for helping couples learn to negotiate intimacy have been devised. One is based on a straightforward linear educational model that follows the general principles of structured enrichment programs (Sloan & L'Abate, research in progress). The other, based on more circular, cryptic, and therapeutic principles follows the general guidelines of paradoxical psychotherapy elaborated by Weeks and L'Abate (1982). This strategy is communicated in a letter to the couple from the therapist. Essentially in this letter:

1. Defeats are positively reframed and prescribed in terms of their being the glue that holds the marriage together and that helps both partners avoid intimacy.
2. Intimacy is described as a dangerous and difficult task that is almost impossible to obtain in a lifetime.
3. Skepticism is expressed about the changes the couple may have to undergo in reaching a satisfactory resolution of intimacy.

Even though the themes and tenor of the letter are the same for all couples, some variations are made to particularize each letter to the specific couple. This tailoring is done toward the end of the letter while the reframing of defeats remain intact for all letters. Five case studies wherein this letter was used follow. The details describing each couple have been changed to protect their identities.

Facsimile of Letter

Dear Mary and Joe:

After working with you for so long, I am fairly convinced that you need to defeat each other to avoid getting too close. Intimacy can be a very scary and dangerous condition, and I can understand how it affects you in that way. For some people, intimacy means loss of control, loss of mind, loss of self, loss of strength, and in some cases, loss of life. Therefore, I have no recourse but to recommend that you keep defeating each other, as much as you can, so the defeats will allow a certain amount of distance between you. That distance will protect you from risking hurt to some degree, but if you are not willing to risk hurt, you can also protect your partner from the threat of closeness. Part of the way that you folks have managed this distance is by allowing your family's depression to continue its current course. It may be that your relationship is so comfortable that you will want to continue on the present course for a while longer.

· ·Joe, please read this letter aloud to Mary each Monday, Wednesday, and Friday for the next six weeks.

COUPLE ONE

This couple consisted of Jerry, a 32-year-old male, and Barbara, a 33-year-old female. The therapist had seen Jerry to deal with his sometimes severe depression before he was married. This was a problem he had dealt with for years, but was also connected with his up-and-down relationship to Barbara who was living in another city at the time. Jerry had been in therapy before. Learning to use his depression, he had made significant progress in seeing his depression as a friend and in controlling it (L'Abate, submitted for publication).

The couple had been seen for several sessions before they were married and were encouraged to undertake more pre-marital counseling, but they felt everything was okay. Approximately one year later, Jerry called and said he needed help.

When the therapist talked to Jerry, he reported feeling trapped and wanted to run away. He indicated that he felt forced into the marriage because Barbara was in another city and he wanted to be with her. He also felt guilty because they had had sex before marriage and, therefore, he felt obligated to marry her. He felt frustrated during the entire marriage because of financial problems and Barbara's frequent threats of going home. She was often depressed as well. They were seen together for several weeks in an effort to deal with the depression and financial situation. After some initial, limited progress, their relationship grew steadily worse.

What Led to the Letter

It gradually became clear that therapy was not helping this couple because they were protecting each other by not expressing their real feelings, both at home and in the therapist's office. This process prevented therapy from being helpful by not being intimate. The therapist dealt with the couple for several sessions by concentrating on intimacy, including its paradoxes. However, these efforts produced limited gain and led to the therapist's writing the intimacy letter during a session in his office.

Outcome

When the therapist talked to the couple about the letter three weeks later, Jerry said that it was accurate—he had become very aware that being intimate did make him feel he was going to lose control. Barbara replied that she did not think the letter was accurate, and that it made her angry. Both reported that they had argued very little recently, and that they felt better about their relationship.

Several months later their relationship was vastly improved. They were seen less frequently. However, some problems remained. Jerry is experiencing great anger that he has difficulty in controlling, but is now expressing this appropriately to Barbara. He no longer is keeping it inside. In addition, he seems to realize that often the anger needs to be projected toward its source rather than his wife.

COUPLE TWO

Tim was a 31-year-old male; his wife, Dot, was also 31. Dot was the idenitified patient, with depression as the presenting symptom. Initially the couple was seen together. However, after some marital issues were dealt with, the wife was seen alone for quite a while. Treatment continued for 18 months. Sessions during most of this time were held about every two or three weeks.

Several issues were explored that seemed to be somewhat helpful in treatment: (a) Applying appropriate parenting skills; dealing with guilt that Dot learned in her role as a parental child in the family; and (b) dealing with some unhealthy ideas about religion.

The most substantial gain was a reduction of depression, when after about a year of treatment, the client revealed that there had been an incestuous relationship with her father for about a year when she was around 12 years old. She felt extreme guilt about this experience and having told someone about this trauma for the first time proved very helpful. More of the guilt and depression left as we explored some of the facts about incest as well her guilt and anger toward her father. This led into family-of-origin work and included a letter to her father, which she was not able to mail. Nevertheless, the letter helped her to work out some of her anger.

92

What Led to the Letter

After making consistent progress with her depression over a period of months while dealing with the above issues, a period of regression set in. For a while the depression was severe. It began to seem that the substantial progress Dot had made was about to be lost. After some insisting on the therapist's part, she agreed that we needed to work with both her and her husband again. Much of this work focused on the inability of either party to express feelings. Though the couple listened to what the therapist had to say about this lack of intimacy, it did not produce much change in the relationship. Consequently, the intimacy letter was written.

Outcome

After only two weeks, both partners reported that the letter helped them realize they really did not know each other. They both said that as they did their regular assignment of reading the letter, they felt strange about not realizing that they did not know each other.

Two months after writing the letter, Tim reported that they were very happy and that Dot was not depressed at all. He further indicated that they had been to see Dot's family and that she had not gotten upset at all (which was a departure from previous experiences). She reported that she was even able to relate better with her dad.

Six months after the letter, the therapy was terminated. They reported in a phone conversation that they were still talking and not hiding their feelings from each other as they once had done. Tim said, "We can really tell each other things we don't like." After six months, Dot's depression continued to be well controlled.

COUPLE THREE

This couple was referred after severe marital conflict that included homicidal and suicidal threats by the husband. He said that she was threatening to leave and take the children. He also said that she was not sharing sexually nor was she very open with her feelings. He was very jealous, which had some basis in that just recently she had had a brief affair. She indicated that he was a perfectionist and it was impossible to please him regardless of how she handled their relationship. It was impossible for her to be happy with someone who hit her and threw temper tantrums.

This couple was seen first on a weekly basis and then every other week for approximately four months. Early in treatment it was obvious that a primary problem was the wife's low self-esteem which led to

93

many placating responses on her part, although admittedly he took an active part in their system. Initially this insight seemed helpful but the couple gradually regressed back into the blame game. At this point the therapist suggested that if the husband was going to be accused of blaming, he might as well do it right. Again some progress was made but again it was short-lived.

What Led to the Letter

It was obvious that the wife continued to have difficulty expressing her feelings, which angered her husband. However, when she did express her views, he was often critical. This, of course, reduced the frequency of such expressions. It was obvious that since this game consistently prevented the couple from achieving intimacy, the intimacy letter would be dictated and assigned—to be read Monday, Wednesday, and Friday.

Results

The couple resisted reading the letter regularly over the course of the next month. The therapist tried various techniques to get them to read the letter but excuses always prevailed. Finally he framed the lack of response as fear of intimacy and suggested they not read the letter because it might be too frightening for them. The couple continued in therapy several more weeks until the husband suggested they stop coming. His wife wished to continue but when he became more insistent, the therapist suggested that the wife stop as well.

When the therapist called and talked to both of them about six months later, they were together but problems remained even though they indicated that progress had been made. The therapist's feeling was that the intimacy letter had helped underline for this couple their need for but fear and avoidance of intimacy.

COUPLE FOUR

This couple consisted of a 30-year-old male and his 26-year-old wife. Their basic concerns in coming to therapy were his insecurity, as well as his dependence on his wife. He indicated that he wanted to learn to be more assertive. His wife admitted being domineering and manipulating him much of the time. He also admitted that problems had resulted from his frequent bringing up the past. She was not satisfied with their sexual relationship in that she felt the foreplay was inadequate and that he did not seem interested in her needs in general.

Initially, a good deal of attention was given to the husband's self-sacrificing behaviors. We discussed priorities in the relationship and he agreed he needed to consider himself first in the relationship more often. He agreed that he behaved in this way to avoid rejection.

We used this issue to begin focusing on appropriate assertiveness. Both learned to use "I statements"; she learned to avoid manipulation and the need for him to be intimate in order to meet his own needs and express his real feelings. Both made some progress in this area, though his was identifiable in the way he related more to their son than to his wife. Before this training he had consistently given in to their five-year-old son and never disciplined him. After the training, the son was no longer able to use temper outbursts to control his father.

What Led to the Letter

During the seventh session the husband expressed a good deal of dissatisfaction about being forced into a mold in which he felt uncomfortable. Much of this dissatisfaction seemed to revolve around a disagreement the couple was having about spending money on house repairs. It appeared that he had not expressed his feelings very openly and this difficulty was framed as the couple having difficulty being intimate. We talked further about how power struggles can block intimacy.

The husband did not show up for the next session. His wife reported that counseling was making him nervous and that he felt he really wasn't changing that much. The therapist felt that his not coming probably was a result of his fear of intimacy, and that the intimacy letter would probably be a good way of following up on the previous session as well as consolidating gains that had already been made. It was also felt that this would be a way of including him in the session and getting him to return. If not, it could serve as a termination tool.

Results

At the next session the wife reported that he had read the letter regularly as assigned and had talked about it a great deal. She indicated that he really was working hard at the relationship but was still not sure he wanted to return. The therapist continued to work with her for several more sessions on family-of-origin issues and talked with both of them by phone about six months later. They reported that they felt good about where they were and that therapy was really helpful.

COUPLE FIVE

This couple was separated when they were first seen. He seemed critical and she played helpless to do anything about it. He said he did not like her friends, that she drank too much, did not clean the house, and cried for attention. She indicated she was angry because he was so critical of everything she did, had said he would work and did not, had threatened her by not doing things he promised to do, and regularly put her down in various ways.

Progress was slow initially but she did agree to move back in with him after about three weeks. Both linear and circular interventions were used but paradoxical tactics seemed to work best. This couple really seemed to fit the Victim-Persecutor-Rescuer triangle but gained little from talking about this difficulty until the therapist suggested that since they liked doing this so much maybe they should do it more often. The husband seemed to make some progress at this point, not only in giving up some of the persecuting, but also in doing some linear assignments to show his wife he did love her, such as taking her out and being affectionate other than sexually. However, she continued to be afraid of being victimized and therefore was not able to share her feelings with him. This infuriated him, and the situation grew progressively worse.

What Led to the Letter

Her inability to share her feelings made him feel rejected and unloved which prompted him to return to his old persecuting habits. The therapist framed their behavior as protecting each other because they were each afraid of feelings. This and other tactics met little success so the therapist decided to use the intimacy letter.

Results

The effectiveness of the letter was first sabotaged by the husband's unwillingness to read it aloud. The therapist then asked the wife to make a copy for both of them (which she failed to do for three weeks). He came to one more session but then said he was unwilling to come any longer because she was not trying. At this point she gave him his copy of the letter. One week later she reported things being somewhat better. However, the following week she said he had gone back to being critical and that she was filing for divorce. He finally said he would come back to counseling but by this time she would not reconcile. They were divorced a couple of months later.

In this case the letter may have helped the wife see their unending defeat of one another and given her the courage to face a dreaded divorce, though this was not the therapist's intention. Later conversations with each of them revealed that it helped both of them to be aware of their fear of intimacy.

On the basis of these case studies, it would seem that intimacy letters, as an invariable prescription, may be useful whenever the therapist feels defeated and unable to continue the therapy. These letters provide the therapist with a tool for promoting change in couples' avoidance of intimacy.

REFERENCES

Jessee, E., & L'Abate, L. The paradoxes of marital depression: Theoretical and clinical implications. *International Journal of Family Psychiatry* (in press).

Jessee, E., & L'Abate, L. Intimacy and marital depression: Interactional partners. *International Journal of Family Psychiatry* (in press).

L'Abate, L. The paradoxical treatment of depression (submitted for publication).

L'Abate, L. *Enrichment: Structured interventions for couples, families and groups.* Washington, D.C.: University Press of America, 1977.

L'Abate, L. Intimacy is sharing hurt feelings: A reply to David Mace. *Journal of Marriage and Family Counseling,* 1977, *3,* 113-46.

L'Abate, L., & L'Abate, B.L. Marriage: The dream and the reality. *Family Relations,* 1977, *3,* 13-16.

L'Abate, L., Weeks, G.R., & Weeks, K. Of scapegoats, strawmen, and scarecrows. *International Journal of Family Therapy,* 1979, *1,* 86-96.

Selvini-Palazzoli, M., Boscolo, L., Cecchin, G., & Prata, G. *Paradox and counterparadox.* New York: Jason Aronson, 1978.

Sloan, S.Z., & L'Abate, L. *Intimacy Workshops* (research in progress).

Waring, E.M., McElrath, D., Mitchell, P., & Derry, M.E. Intimacy in the general population. *Canadian Psychiatric Association Journal,* 1981, *26,* 167-172.

Weeks, G., & L'Abate, L. *Paradoxical psychotherapy: Theory and practice with individuals, couples, and families.* New York: Brunner/Mazel, 1982.

Weeks, G., Wagner, V., & L'Abate, L. Enrichment and written messages with couples. *American Journal of Family Therapy,* 1980, *8,* 36-44.

CHAPTER 9

BEYOND PARADOX: ISSUES OF CONTROL

LUCIANO L'ABATE
Georgia State University

The purpose of this paper is to clarify any possible misinterpretation of paradoxical treatment by reducing it to two major sets of issues: issues of positive reframing, and issues of control. Since issues of circularity and positive reframing have been considered at length and in detail in other sources, issues of straightforward control will be considered here in greater detail than in the past. The major characteristic of symptomatic behavior is its uncontrollability. After consideration of certain paradoxes about control, guidelines to achieve control are given. The goal is to obtain control and give it away to families. The notion of control is considered within the context of positive reframing, which may be the only "circular" procedure in the whole process of intervention.

One of the most important issues in family therapy is control. Who is in control of the therapy? Who is in control of the family and who should be? How much control should the therapist have and why? It will be argued that: (a) the therapist needs to be in control, in order (b) for the families to learn to achieve control (c) eventually not only over the symptom but also over their lives.

What does it mean to control? Control is an expression of authority and power. To control is to determine how, where, when and for how long people will behave. How can one be in control without being coercive? Can one achieve control without coercion? To avoid any implication of coercion, in this paper control means *being in charge*, a notion that implies responsibility. Without coercion, it is virtually impossible, philosophically, empirically, and existentially, to control anybody *unless they let us*. At best, we can control ourselves but not others. It is important for therapists to achieve control so that, and to the extent that, they can help others learn to control themselves. The family is not going to carry out instructions that are contrary to its world view. For instance, a religious family should not be told not to go to church or to use profane language. However, when symptomatic behavior is positively connoted, it is easier for the family to accept control over the symptom and to carry out assignments. Whether positive reframing is a *sine qua non* for control remains to be seen. In fact, if control can be achieved, positive reframing may not be necessary.

It will be argued that the major circular paradoxical intervention is indeed positive reframing. Once positive reframing of the symptom has taken place, the rest of the intervention is mainly linear. Since a great deal has been said about positive reframing (Hansen & L'Abate, 1982; Weeks & L'Abate, 1982), it will not be discussed here. What will be considered are issues of control, their paradoxes, and conceptual and practical guidelines for achieving control.

Control is a major issue in therapy because it is a major issue in life. To the extent that we control ourselves as persons and as therapists, to that extent we can be successful in intervening helpfully in other people's lives. Issues of control have, of course, been considered by many sources (e.g., Gibbs, 1982; Hunt, 1971; Langer, 1983). Behaviorists, particularly, have given control a great deal of attention (Sidman, 1960; Skinner, 1974). However, they have emphasized contingencies and consequences that reinforce behavior noncontextually. Their contribution, though relevant for an understanding of the etiology of symptoms, is too limited to encompass all the issues of control reviewed here.

Fagan (1970) devotes a great deal of attention to the task of control for the therapist: "He must be able immediately to exercise control or nothing else can follow." She defines control as the therapist "being able to persuade or coerce [sic!] the patient into following the procedures he has set . . . unless patients do some things that the therapist suggests, little will happen . . . " In addition to the importance of achieving control, Fagan also sees dysfunctional behavior as a form of control:

> Part of the importance of control is that all symptoms represent indirect ways of trying to control or force others into certain patterns of behavior. The therapist has to counter being controlled by the patient's symptom and also establish the conditions he needs to work. (p. 92)

Fagan emphasizes that issues of control are important at the beginning of therapy. Controllability is one of the factors in the two dimensions of coherence and meaning within the comprehensive model of family functioning developed by McCubbin and Patterson (1983).

THE UNCONTROLLABILITY OF DYSFUNCTIONS AND SYMPTOMS

That dysfunctions and symptoms are uncontrollable is supported by literature on psychopathology too extensive to be cited here.

Powerlessness. One of the major characteristics of troubled families lies in their feelings of being unable to control the undesirable or symptomatic behavior. The concept of uncontrollability relates to Rotter's (Rotter, Chance & Phares, 1972) concept of external locus of control (it controls us rather than we control it) or similar conceptions like "learned helplessness."

Involuntariness. The symptom is not under the voluntary control of the family, that is, the dysfunctional behavior or symptoms are outside of the conscious awareness of control by the family. This particular quality of the symptom brings about the third characteristic, that the symptom is no one's responsibility.

Irresponsibility. A good deal of dysfunctionality is related to a lack of awareness of contextual factors which may have determined the particular dysfunction, that is, there is no awareness that any one is responsible for the symptom. How can anybody be responsible when no one has the power to do anything? There is no awareness that the family environment in one way or another multiply determines a particular behavior.

Unexplainability or Unintelligibility. A good deal of pathology is supposedly unexplained or unexplainable. This aspect of mysteriousness is present because there is no understanding of how and why a particular symptom has arisen, also because of the previous characteristics mentioned—powerlessness, involuntariness, lack of responsibility. All of these factors together bring about the fact that there is no "rational" explanation of why the symptom should take place at a particular time or at any other time.

THE PARADOXES OF CONTROL

Control is not the goal of the therapist. There is no need to be in control, except that being in control allows the therapist to be effective. To the extent that the therapist can be therapeutic, to that extent, s/he needs to be in control.

Why should we achieve control? We need to help families achieve control, and we need to have control in order to give it away. How is control to be achieved? There are many ways of achieving control.

It is important to remember that control cannot be achieved unless the symptom is positively reframed. However, whether the symptom needs to be positively reframed in order to be prescribed remains an hypothesis to be tested. How can one prescribe a negatively described behavior, as the family sees it? It is important to prescribe behavior that is nondestructive and positively connoted. Once it is positively reframed, it is important that the symptom then be prescribed. The prescription of the symptom is the basis for achieving control. To be in control for control's sake means absolutely nothing from a therapeutic viewpoint. Consequently, we shall discuss five seeming paradoxes that pervade the nature of control.

Control without Appearing to Control

It is important to be in control; however, it is not necessary to be autocratically or dictatorially mindful of such a need. One can be in control without having to appear in control. In many cases, even though therapists may allow themselves a loss of control, it is important that they be in control, that is, in charge of themselves, since it is clear that an individual cannot control what others do. In fact, one could argue that no one can control anybody. At the most, one can control oneself. That in itself is a very difficult goal to achieve.

Take Control to Give It Away

It is important for the therapist to have control, but the only purpose of achieving this control is to let the family have it. A major goal of therapy is to give the family the feeling that they are in charge of themselves and of their destiny, and that they are indeed able to control the symptom. In the first place, it is important for the therapist to be in control in order to model how to be in control. In the second place, it is important to give the control away. If the therapist does not know how to be in charge, to achieve control, how can s/he teach families how to be in control? Strong and Claiborn (1982) have summarized the same point as: "Control of others is gained through yielding control to them" (p. 39).

101

By "it" is meant dysfunctional behavior or symptoms. The symptom needs to be controlled, and in order to control it, we need to join it rather than to fight it (Weeks & L'Abate, 1982). It is very important to ask the symptom bearer and the surrounding system whether, indeed, they want to achieve control. Without their permission and without their stated clear consent there is no point in the therapist trying to teach the family to achieve control. Therefore, one has to ask directly: "Do you want to achieve control?" Only if and when the family emphatically states that indeed they do want to be in control can the therapist proceed accordingly. To proceed accordingly, the therapist has to be aware of two other paradoxes, which follow.

Start It If You Want to Stop It

The behavioral literature has forced us for the last 20 years to look at the consequences of behavior. We have been so taken by this particular position that we have forgotten that there are other ways of achieving control. One method of control can be stated: If we really have control of a certain behavior, we can start it. A great deal of what's behind the paradoxical literature (Weeks & L'Abate, 1982) is the notion of simulation, that is: The symptom needs to be started. This is one of the major points of the Madanes (1981) "pretend" technique, role-playing à la Satir (1972), the reenactment of Minuchin (1974) and many other similar techniques, which essentially all have the same characteristic, namely, starting a symptom in order to control it. Once the family is aware that they can indeed start the symptom, that is a step toward the awareness that perhaps they have something to do with its maintenance. Starting it is an important way of communicating to the family the fact that they are not as powerless as they say they are, that they do have some degree of control, and that *perhaps* they even have some responsibility over who is in charge of the symptom.

Therapists achieve control through prescription of the symptom. It is the most readily available behavior, and the easiest behavior to learn because it is the most prominent and preeminent. In prescribing the symptom we are essentially telling the family to *start* the symptom instead of stopping it. If you cannot start it how can you stop it? Consequently, we achieve control by starting a symptom. After all, how do we achieve control over our environment? By stimulating uncontrollable behavior in the laboratory and, in our case, at home. Scientists achieve control by making the behavior they want to control happen "under controlled conditions." What does that mean? It means varying all of the independent variables to obtain the desired or hoped-for outcome. Since a rigorous method of control is not possible or even desirable in real life with families, we need to limit ourselves to a more realistic level. Perhaps, the best analogy for our procedure can be found in the practice of lobbing explosives into snow banks to produce an avalanche. Thus, an avalanche is started artificially (under controlled conditions), when it will do less damage, to prevent an avalanche occurring unexpectedly, when it would do the most damage.

Make It Happen When It Is Naturally or Spontaneously Happening

Make the undesirable behavior take place where and when it is usually or naturally occurring. By applying this principle by means of positive reframing and ritualistic prescriptions we can help families learn how to achieve control. One way to do this, of course, is to have dysfunctional behavior enacted in the office. Another is to give instructions or homework that tell the family how to do it. Homework can be used to prescribe the symptom. First of all, prescription of the symptom covers the starting paradox, i.e., it makes the symptom occur in a different cognitive context because the family *makes* it happen when it would usually happen. The first step is to approximate and make the symptom take place when it occurs most frequently. For instance, if two siblings are fighting, it is important to make the fighting take place when it usually occurs. It is important to approximate as much as possible the natural conditions surrounding the symptom. However, by prescribing the symptom, it no longer takes place naturally or spontaneously, as the family thinks it does. Essentially, one transmits to the family the feeling that there is no spontaneity in the symptom and there is a good deal of voluntariness and even lawfulness in how the symptom arises. The next step is to make the symptom happen when it would not usually or spontaneously happen.

From the preceding paradoxes of control, one can go on to more specific guidelines for control.

GUIDELINES FOR CONTROL

We achieve control when we can specify the place, time, duration, and frequency of the behavior we want to learn to control. Once we are able to specify and prearrange what, where, when, and how, we have taught the family how to be in control by accepting the symptom as a friend rather than an enemy. In other words, the primary prerequisite for prescribing behavior is to label it positively. We do not or cannot prescribe negative or negatively connoted behavior for obvious ethical and practical reasons. However, we can prescribe behavior that has been labelled positively, as "caring," "protection," "sensitivity," and so forth.

Achieving Control

By determining how, where, when and for how long behavior, whether desirable or undesirable, is to take place, we achieve control. By reframing symptomatic behavior positively and prescribing it ritualistically and systematically, we achieve control. The concept of control is specific to ritualistic prescriptions. By determining beforehand where, when, and for how long the behavior is to take place we are defining its spatial and temporal parameters.

There are three major characteristics to achieving control. We are in control when we know 1) where the behavior is going to take place, 2) when it is going to take place, and 3) what is going to take place.

Controlling Space (Where)

It's important to detail where the symptom is to take place—whether it is going to take place in the office, in the home, or outside the office or home. The primary requirement for control is to specify that space—the familiar physical setting where the symptom is most likely to take place. The best place to assign is where the behavior we want to control usually takes place. It may be the bedroom, the living room, the kitchen, or the bathroom. However, for the sake of drama or of practical considerations, it may be helpful to choose a place that is new or not thought of, for instance, the basement for temper tantrums or fights.

Controlling Time (When)

It is important to conceive of time in terms of frequency, duration, and intensity. These three characteristics need to be dealt with in three different ways. The therapist should specify: 1) when the behavior should start, 2) how long it should last, and 3) how frequently it should take place (once a week, twice a week, three times a week, or every day).

Frequency. First of all, the frequency of the symptom has to be prescribed in terms of ritualized times. It should be performed where a clock can control the time rather than this impersonal chore being someone's responsibility, making it an emotional issue.

Duration. It's important to have an awareness of how long the symptom should occur. Consequently, the duration should be specifically given in minutes, i.e., 5, 15, 30 minutes, or one hour at the most.

Intensity. Intensity is difficult to control but it is important always to make clear how often this prescription is to be executed over an extended period of time, whether it should be done for a week, two weeks, and so forth.

Controlling Content (What)

The behavior most available and familiar to the family is the symptom. It is the clearest frame of reference for their referral, and the desire to control the symptom is the reason for their coming to therapy. However, the issue of *what* to control remains a thorny one. Controlling the symptom is not enough. It serves the purpose of reducing conflict and anxiety but, although necessary at the outset, it is not sufficient. Symptomatic relief is but the first stage of therapy, even though there are therapists who conceive of it as the goal of therapy (Hansen & L'Abate, 1982). There is more to family therapy than symptom reduction and relief. Another goal is teaching families how to negotiate whatever issues they may face in the future.

The content of what needs to be controlled involves two major aspects: *negotiation*—power sharing, decision making, problem-solving skills; and *issues of being*, also called *intimacy skills*—the ability to share one's neediness and fallability, one's fears of being hurt and being found unlovable.

Clearly, the therapist, the one in control, can teach the negotiation process. One can start with the simple aspects of what the family is doing and what things need to be done. When children are involved, *having* things and possessions needs to be negotiated. Eventually, though, what needs to be negotiated in therapy is the whole issue of being (L'Abate et al., 1983). How do we choose to be with one another? This is something that dysfunctional families do not seem to be able to do. Many of these families *have* enough possessions, *have* enough money. Many of them are employed, they perform services, they *do* things. Yet, they do not seem to know how to love each other and feel important with each other. Therefore, what they need to learn is how to *be* with each other, how to negotiate feelings, how to express feelings properly without judgment, how to learn problem solving, and how to deal with intimacy.

HOW TO ACHIEVE CONTROL

There are at least six specific ways of achieving control. Some of these are commonsensical, some have been covered in the literature, and some may be new. They are: 1) change the context of the symptom; 2) change the direction of the symptom; 3) limit information flow; 4) control through planning; 5) control through appointments; and 6) control through writing.

Change the Context of the Symptom

There are many ways of changing the context of the symptom, as suggested originally by Haley (1976). One way he suggested was to change the caretaker who was most involved with the symptomatic individual. Change the overinvolvement by putting someone who is less involved in charge of the symptom or the symptommaker or identified patient. Changing this particular involvement changes the context. If the mother is overinvolved with the symptom bearer, get her to become uninvolved and choose someone else to take her place, father, grandmother, etc. *We change the context by changing the pattern or configurations of relationships in the family.*

This is not the only way to change context. We can change the context *behaviorally* by giving the family new activities to do. For instance, prescription of homework assignments that involve the family coming together for specific periods of time, something they have never done before.

We can change the context *cognitively* by the positive reframing of the symptom. When the symptom, instead of being attributed negative qualities, is now attributed positive valances, the family learns to see it in a different light. We can reframe the symptom in writing as the Milan group does (Hansen & L'Abate, 1982). We can reframe the reasons for referral, as done by L'Abate (1983).

Kempler (1982), Satir (1972) and existential therapists change the context *emotionally*, by having people relate emotionally to each other in a different way than they have done before. Kempler (1982) changes the context by making himself available as an individual instead of as an "expert."

Change the Direction of the Symptom

In addition to changing the context, we can also change the direction of the symptom, as for instance, in the case of depression. Instead of working from the depressed person to the intimate other, i.e., the spouse or the parent, we can change the direction by asking the spouse to remind the depressed person to be depressed on schedule, at a certain time, for a certain duration, in a specific place, and according to specified routines. In other words, we achieve control when we take responsibility for making the behavior (desirable or undesirable) take place according to preestablished, prearranged plans and prescriptions. Other ways of changing the direction of the symptom are:

From the Controller to the Controlled. The caretaker is put in charge of the symptom rather than reacting to the symptom. For instance, the child with temper tantrums controls the parents if the parents react every time the child has a temper tantrum. But when the parent is told to make sure that the temper tantrums occur at a certain time, on certain days, at a certain hour, for a certain length of time, the controlled becomes the controller. The caretaker now has control of the symptom and the former controller, that is, the identified patient, no longer has the power to control everybody through the symptom.

Generational and Hierarchical Redress. Usually the weakest and the youngest are the symptom bearers. By putting the oldest in charge of the symptom, one redresses hierarchical barriers and essentially puts the power (authority and responsibility) where it is supposed to be. It's important to follow generational lines and

105

make sure one redresses the power structure of the family system according to age-appropriate criteria.

Breaking the Deadly Drama Triangle. A triangle, consisting of a victim, a persecutor, and a rescuer seems to be the beginning of most psychopathological dysfunctions (L'Abate, 1976). If and when that drama triangle is evident, it should either be prescribed as is or it should be broken indirectly through other kinds of homework assignments.

Limit Information Flow

We achieve control by limiting information either from the therapist to the family or between family members, i.e., between parents and children. An example is asking parents to leave the children with a baby-sitter without telling the children where the parents are going or what they are doing.

By not telling the family what it is supposed to do, by just giving them an assignment, by not giving all of the information necessary, the therapist can be in charge as an authority. This, of course, is a favorite approach of bureaucrats, politicians, and intelligence spies. Personally, I feel it's better to inform the family straight out and straightforwardly what the purpose of each exercise or assignment is, once it is agreed that control is the goal to be achieved. However, one can think of various examples or possibilities where indeed the therapist may want to limit either the information flow from the therapist to the family or may give information to the older generation and have them limit the flow to the child. It may be important to achieve control through limiting the information flow, even from the therapist to the family or within the family system.

Control through Planning

If the therapist can plan an intervention, if what stance to take and what to prescribe to the family is clear, if the therapist has a clear sense of direction after being allowed to proceed by the family, then the planning itself indicates the level of competence of the therapist. The therapist must plan the various steps of an intervention and have some degree of rationale that is specific to the needs of the family. Planning and assignments that follow clear stages and steps indicate to the family that the therapist is competent. The planned intervention indicates that the therapist is in control.

Control through Appointments

Progress and change often occur in real life among adults through appointments. Fighting by appointment (Bach & Wyden, 1968), having marriage and family conferences, and so forth, leads to resolution. In other words, the world progresses according to two procedures: 1) appointments—meeting at certain preestablished times, and 2) a running record that allows a check on progress.

By asking and demanding that the assignments be carried out on preestablished and agreed-upon times by the family, the therapist achieves control. By carrying out the assignment according to the therapist's plan, the family itself learns to achieve control, because they are carrying out the assignment themselves on their own. It is important that assignments be followed so that the family has an appointment on a regular basis at home for marriage or family conferences, and that these conferences be recorded.

106

It is very important for families to keep running accounts of contracts, of conferences, of when they are depressed, of sibling rivalry, of temper tantrums, and so forth. By putting it in writing the family learns to be in charge of itself. With a record they can remember and derive some lessons. Without a written record to improve upon, forgetting, distortion, and suppression will continue the upset in the family.

CONCLUSION

Instead of considering the paradox as possessing mystical powers and involving mysterious processes of a circular nature, most paradoxical interventions can be and should be linear, step-wise, gradual approaches to working with families. Once the problem is reduced to issues of control, the mystique of the paradox can be reduced essentially to positive reframing. Here is where circularity is indeed present and needed. Once positive reframing has been made, the prescription and assignment of heretofore dysfunctional behavior becomes a gradual, step-wise, linear matter of control. Consequently, there is nothing about the paradox that cannot be reduced to (a) positive reframing, (b) prescription of the symptomatic behavior, and (c) control that when taken by the therapist is given to the clients.

REFERENCES

Bach, G. R., & Wyden, P. (1968). *The intimate enemy: How to fight fair in love and marriage.* New York: William Morrow.

Fagan, J. (1970). The tasks of the therapist. In J. Fagan & I. L. Shepherd (Eds.), *Gestalt therapy now: Theory, techniques, applications.* Palo Alto: Science and Behavior Books.

Gibbs, I. P. (1982). *Social control: Views from the social sciences.* Beverly Hills: Sage Publications.

Haley, J. (1976). *Problem-solving therapy.* San Francisco: Jossey-Bass.

Hansen, J. D., & L'Abate, L. (1982). *Approaches to family therapy.* New York: Macmillan.

Hunt, W. (Ed.) (1971). *Human behavior and its control.* Cambridge: Schenkman.

Kempler, W. (1982). *Existential family therapy.* New York: Gardner Press.

L'Abate, L. (1976). *Understanding and helping the individual in the family.* New York: Grune & Stratton.

L'Abate, L. (1983). Styles in intimate relationships: The A-R-C model. *The Personnel and Guidance Journal, 63,* 279–283.

L'Abate, L., Sloan, S., Wagner, V., & Malone, K. (1983). The differentiation of resources. In L. L'Abate (Ed.), *Family psychology: Theory, therapy, and training.* Washington, DC: University Press of America.

Langer, E. J. (1983). *The psychology of control.* Beverly Hills: Sage Publications.

Madanes, C. (1981). *Strategic family therapy.* San Francisco, CA: Jossey-Bass.

McCubbin, H. I., & Patterson, J. (1983). The family stress process: The double ABCX model of adjustment and adaptation. In H. I. McCubbin, M. B. Sussman, J. M. Patterson (Eds.), *Social stress and the family: Advances and developments in family stress, theory, and research.* Marriage and Family Review, 6(1/2). New York: Haworth Press.

Minuchin, S. (1974). *Families and family therapy.* Cambridge: Harvard University Press.

Rotter, J. B., Chance, J. E., & Phares, E. J. (1972). *Applications of a social learning theory of personality.* New York: Holt, Rinehart, and Winston.

Satir, V. (1972). *Peoplemaking.* Palo Alto: Science and Behavior Books.

Sidman, M. (1960). *Tactics of scientific research: Evaluating experimental data in psychology.* New York: Basic Books.

Skinner, B. F. (1974). *About behaviorism.* New York: Knopf.

Strong, S., & Claiborn, C. D. (1982). *Change through interaction: Social psychological processes of counseling and psychotherapy.* New York: Wiley-Interscience.

Weeks, G., & L'Abate, L. (1982). *Paradoxical therapy: Theory and practice with individuals, couples, and families.* New York: Brunner/Mazel.

Chapter 10

The Practice of Programmed Family Therapy

A Radical Proposal

Luciano L'Abate

Abstract

This chapter presents a rationale for the practice of programmed family therapy. In addition to the contribution of the therapist, this practice relies heavily on written homework assignments, which allow a more verifiable assessment of the effectiveness of therapeutic interventions than would otherwise be possible. From a public health viewpoint, these assignments, combined with structured enrichment or psychoeducational programs, would permit enlarging the scope of family therapy to deal with families and individuals who cannot be reached by traditional family therapy practices.

Many family therapy theories, techniques, and practices are not verifiable and remain untested and untestable (see chapter 1; Hansen & L'Abate, 1982; L'Abate, 1986a; Levant, 1983). Moreover, current family therapy practices follow a crisis and private practice model that limits the number of families that can be reached and helped.

In this chapter, I propose a radical departure from existing theories and models of practice, one that may reduce some of the problems already mentioned. This departure is based on the laboratory method in clinical psychology (L'Abate, 1968, 1973, in preparation). The cornerstone of this method is standard operating procedures in the hands of paraprofessionals under the direction and supervision of a professional. This method has been applied to the evaluation of children, couples, and families (L'Abate & Wagner, 1985), to monitored play-therapy with children (L'Abate, 1973), and to structured enrichment with functional and semifunctional couples and families (L'Abate, 1986b). The same laboratory approach is now being applied to family therapy (L'Abate, 1986a).

It is possible to operate therapeutically and at the same time collect cumulative records that attest to the validity of a given viewpoint. Instead of being in favor of one diametrically opposed conceptual position, for instance, the aesthetic over the pragmatic, one can operate in ways that combine both positions (L'Abate, 1986a). One can be a practitioner and use stylistically personal ways of intervening and, at the same time, be a scientist, collecting repeatable data, without doing injustice to and diminishing the importance of one position at the expense of the other. It is possible to create written homework assignments that derive either from theory (L'Abate, 1986a) or from practice. When these written homework assignments are coupled with the help of subprofessional personnel and psychoeducational programs, one can or should obtain verifiable results at a much lower cost than in traditional family therapy practices. Instead of research and practice remaining two separate enterprises, as they are now, the use of the laboratory method makes it possible to combine research and practice without doing injustice to either.

The Notion of Verifiability

The very concept of verifiability is not even considered a criterion for either theorizing or practicing in family therapy (Hansen & L'Abate, 1982; Levant, 1983). Theories, techniques, and practices follow a chaotic state of affairs, in which one guru's word is as good as another guru's, depending on the charismatic influence of a particular guru. Some gurus are more charismatic than others and thus command more influence and credibility (see chapter 2). Under these chaotic conditions, it is doubtful whether family therapy can progress in its theories or in its practices. As long as the criterion of success seems to be the popularity of the particular theorist, his or her charisma, and the seductive plausibility of his or her theory or technique, no progress can take place. No one seems to ask whether, in addition to popularity and plausibility, other criteria for theory or practice are necessary.

One criterion that has been considered a sine qua non for a theory is verifiability; that is, the extent to which a theory or practice is reproducible and repeatable, with a minimum of variability from one therapist to another and regardless of what a therapist says she or he did or thinks she or he did (L'Abate, 1986a). Before indicating how this concept can be applied directly to the therapeutic process, I think it is important to consider the current status of theory, techniques, and practices in family therapy.

The Status of Theory in Family Therapy

The theory that has characterized the field, above and beyond "theorettes" and models, has been the so-called general systems theory, which has been translated in family therapy as family systems, which are based mostly on the contributions of Bateson, von Bertalanffy, and others. This theory has not only been taken over as the encompassing Zeitgeist of the field but has become an accepted metaphor that transcends all other models. Until now, it has been accepted lock, stock, and barrel, without question and without criticism. No one claims the title "family therapist" unless he or she can spout terms such as feedback, homeostasis, circularity, hierarchy, and other buzz words that help establish one as a member of the group. Instead of remaining what it was and is, just a metaphorical metatheory, it has achieved the status of a cult, an entry and status ticket into the field (see chapter 2).

Fortunately, a trend toward critical appraisal has begun, suggesting that family systems thinking may pass at best as a metaphor or a metatheory or at worst as the cruelest intellectual fraud ever perpetrated on an unsuspecting profession and on an even more unsuspecting public. Some criticisms have been focused on the high level of abstraction, which makes this metaphor untestable and distant from the evidence gathered from the science of psychology, especially developmental psychology (see chapter 1).

Falser (1986), in a critique of these theoretical foundations, even though recognizing the historical, evolutionary importance of the "cybernetic metaphor . . . as an heuristic device," concluded:

> I will suggest that any effort to establish a dominant approach to family therapy is ill-founded. I will argue that epistemology and cybernetics provide an insufficient understanding of families and family therapy and should be rejected as a foundation for the field. . . . I will suggest that the quest for a logical foundation, that is, for a base of fundamental knowledge about what constitutes families and family therapy, be abandoned altogether. (pp. 355, 358)

These are harsh conclusions about a metatheory that has dominated the field for so long with so few disagreements or even criticisms. It has filled a conceptual vacuum left by the disinterest in the family that has been shown by psychology as a science and as a profession (see chapter 22). Most family therapists have shown either ignorance or lack of interest in sociological theories of the family (see chapter 2). Such conclusions, however, beg the question: Should therapeutic practices have a foundation of any kind? If the answer is no, one need go no further. If the answer is yes, one must expect empirical evidence, no matter how flimsy or contradictory, to be the fundamental basis for theory construction, theory testing, and clinical practice (see chapter 22; L'Abate, 1986a).

Thus, the theoretical underpinnings of current therapeutic practices are now beginning to crumble under closer critical scrutiny. What about clinical practices? Can they be any better than the theory that underlies them?

The Status of Therapeutic Practices

When one looks at the range of therapeutic practices (Sherman & Fredman, 1986), one discovers that most of them consist of ad hoc gimmicks and nonrepeatable procedures. These contributions cannot even differentiate between a technique and a method! The individual style of the therapist, which is nonrepeatable behavior, is confused with the demonstrable and pragmatic methodological contribution of the therapist, which should go beyond individual style

(L'Abate, Ganahl, & Hansen, 1986).

These critical remarks are made to indicate the lack, if not totally, certainly in great part, of verifiability in family therapy. The field seems to pay little or no attention to other important issues, such as the cost-effectiveness of therapeutic procedures and the need for large-scale, possibly mass-oriented, practices.

The Costs of Doing Therapy

Although mystery seems to shroud this topic, one can surmise that the fee for one hour of therapy may range from $10 or $15 for a student intern to 10 times that much for an experienced practitioner. No one seems to wonder whether these costs might be reduced without reducing effectiveness. How can a therapist's effectiveness be improved without reducing the workload? How can a therapist improve effectiveness and at the same time test the validity of one or more theoretical positions?

There is no way in which family therapy, no matter how strong the number or quality of practitioners and organizations, can take care of the millions of families who, in one way or another, need help. Instead of a crisis-oriented, private practice model, which is limited to a relatively small number of families, a public health model needs to be considered. To deal with the problems of the American family (Kahn & Kamerman, 1982), a radically new perspective will be necessary to reconcile preventers (L'Abate, 1986b) and therapists. Not only do they not talk with each other, they use mutually exclusive practices that weaken the whole enterprise of helping families (L'Abate, 1986b; L'Abate & Milan, 1985; Levant, 1986).

Can we find ways of reconciling both sides along the spectrum of functionality-dysfunctionality rather than limiting ourselves to families in crisis? Is it possible to produce reproducible and verifiable methods that can be used by therapists, preventers, and family life educators? The answer to both questions is yes. In the rest of this chapter, I suggest how such a reconciliation can be achieved.

Programmed Homework Assignments

Systematic homework assignments for couples and families have been published (L'Abate, 1986a).1 The assignments deal first with marital or family depression, then progress to negotiation skills and, ultimately, to the achievement of intimacy.

Subsequently, I developed additional written homework assignments to help families deal with resistant patterns such as arguments or fights, sibling rivalry, temper tantrums. For each of these problems, a series of three assignments focuses on (a) a description of the behavior (frequency, duration, and intensity); (b) a list of multiple, positive reframings of these behaviors; and (c) guidelines, sometimes paradoxical, prescribing the behaviors.2   These resistant patterns need to be taken care of at the outset of therapy.   Once they are brought under control, one can deal with possibly underlying depressive patterns or go on to use negotiation and intimacy homework assignments.

Resistant Family Patterns

There are at least three repetitive, often strongly and rigidly resistant, family patterns that are very difficult to eliminate for good before real therapy can be initiated.   These patterns are arguments or fights, sibling rivalry, and temper tantrums.   (For background on these patterns and the paradoxical strategies to deal with them, see chapter 7; L'Abate, Baggett, & Anderson, 1984; L'Abate, Ganahl, & Hansen, 1986; Weeks & L'Abate, 1982).

The issue here is whether one can produce and reproduce standard operating procedures to be followed with couples or families who exhibit these resistant patterns.   These standard operating procedures consist of descriptions, explanations (multiple positive reframings), and guidelines (prescriptions) that are administered in writing (see chapter 11).   The written word ensures that all the details necessary to carry out the assigned steps are available beforehand.   The written form saves time and energy for everybody (including the therapist) and avoids misunderstanding, avoidance, or distortions. The similarities and repetitiousness of these patterns from one family to another led to putting instructions in writing yet allowing for individual idiosyncrasies within families.

Before using these guidelines, the therapist must be sure that straightforward, linear methods have failed and that a more circular, indirect approach seems appropriate.   Also, before administering these guidelines in writing, one needs to be sensitive to a necessary, preliminary step: discounting the procedures themselves or the author of them.

Discounting procedures or discounting the author. It is usually helpful to minimize the role of these potentially powerful procedures. They may be presented as "experimental."   "It is doubtful whether they will do any good"; "I really do not know what else to do"; "I am quite baffled by what is going on and these procedures probably will not help." By the same token, the therapist can give a completely contradictory message by supporting their successful use with other families but doubting "whether they will be of help in your case." Thus, the administration of these procedures may be tentative, nondogmatic, and colored by misgivings and doubts: "I doubt whether they will work, but let's try them for the next 2 weeks or so and see what happens."   The rationale for such tentativeness can be found in Weeks and L'Abate (1982).   If these guidelines do work, the therapist may need to show surprise, sometimes even chagrin or indignation: "I really do not understand how they worked for you!"

Descriptions. The first lesson in a series of three consists of completing a form, which is made up of detailed questions designed to elicit specific information concerning the frequency, the duration, and the intensity of a particularly resistant pattern. The form also elicits information on how these arguments, sibling rivalry, or temper tantrums take place, how often and how intense they are, and the main repetitive issue(s) around which these patterns take place. Each person who can read and write and who is involved in the pattern (both spouses, both parents, parent-child dyads) answer in writing, without checking with the other person. This individual assignment is done to flush out any possible (quite common) discrepancies in perceptions of the pattern.

After completing this form individually, the family members are to meet at home at an appointed time (preferably agreed upon in the presence of the therapist) to discuss their answers with each other and with any family members who have not completed the form. After obtaining relevant information about the patterns of the behavior, one can proceed to the explanations for and the prescription of the behavior.

Explanations: Multiple positive reframings. The rationale for the use of multiple reframings can be found in L'Abate (1986a), especially in regard to marital depression. In brief, it is doubtful (and documentation is lacking) that a single positive reframing, no matter how tailored to a particular family, is sufficient. It seems more appropriate and useful to give families a variety of positive reframings.

They are asked to spend one home session discussing and ranking the reframings in terms of how they apply specifically to the family, ranking first the one that seems to apply best, then ranking the 2nd best, 3rd best, until all the explanations have been ranked from 1 to 10 (10 being the one that does not apply at all). If the family believes that none of the reframings apply, they can come up with an explanation that seems to apply better to their family.

Guidelines: Prescriptions. After ranking and discussion have been completed, the family is ready for the guidelines (the prescription). The explanations lead, ideally, toward a prescription of the behavior. If no connection can be made between explanation and prescription, one can still justify the use of the explanations and the guidelines on the basis of pragmatism rather than on the basis of rational explanation ("It would take 6 months to find out how this pattern came about. It may take a few weeks to bring this pattern under control. Which do you prefer?").

Fighting, or arguing, is the most frequent, pervasive, and intense of the symptoms that I have seen in 30 years of practice. It is also one of the most difficult to control and to turn into constructive discussions. Unless steps are taken from the outset of therapy, this pattern may derail and defeat the process of therapy. At the beginning, ask the family to define argument or fight (or sibling rivalry or temper tantrum) as it applies to their family.

The main discovery that results from the administration of these guidelines is that under these conditions no constructive argument or fight can really take place. The couple (or the parent-child dyad) who tries to follow these guidelines will soon find out (on their own!) that many of these guidelines mimic what they have been doing for years. New structures and guidelines need to be developed first on how to argue and then on what to argue about.

What the family needs to continue to follow from these guidelines, however, is the importance of arguing (i.e., discussing issues) by appointment and in writing; that is, to be in charge of ourselves and our arguments we need to set temporal and spatial limits on when, how long, and how these discussions are to take place. This requirement needs to be coupled with a second requirement--a written record of what goes on (L'Abate, 1986a). Without a written record, little progress can take place, because writing helps improve reflection and control. From the guidelines, families very quickly learn that to have a successful discussion, they need to do the opposite of what is requested of them in each point.

Thus, the guidelines are designed to help couples and families find out, on their own, that the unwritten and unspoken processes they have been following in their arguments or fights are self-destructive (i.e., "suicidal") and useless. They can come to this realization once they become aware that these guidelines highlight the uselessness and destructiveness of past processes and that new, more constructive processes need to be developed. These new processes are implicit in doing the opposite of what the guidelines require.

Just like arguments and temper tantrums, sibling rivalry suggests a failure of leadership on the part of parents. It is important that the guidelines be followed by both parents together or, if necessary, adopted by the parent who is less involved. After this pattern is brought under control, one needs to pay attention to underlying, unspoken patterns that the family is either unable or unwilling to bring up, usually a pattern of marital depression, which needs to be considered as a second step in therapy (L'Abate, 1986a).

Temper tantrums are most likely to occur and to come to the attention of the therapist when one of the children is still young, usually before school age. Consequently, it is doubtful that the child will understand what is discussed with the parents. The child should be congratulated for his or her behavior because of its many positive results. Again, before using this procedure, the therapist must obtain all pertinent information about this pattern and attempt to eliminate it by using linear procedures. If these linear procedures fail, the therapist may try the procedures outlined here.

The procedures just described precede all the assignments to teach families how to deal with depression, learn negotiation skills, and learn the sharing of intimacy. They are often used at the beginning of therapy when the referring symptom is fighting, sibling rivalry, or temper tantrums, or when it is found, during the initial interview, that one of these patterns is prominent.

Dealing with these recurring patterns is relatively easy. What remains more difficult is to find the underlying condition that is producing these patterns in the family. More often than not, in my experience, these patterns express an underlying deficit in the marital partnership. If the partnership is not working well, it is difficult to become and be a competent parent. This underlying deficit is usually related to marital depression, which women readily admit but which men usually deny and avoid (an issue discussed in chapter 13).

If progress in therapy is not taking place, the father is usually responsible for failing to cooperate in the treatment. Sometimes the sabotage is very covert and indirect. Sometimes one finds a pattern of driven behavior (alcoholism, drug usage, workaholism, gambling, running around) that the father is refusing to give up or to bring up. Under these conditions, one needs help in the form of medication, AA, or limiting treatment goals strictly to symptom reduction.

In conclusion, resistant patterns of arguing, sibling rivalry, and temper tantrums can be brought under control by following written descriptions, positive reframings, and guidelines. After this initial step in therapy has been successfully completed, a more difficult step follows--helping families learn to negotiate and to love.

Individual Patterns

In addition to written procedures for resistant family patterns, I have developed two self-paced programs for two different populations: (a) acting-out individuals and (b) cooperative individuals who cannot afford lengthy therapeutic sessions.

The purpose of the Social Training program is to train individuals who have deficits in the comprehension of social situations, which are expressed in impulsivity and acting out, either potential or actual. More than likely, these individuals need to be under a court order, on probation or parole, or incarcerated. Without these restrictions, it would be difficult to obtain their cooperation.

This program is based on principles of semantic reconditioning that recognize and stress the power that certain key words (e.g., self, control, law, love) have over our behavior. The 16 lesson are programmed in a stepwise sequence that eventually leads the person to reflect on his or her behavior. Each lesson, however, ends with homework assignments that need to be completed before the person is allowed to go on to the next lesson. For people who cannot read and write, this program could be the outline of a group discussion course, possibly lead by someone who has successfully completed this program in writing.2

The Social Growth program has been written with the goal of creating an additional therapeutic experience for individuals, either as an adjunct to therapy or as a substitute for therapy for individuals who cannot afford weekly sessions but who are motivated to learn and to change, with a minimum of professional feedback and help. It consists of 13 lessons, which each individual has to answer in writing, concerning a variety of issues that we all have to face in life, for instance, family of origin, achievement, sexuality, relationships with the opposite sex. These lessons were revised from an interview schedule developed by Kagan and Moss (1972).3

Structured Enrichment

In addition to the written homework assignments, usually to be administered by the therapist, my co-workers and I (L'Abate & Weinstein, 1986; L'Abate & Young, 1987) have produced a library of 50 structured enrichment exercises dealing with myriad topics both from a developmental life cycle and a structural perspective. These programs have been used for the past 16 years to train first-year graduate students, who learn to work with functional families first, then go on to work with semifunctional and dysfunctional families (Jessee & L'Abate, 1981). Since the instructions for these programs are given verbatim, subprofessional and paraprofessional intermediaries can learn relatively quickly to administer them under the supervision of a more experienced family therapist or preventer and at much lower cost than if a full-fledged professional were to administer them. Unpaid volunteers in a mental health clinic were trained to work successfully with families who had recently terminated crisis-oriented family therapy (see chapter 26). Furthermore, L'Abate, O'Callaghan, Piat, Dunne, Margolis, Prigge, and Soper (1975) have demonstrated that the combination of therapy at the outset and enrichment at subsequent stages can be feasible, productive, and cost-effective.

The Need for a Hierarchical Structure
Among Family Facilitators

The potential application of combining written homework assignments with structured enrichment or other psychoeducational programs suggests a hierarchical structure of family facilitators. The more experienced professional, possibly or preferably a family therapist, can supervise a second tier of less experienced family therapists. These therapists, in addition to seeing families directly, can supervise subprofessional (A.A. or B.A. degree) personnel who

117

are administering a plethora of structured enrichment programs or other psychoeducational programs currently available (L'Abate, 1986b; L'Abate & Milan, 1985; Levant, 1986).

Each family who is seen for crisis-oriented family therapy, after the crisis or symptom has been taken care of for the short haul, can enter a second stage of therapy in which they can learn better ways of problem solving and communicating with each other for the long haul. This stage can consist of psychoeducational programs applied by subprofessional personnel under the direction and supervision of a more experienced family therapist, who may intervene toward the termination stage of therapy.

The Family Therapist as a Team Leader and Supervisor

This hierarchical structure would require a much more responsible and expanded leadership role for the family therapist than that envisaged up to now. She or he would need to be a therapist as well as a preventer, since any family who enters family therapy is at risk for relapse (Leff & Vaughn, 1985). Further psychoeducational training should decrease the possibility of such a relapse. It is possible to train such leaders. Training begins with psychoeducational programs and progresses gradually to less structured (and more complex) family therapy methods (see chapter 22; Kochalka & L'Abate, 1983).

Conclusions

This proposal is not as drastic or radical as it may seem at first blush. Anderson (1983) and her coworkers (Anderson, Reiss, & Hogarty, 1986), as well as Falloon (Falloon, 1985; Falloon & Liberman, 1983), have shown how important and beneficial psychoeducational teaching can be to families with members who have been labeled schizophrenic. These programs are cost-effective and can be administered by lesser trained and experienced personnel under the direction of a more experienced supervisor.

Homework assignments and structured enrichment or psycho-educational programs rely on the written word, either on the part of the family or on the part of the enricher. They can be duplicated, replicated, and repeated endlessly. In short, they are verifiable procedures. In addition, the validity of the therapist's underlying theoretical assumptions, the usefulness of this methodology, and its cost-effectiveness can be verified. If they do not work well, they can be corrected, changed, and improved. Therapists cannot be controlled, improved, or verified, as can the standard operating procedures of the laboratory method, which I have used for more than 20 years.

Footnotes

[1]The systematic homework assignments are available from the publisher, Brunner/Mazel, 19 Union Square, New York, NY 10003.

2The guidelines for helping families deal with resistant patterns may be obtained directly from Social Training, P. O. Box 450843, Atlanta, GA 30345.

3The Social Training and the Social Growth programs may be obtained directly from Social Training, P. O. Box 450843, Atlanta, GA 30345.

References

Anderson, C. M. (1983). A psychoeducational program for families of patients with schizophrenia. In W. R. McFarlane (Ed.), Family therapy in schizophrenia (pp. 99–116). New York: Guilford.

Anderson, C. M., Reiss, D. J., & Hogarty, G. E. (1986). Schizophrenia and the family: A practitioner's guide to psychoeducation and management. New York: Guilford.

Falloon, I. R. H. (1985). Behavioral family therapy: A problem-solving approach to family coping. In J. Leff & C. Vaughn (Eds.), Expressed emotion in families (pp. 150–171). New York: Guilford.

Falloon, I. R. H., & Liberman, R. P. (1983). Behavioral family interventions in the management of chronic schizophrenia. In W. R. McFarlane (Ed.), Family therapy in schizophrenia (pp. 117–137). New York: Guilford.

Falser, P. R. (1986). The cybernetic metaphor: A critical examination of ecosystemic epistemology as a foundation of family therapy. Family Process, 25, 353–363.

Hansen, J. C., & L'Abate, L. (1982). Approaches to family therapy. New York: Macmillan.

Jessee, E., & L'Abate, L. (1981). Enrichment role-playing as a step in the training of family therapists. Journal of Marital and Family Therapy, 7, 507–514.

Kagan, J., & Moss, H. (1972). From birth to maturity. New York: Wiley.

Kahn, A. H., & Kamerman, S. B. (1982). Helping America's families. Philadelphia: Temple University Press.

Kochalka, J. A., & L'Abate, L. (1983). Structure and gradualness in the clinical training of family psychologists. In L. L'Abate, Family psychology: Theory, therapy and training (pp. 287–299). Washington, DC: University Press of America.

L'Abate, L. (1968). The laboratory method as an alternative to existing mental health models. American Journal of Orthopsychiatry, 38, 296-297.

L'Abate, L. (1973). The laboratory method in clinical child psychology: Three applications. Journal of Clinical Child Psychology, 2, 8-10.

L'Abate, L. (1986a). Systematic family therapy. New York: Brunner/Mazel.

L'Abate, L. (1986b). Prevention of marital and family problems. In B. A. Edelstein & L. Michelson (Eds.), Handbook of prevention (pp. 177-193). New York: Plenum.

L'Abate, L. (in preparation). The laboratory method in clinical psychology.

L'Abate, L., Baggett, M. S., & Anderson, J. S. (1984). Linear and circular interventions with families of children with school-related problems. In B. F. Okun (Ed.), Family therapy with school-related problems (pp. 13-27). Rockville, MD: Aspen Systems Corp.

L'Abate, L., Ganahl, G., & Hansen, J. C. (1986). Methods of family therapy. Englewood Cliffs, NJ: Prentice-Hall.

L'Abate, L., & Milan, M. (Eds.). (1985). Handbook of social skills training and research. New York: Wiley

L'Abate, L., O'Callaghan, B., Piat, J., Dunne, E. E., Margolis, R., Prigge, B., & Soper, P. (1975). Enlarging the scope of intervention with couples and families.: Combination of therapy and enrichment. In L. R. Wolberg & M. L. Aronson (Eds.), Group therapy 1975--An overview (pp. 62-73). New York: Stratton Intercontinental Medical Book Company.

L'Abate, L., & Wagner, V. (1985). Theory-derived, family-oriented test batteries. In L. L'Abate (Ed.), Handbook of family psychology and therapy (Vol. 2, pp. 1006-1031). Homewood, IL: Dorsey Press.

L'Abate, L., & Weinstein, S. (1986). Structured enrichment programs for couples and families. New York: Brunner/Mazel.

L'Abate, L., & Young, L. (1987). Casebook of structured enrichment programs for couples and families. New York: Brunner/Mazel.

Leff, J., & Vaughn, C. (Eds.). (1985). Expressed emotion in families. New York: Guilford.

Levant, R. F. (1983). Family therapy. Englewood Cliffs, NJ: Prentice-Hall.

Levant, R. F. (Ed.). (1986). Psychoeducational approaches to family therapy and counseling. New York: Springer.

Sherman, R., & Fredman, N. (1986). Handbook of structured techniques in marriage and family therapy. New York: Brunner/Mazel.

Weeks, G. R., & L'Abate, L. (1982). Paradoxical psychotherapy: Theory and practice with individuals, couples, and families. New York: Brunner/Mazel.

Chapter 11

Therapeutic Writing Through Homework Assignments

Luciano L'Abate

Abstract

Therapeutic writing, the use of homework assignments devoted to writing on a specific topic, has been around for quite some time. In spite of its many advantages, such as saving time and cutting costs, it has not received the attention it deserves from the psychotherapeutic community. Background, rationale, and specific applications are discussed. Even though more empirical evidence needs to be gathered to support the wider applicability of therapeutic writing, the applications and consumer satisfaction seem to support increased use under controlled conditions.

In this paper I present the background and rationale for the use of therapeutic writing, that is, the assignment of writing at home, focused on specific topics relevant to the individual's, the couple's, or the family's life. Even though my experience is thus far strictly impressionistic (L'Abate, 1986), I have been impressed by its usefulness in helping to deal with specific problems that usually require more time and higher costs.

My purpose, therefore, is to lay the groundwork for a systematic, therapeutic use of writing as an alternative or as an additional form of communication between therapists and clients. Its application in psychotherapy is based in part on the following rationale. First, if a topic is important enough to talk about, it is important enough to be written down (another way of saying that talk is cheap). Writing is also a way of finding out whether a client's verbal claims of change are supported and paralleled by performance. Writing forces the client to <u>do</u> something rather than just talk about it. It puts the client on the spot, so to speak, to produce and to perform. If talk is therapeutic in and of itself, why not add another dimension to it? It helps in evaluating directly and swiftly the motivation for change, beyond the oral level. The client who is really motivated to change is willing to work for change directly.

The vast and as yet untapped possibilities of writing as a third therapeutic modality, in addition to the traditional verbal-nonverbal dichotomy, are not even mentioned in encyclopedic treatises on psychotherapy (Garfield & Bergin, 1978; Norcross, 1986). This modality, then, could conceivably be used with individuals who have been consistently resistant to and untouched by therapeutic interventions based on talking, for instance, psychopaths, juveniles, and acting-out individuals. (A rationale for a self-administered social training

123

program for acting-out individuals is in preparation.)

Second, therapeutic writing raises some questions about streamlining existing therapeutic procedures without a loss of therapeutic effectiveness. Psychotherapy is expensive. Billions of dollars are spent every year in this enterprise. In spite of its successful institutionalization and widespread use, it cannot reach many of the individuals who could profit by it. Therapeutic writing may be a way of increasing therapeutic effectiveness, decreasing costs, and enlarging the circle of needy people who can be helped therapeutically.

Third, therapeutic writing is a record-keeping function. If progress is to be made, record keeping is essential, as in any human enterprise, to orderly progress. The therapist, instead of keeping records only for and by himself or herself, has records of what the client is doing, as well as what the client is saying.

Fourth, therapeutic writing can bring about the expression of pent-up feelings, or, especially in couple and family therapy, it can help hold in check explosive emotionality and uncontrolled feelings. One can express in writing many feelings that are difficult to express orally (of course, the reverse may also be true).

In spite of these advantages, therapeutic writing has limitations. It cannot be used with people who cannot read or write. By the same token, how many people who cannot read and write are helped by oral psychotherapy? These persons can use a tape recorder, which is also an option for those who become tired of writing and want a medium of expression in addition to writing.

Historical Background

In reviewing the brief, or short-term, therapy literature (Barten, 1971; Barten & Barten, 1973; Buchman, 1981; Malan, 1976; Small, 1971; Wolberg, 1980) on innovations in psychotherapy (Abt & Stuart, 1982; Corsini, 1981; Usdin, 1975), I have found only one reference to the potential use of therapeutic writing. Small (1971), in one paragraph, referred the reader to the pioneering work of Phillips and Wiener (1966). Actually, years earlier Ellis (1955, 1965) and Pearson (1965) devoted a whole American Psychological Association symposium to this topic (Burton, 1965; Raimy, 1965).

The historical roots of therapeutic writing can be found in the use of written autobiographies by college students (Riccio, 1958; Shaffer, 1954); the earliest reference to its clinical usefulness can be found in Landsman (1951), followed by Messinger (1952) and then by Farber (1953). However, the most important work on its therapeutic effectiveness remains the study by Phillips and Wiener (1966, pp. 130-135, 159-185), who investigated therapeutic writing under controlled conditions. Referring to a master's thesis by Test (1964) and an abstract by Phillips, Test, and Adams (1964), they evaluated three

124

different groups, using the Minnesota Multi-Phasic Inventory (MMPI), the Edwards Personal Preference Schedule, the Butler-Haigh Q-Sort, the Otis Self-Administering Intelligence Test, and a personal data sheet, all of which were used before and after treatment. All the students were drawn from the same population--applicants at a university counseling service. One group (n = 11) received group therapy, a second group (n = 8) received individual therapy, and a third group (n = 12) received what they called "writing therapy"; that is, all communication between the student and the therapist took place in writing without any visual or oral contact between the two. The student communicated with the therapist through written notes about his or her problems, and the therapist answered in writing. The subjects in each group received an equal number of sessions (10), and a control (no therapy) group was evaluated on a pre-post basis. The control group (n = 16) showed the greatest number of dropouts (n = 8), a 50% attrition rate. In the other three experimental groups the attrition rate was 16%.

In terms of results the group therapy subjects did not show any reliable changes on the MMPI or on the Butler-Haigh Q-Sort; on the Edwards, significant pre-post changes were found on Deference (p > .05) and Aggression (p > .01). Somewhat less reliable improvements (p > .05) were found on the Affiliation and the Endurance subscales. There was also a reliable (p > .01) improvement in grade point average (from C- to B-). The individual therapy group showed significant changes on the Depression, Psychasthenia, and Schizophrenia subscales of the MMPI; on the Edwards there were changes on the Aggression, Endurance, Abasement, Dominance, Succorance, and Autonomy subscales at various levels of significance. "The largest number of changes, and the most significant ones, were in the third formal therapy group--those involved in writing therapy" (Phillips & Wiener, 1966, p. 132). On the MMPI, significant improvements were found on the Depression, Psychasthenia, Psychopathic Deviate, Schizophrenia, and Social Introversion subscales. On the Edwards, changes were obtained on the Heterosexuality and the Abasement subscales; on the Butler-Haigh Q-Sort, there were changes in increased congruence and a shift in self-ideal discrepancy. Unfortunately, the control (no-therapy) group also showed significant changes on these paper-and-pencil tests, decreasing considerably the validity of the results. The authors rationalized these changes in terms of the fact that the eight dropouts were not included in the analysis and speculated that the remaining eight controls may have been psychologically "healthier" and thus may have improved without intervention.

On the basis of this admittedly exploratory study and the tentative, if not questionable, results, Phillips and Wiener (1966) considered writing therapy "a new approach to treatment and training" (chapter 9).

If we can demonstrate that therapeutic writing increases therapeutic effectiveness (i.e., therapy takes less time and therefore costs less), a significant therapeutic adjuvant may become available. As Phillips and Wiener concluded: "Writing therapy has been used in several forms as an adjunct tool, or as a replacement for, more formal, oral therapy, especially where the latter was not possible or practicable. Like much of the reporting on short-term therapy, the existing literature on writing therapy consists mostly of clinical impressions" (pp. 151-162). After 20 years this conclusion still stands unchallenged, even though therapeutic writing (in the form of diary keeping) as an adjuvant to meditation has received the endorsement of Progoff (1975, 1980) and of Reiner (1978).

In fact, Howard and Barton (1986) stated that "writing is thinking," proposing that (a) writing is a symbolic activity of meaning-making, (b) writing for others is a "staged performance, and (c) writing is a tool of understanding as well as of communicating. "Writing is always mediated thought. . . . the act of writing becomes father to the thought itself" (pp. 21, 24). These authors also proposed that the act of writing involves a process of discovery, exploration, speculation, imagination, and the generation of ideas that need composition and eventual expression.

Applications

At the end of their chapter, where they presented case studies of writing therapy, Phillips and Wiener (1966) gave guidelines for the use of writing therapy. I have paraphrased them freely to include guidelines that can be helpful in any practice, provided therapeutic writing is additional to individual, marital, or family therapy (L'Abate, 1986).

1. Writing should be done at set times (e.g., every other day, at 9:00 p.m.) for a constant length of time (half an hour, an hour, depending on topic to be explored and its pre-eminence in the individual's life). For instance, if depression is to be controlled (L'Abate, 1986), the client may need to write about it every day for at least an hour when the depression is severe. In less extreme cases, once every other day may be sufficient.

2. It is usually helpful to suggest a specific topic so that the client focuses energy and concentrates on one topic at a time. Once the topic has been suggested, the client should be encouraged to write freely, without paying attention to sentence structure, grammar, or logic.

3. If writing is difficult because of educational level or other factors, the client can be encouraged to speak into a tape recorder.

4. If a rationale is to be given, issues of control (L'Abate, 1986) can be considered ("Do you want the depression to control you, or do you want to learn to control the depression?"). In addition to control issues, one can consider that therapeutic writing

helps get obsessive thinking "out of the head" and onto a piece of paper (i.e., from the inside to the outside), where it can be evaluated.

5. Another rationale for therapeutic writing (already mentioned) is record keeping. (Progress in our world is generally recorded; without records we would not be able to evaluate change or progress.)

6. The notes can be read during the therapy session, or they can be read afterward by the therapist and brought up for discussion during the next session.

Research Possibilities

Another line of inquiry that offers empirical and theoretical support for therapeutic writing can be found in writing research (Nystrand, 1986). Instead of reviewing the literature, I think it will be sufficient to show how this area could furnish the theoretical and empirical support that therapeutic writing will need to achieve a certain degree of legitimacy in the therapeutic community. Nystrand (1986) had this to say about written communication:

> Researchers see both writing and reading as constructive, interpretative activities in which both writer and reader test hypotheses about possible meanings. . . . Writers are said to represent and evaluate their intentions continuously in the conventions of written text. . . . What is not always recognized, however, is that writers and readers interact not only with the text but also with each other by way of the text. . . . Communications between writers and readers require that the text they share configure and mediate these respective interests and expectations. . . . More fundamentally, each [writer and reader] presupposes—indeed counts on—the sense-making capabilities of the other. There is a condition of reciprocity between conversants that undergirds and continuously regulates discourse at every turn. (p. ix)

This condition of reciprocity between the writer and the reader is elaborated further by Nystrand:

> The principle of reciprocity is an essential key to understanding the interactions and negotiations of writers and readers. Most research on writer-reader interaction has focused on (a) the effects of reflection, for example, when writers reread what they have written . . .; (b) concrete response . . .; (c) projection. . . . Much of this research works from the premise that writers and readers ultimately collaborate via the internal representation of meaning created in the process of writing and reading. (p. 14)

Nystrand, then, considers writing a social interactional process based on the principle of reciprocity and a way to achieve an improvement in meaning transmission: "Writing is no less interactive than speech in either principle or practice. As discourse, writing is nonetheless an interactive medium even if the reader does not know the writer. ... As long as writers and readers collaborate in their complementary and reciprocal tasks of composing and comprehending ... the result is coherent communication" (pp. 40-41).

Thus, Nystrand's book and the research cited in it can be used as the basis for a theoretical understanding of therapeutic writing. Of course, further research on clinical and therapeutic effectiveness is crucial.

Advantages

On the basis of my experience, I see therapeutic writing as a valuable adjuvant to therapy because of the following advantages:

1. Therapeutic writing increases a sense of self-mastery. For instance, by keeping appointments and concentrating on a single task, the client begins to feel that he or she is doing something worthwhile for and by himself or herself.

2. It improves self-knowledge because the client no longer ruminates and obsesses but is able to get these thoughts out of the self so that the client and the therapist can look at them.

3. It increases the process of introspection, reflection, and mediation, especially in considering previously impulsive and repetitive behaviors.

Therapeutic writing can be classified into two different classes of activities that represent extremes on a continuum of structure. At the extreme of openness and little structure, the instructions may be merely "Write anything that comes to your mind." The next step in an increase of structure is "Write anything that comes into your mind when you are depressed [anxious, fearful, tense]." From here one goes into much greater structure, such as series of written questions and instructions focused on a particular topic, such as loneliness, dependency, deception. I have developed written homework assignments that deal with (a) depression, negotiation, and intimacy in couples (1986); (b) written paradoxical procedures to deal with arguments or fights, sibling rivalry, and temper tantrums in families (see chapter 10); and (c) a workbook to work with acting-out juveniles on parole or with incarcerated criminals who have low social comprehension (L'Abate, 1987b), and (d) a workbook to facilitate awareness and increase growth in individual psychotherapy (L'Abate, 1987a). Homework assignments on depression have been administered in a pilot project to nursing students in an abnormal psychology class. According to scores on the Beck Depression Scale, these assignments lowered significantly the level of depression of the students who scored in the medium and high ranges of depression. Unfortunately, there was no control group. However, Levis (1987) is using the same assignments to compare their effectiveness with the effectiveness of written homework assignments based on Beck's cognitive therapy. The rest of the evidence supporting the clinical effectiveness of these procedures is strictly impressionistic and needs to be bolstered by forthcoming empirical evidence.

The topics on which one can write are as varied as the immense range of the human condition. Nevertheless, certain topics seem to repeat, especially in cases of symptomatic behaviors, such as anxiety and depression, dependency, denial, deception. To deal with issues of identity, I have found it helpful to have clients write about their five major roles--child, single adult (personhood), married adult (partnership), parent, and parent to one's parents, under three temporal conditions (past, present, and future).

The relationship between degree and specificity of structure is represented in Table 1, in which three different degrees of structure are related to three different types of therapeutic writing.

As for disadvantages, we have found no side effects. Of course, therapeutic writing can best be used when the client is optimally motivated toward change, so that any therapeutic contract would as a matter of course include weekly meetings with the mate, or the family (L'Abate, 1986).

Implications

There are at least three kinds of implications in the practice of therapeutic writing: (a) conceptual, (b) practical, and (c) empirical.

Conceptual Implications

Conceptually, therapeutic writing is related to three areas of endeavor: (a) education, (b) business, and (c) cognitive psychology. In the case of education, one needs to be mindful that the educational process is responsible for changing more attitudes of more people than any other process. This change is predicated on the acquisition of knowledge through reading and writing. Reading consists of textbooks, articles, and notes. Writing consists mostly of examinations and term papers or the like. A great many attitudes change during the educational cycle from kindergarten to postdoctoral specialization. A great deal of the process requires the evaluation of performance in writing. The reader acquires and accumulates knowledge, then gives an idea of how much she or he has learned through written examinations and papers. This output is the basis on which the evaluator judges how much knowledge has been mastered and how well it has been mastered.

129

Table 1
A Beginning Classification for Therapeutic Writing

	Minimal	Medium	Maximal
Degree of structure	Minimal	Medium	Maximal
Specificity of structure	Open-ended	Focused	Programmed
Type of writing	Diaries and journals	Topical assignments (e.g. "depression")	1. Written procedures (see chapter 10) 2. Systematic homework assignments 3. Workbooks (L'Abate, 1987 a & b)

Hence, education is the cheapest, mass-produced form of attitude change that is based mostly on the written word. Reading is processed into writing. The writing is the basis for passing or failing and for more specific evaluation of how well one does on a particular topic.

In emphasizing the importance of writing and writing skills, Boyer (1983) concluded that "Clear writing leads to clear thinking: clear thinking is the basis of clear writing. Perhaps more than any other form of communication, writing holds us responsible for our words and ultimately makes us more thoughtful human beings. . . . Writing is an essential skill for self-expression and the means by which critical thinking also will be taught" (pp. 90, 176).

In commenting on these quotations, Quellmalz (1987) concluded, "Therefore, evidence is accumulating that our students need instruction on higher-order skills and that writing and sustained discussion are essential activities for fostering critical thought" (p. 87). We now need to accumulate evidence that not only students but also our clients can use writing as a therapeutic mode of experiencing, expressing, sharing, and learning to cope. Baron (1987) elaborated on this and earlier conclusions: "As a sustained activity, writing has the potential to develop many of the dispositions associated with the development of thinking skills. Certainly it can foster persistence and precision in both thought and the use of language. Therefore, writing provides opportunities for evaluating many of the dispositions and abilities that accompany good thinking" (p. 232).

In addition to education, progress in many other fields of human endeavor is based on the written rather than on the spoken word. No business, no political forum, no human enterprise, can flourish and advance without a written record of its transactions. Congress publishes a record of its acts. Businesses keep minutes of their meetings. Science progresses on the basis of published results. The progress of human enterprise as a whole is based on the written word. Psychotherapy and psychotherapeutic practices are one of the few enterprises in which process and assumed progress are based on the spoken word.

If thinking is at the basis of most behavior, as cognitive theorists and therapists like to stress, faulty thinking is at the basis of inappropriate behavior. Criminals and psychopaths, for instance, show a consistent deficit in the Comprehension subscale of the Wechsler Adult Intelligence Scale, with a parallel decrease in verbal intelligence and a relative increase in manual performance (sometimes Picture Arrangement, another nonverbal measure of social comprehension, is also lowered). Most traditional talk therapy with these people seems to fail because they learn what the therapists want to hear and thus talk--without any change in behavior. Some other form of therapy, not based on talk, may be necessary. This is why I have developed a workbook (L'Abate, undated a) that is programmed and

131

self-paced to retrain acting-out individuals of limited educational and intellectual backgrounds to learn bit by bit to think in more constructive and socially acceptable ways. They are asked to answer specific questions with specific answers, in writing, including week-long practice exercises, in which they apply in their behavior what they have written down on paper.

In conventional psychotherapy the only written records are the notes of the therapist. Clients are not required to perform, to produce, to show concrete and specific indications that they are really working on change rather than just talking about it. Relatively little effort is necessary to talk. Everybody does it! It is much more difficult to think and to write; that is, the act of writing implies thinking and reflection that may or may not occur in talking. In using the workbooks already mentioned, the reader is asked to indicate his or her understanding of some key terms that are necessary in daily living. The terms to be defined are, for example, law or any other key term that requires the semantic reconditioning of the individual's thinking habits. The writer needs to define and to elaborate on each term, which means thinking before acting. This process is the reverse of what most acting-out persons usually do (i.e., act before they think). The person needs to be careful about what he or she writes because the answers will be subjected to evaluation and eventual feedback, either in the form of a short response or a longer written reply.

Writing is essentially a cognitive activity that requires thinking, perhaps more thinking than is required by the act of talking. If this is indeed the case, therapeutic writing should be able to produce as much change as talking, perhaps at a lower cost.

Practical Implications

One of the most practical implications of therapeutic writing is its cost. By requiring clients to spend 1 hour writing for each hour of therapy from the very outset, as part of the initial therapeutic contract (after three sessions of evaluation), I am assuming that I am shortening the length of therapy without diminishing its effectiveness. I of course need to support this assumption with hard data, and I am prepared to do so. If one therapeutic approach is as effective as another, the cheapest form of treatment becomes the treatment of choice. If we can demonstrate that therapeutic writing can shorten the process of therapy without lowering effectiveness, a decided advance may be obtained. This advance would mean that we could help many more clients per unit of time than has been possible in the past.

Empirical Implications

Research in therapeutic writing should be easier than in therapeutic talking because a record is given by the client, and there is less need for the transcription and coding of tapes. Therapeutic writing is much more controllable than talk. In my experience, the clients who have rejected writing assignments have eventually dropped out of therapy because of lack of motivation, lack of improvement, or both. The more committed the client has been to work on change through writing in addition to, not instead of, talk therapy, the better the outcome. In some cases the outcome was extremely good. Again, I am perfectly aware that documentation rather than my personal experience will be crucial. Cogswell, Lutz, and I have finished the first research project, in which we used negotiation and intimacy homework assignments with nonclinical couples. This first study will be followed, we hope, by many others.

To evaluate the outcome of these and other treatment and intervention programs, I have constructed a variety of theory-derived, paper-and-pencil tests (L'Abate & Wagner, 1985) as well as a theory-free adjustment inventory that can be used ideographically and nomothetically, and a self-profile chart, based partially and loosely on the work of Wallace (1968).

Conclusion

In conclusion, therapeutic writing has the potential for the following functions. (a) As an adjuvant to verbal psychotherapy, it can become a supplementary form of experiencing and expressing that overlaps little with psychotherapy. (b) It may allow the exploration and elaboration of topics and areas that have not been touched upon during psychotherapy. (c) It may save time (and money) by shortening the process of psychotherapy; if it does not, it may allow the client(s) to deepen it, if that is what is desirable or desired. (d) Some persons who cannot express themselves well orally may be helped by therapeutic writing. (e) Therapeutic writing may be an easier (perhaps cheaper, i.e., cost-effective?) mode of expression to research than oral psychotherapy.

Therapeutic writing, when used within the context of a caring and compassionate therapeutic relationship, can enhance and shorten the process of therapy. In some cases, it has been a real breakthrough in dealing with difficult clinical problems, such as depression, anxiety, obsessions. Clearly, the advantages have not been fully explored, and the disadvantages need to be considered as well. The opinions and impressions I have expressed here are only the beginning step toward the fulfillment of finding external evidence under controlled conditions.

References

Abt, L. E., & Stuart, I. R. (1982). The newer therapies: A source book. New York: Van Nostrand Reinhold.

Baron, J. B. (1987). Evaluating thinking skills in the classroom. In

J. B. Baron & R. J. Sternberg (Eds.), Teaching thinking skills: Theory and practice. New York: W. H. Freeman.

Barten, H. H. (1971). Brief therapies. New York: Behavioral Publications.

Barten, H. H., & Barten, S. S. (Eds.). (1973). Children and their parents in brief therapy. New York: Behavioral Publications.

Boyer, E. L. (1983). High school: A report on secondary education in America. New York: Harper & Row.

Buchman, S. H. (Ed.). (1981). Forms of brief therapy. New York: Guilford.

Burton, A. (1965). The use of written productions in psychotherapy. In L. Pearson (Ed.), The use of written communications in psychotherapy. Springfield, IL: C. C. Thomas.

Corsini, R. J. (Ed.). (1981). Handbook of innovative psychotherapies. New York: Wiley-Interscience.

Ellis, A. (1955). New approaches to psychotherapy techniques. Journal of Clinical Psychology, 11, 208-260.

Ellis, A. (1965). Some uses of the printed, written, and recorded word in psychotherapy. In L. Pearson (Ed.), The use of written communications in psychotherapy. Springfield, IL: C. C. Thomas.

Farber, D. J. (1953). Written communication in psychotherapy. Psychiatry, 16, 365-374.

Garfield, S. L., & Bergin, A. E. (Eds.). (1978). Handbook of psychotherapy and behavior change: An empirical analysis. New York: Wiley.

Howard, V. A., & Barton, J. H. (1986). Thinking on paper. New York: William Morrow.

L'Abate, L. (1986). Systematic family therapy. New York: Brunner/Mazel.

L'Abate, L. (1987a). Workbook: Social growth. Social Training, P. O. Box 450853, Atlanta, GA 30345.

L'Abate, L. (1987b). Workbook: Social training. Social Training, P. O. Box 450853, Atlanta, GA 30345.

L'Abate, L., & Wagner, V. (1985). Theory-derived, family-oriented, test batteries. In L. L'Abate (Ed.), Handbook of family psychology and therapy (Vol. 2, pp. 1006-1031). Homewood, IL: Dorsey Press.

Landsman, T. (1951). The therapeutic use of written materials. American Psychologist, 6, 347.

Levis, M. (1987). Short-term treatment for depression using systematic homework assignments. Unpublished doctoral dissertation, Georgia State University.

Malan, D. H. (1976). The frontier of brief psychotherapy: An example of the convergence of research and clinical practice. New York: Plenum Publishing House.

Messinger, E. (1952). Auto-elaboration: An adjuvant technique in the practice of psychotherapy. Disorders of the Nervous System, 13, 339-344.

Norcross, J. C. (Ed.). (1986). Handbook of eclectic psychotherapy. New York: Brunner/Mazel.

Nystrand, M. (1986). The structure of written communication: Studies in reciprocity between writers and readers. Orlando, FL: Academic Press.

Pearson, L. (Ed.). (1965). The use of written communication in psychotherapy. Springfield, IL: C. C. Thomas.

Phillips, E. L., Test, L., R., & Adams, N. M. (1964). Multiple approaches to short-term psychotherapy. American Psychologist, 19, 475 (Abstract).

Phillips, E. L., & Wiener, D. N. (1966). Short-term psychotherapy and structured behavior change. New York: McGraw-Hill.

Progoff, I. (1975). At a journal workshop. New York: Dialogue House.

Progoff, I. (1980). The practice of process mediation: The Intensive Journal way to spiritual experience. New York: Dialogue House Library.

Quellmalz, E. S. (1987). Developing reasoning skills. In J. B. Baron & R. J. Sternberg (Eds.), Teaching thinking skills: Theory and practice. New York: W. H. Freeman and Company.

Raimy, V. (1965). The use of written communication in psychotherapy: A critique. In L. Pearson (Ed.), The use of written communication in psychotherapy (pp. 47-65). Springfield, IL: C. C. Thomas.

Reiner, T. (1978). The new diary. Los Angeles, CA: J. P. Tarcher.

Riccio, R. C. (1958). The status of the autobiography. Peabody Journal of Education, 36, 33-36.

Shaffer, E. E., Jr. (1954). The autobiography in secondary school counseling. Personnel and Guidance Journal, 32, 395-398.

Small, L. (1971). The briefer psychotherapies. New York: Brunner/Mazel.

Test, L. R. (1964). A comparative study of four approaches to short-term psychotherapy. Unpublished master's thesis, George Washington University, Washington, DC.

Usdin, G. (Ed.). (1975). Overview of the psychotherapies. New York: Brunner/Mazel.

Wallace, A. E. C. (1968). Identity processes in personality and culture. In R. Jessor & S. Feshbach (Eds.), Cognition, personality, and clinical psychology. San Francisco: Jossey-Bass.

Wolberg, L. R. (1980). Handbook of short-term psychotherapy. New York: Thieme-Stratton.

CHAPTER 12

Intimacy and Marital Depression: Interactional Partners

Edgar Jessee
Luciano L'Abate

ABSTRACT: The relationship between marital depression and lack of intimacy in a caring relationship is presented and supported with evidence from the relevant literature. A case example is given to illustrate the therapeutic implications of this viewpoint.

This article is part of a series of publications attempting to relate intimacy to depression (L'Abate & L'Abate, 1979) and to further an understanding of marital depression as distance regulation (Jessee & L'Abate, in press). In that preceding article we elaborated on the paradoxes of depression. It is the purpose of this article to link depression with intimacy or more accurately with the lack of intimacy. We are essentially arguing that depression arises from nonintimate interpersonal marital and familial contexts.

Intimacy and depression are two of the most common psychological terms currently encountered in both theoretical and clinical work with couples. Intimacy has been used primarily to describe an aspect of a relationship between two or more individuals. Depression has most commonly been referred to as a

Mr. Jessee is Clinical Director, Family Therapy and Research Institute, 6225 22nd Ave., Kenosha, WS 53140. Dr. L'Abate is Professor of Psychology and Director, Family Psychology Program, Georgia State University, Atlanta, Georgia, 30303. Reprint requests may be addressed to Dr. L'Abate.

The authors gratefully acknowledge the helpful comments of John Constantine in the preparation of this article.

condition afflicting one individual. Unfortunately, there has been very little effort to relate these interpersonal (intimacy) and intrapersonal (depression) concepts. The purpose of this article is to comment on the interrelatedness of these two terms, and in so doing, suggest a new transactional conceptualization and treatment of depression, i.e., intimacy as an antidote for depression. We certainly would like to avoid universal or cosmic statements or impressions. The field of depression is chock full of theories, theorettes, cures, etc. We are just adding our five cents worth. Of course, there are other antedotes for depression. That is why it is important to specify that we are focusing specifically on marital depression that is; those feelings of despair and hopelessness that are related to the distance and immutability of the marital situation. We want to be specific about what we are dealing with: not all depressions and not all cures!

INTIMACY

In recent years various approaches to understanding the concept of intimacy have been advocated. For instance, Derlega and Chaikin (1975) discussed intimacy in terms of self-revelation to others. Coutts (1973) considered three types of intimacy: (a) intellectual, (b) emotional, and (c) physical. Dahms (1974) expanded this definition into a three-level hierarchy; (Level 1—Intellectual, Level 2—Physical, and Level 3—Emotional) in which emotional intimacy based on mutual accessibility, naturalness, and nonpossessiveness is the highest developmental process. Davis (1973) conducted an in-depth analysis of intimacy and described it as an ongoing interaction between relatively equal individuals who reciprocate numerous intimate behaviors. Davis stated that the four parties who typically achieve some degree of intimacy are: friends, lovers, spouses, and siblings. Feldman (1976) presented a model of intimacy which included five major types of fear of intimacy: (a) fear of merger; (b) fear of exposure; (c) fear of attack; (d) fear of abandonment; and (e) fear of one's own destructive impulses. Perlmutter and Hatfield (1980) described intimacy in terms of "an intimate moment occurs when the ordinary rules of human interactions are suspended, and people begin to talk about their own and their partner's thoughts, feelings, sensations and acts." L'Abate (1977) defined intimacy as "the sharing of hurt feelings and of fears of being hurt." Within

L'Abate's definition there exist three inherent conditions that make the attainment of intimacy difficult: (a) one needs to be separate in order to be close; (b) the ones we love have the greatest power to hurt us; and (c) we must obtain comfort from and be comforted by those we hurt and who hurt us (L'Abate & L'Abate, 1979). These conditions will be elaborated in this article to relate depression to intimacy.

To utilize the concept of intimacy in relationships we have chosen to define it as a reciprocal sharing that can exist on three different levels: Emotionality, Rationality, and Activity (L'Abate & Frey, 1981). The least intimate level is that of cognitive and intellectual intimacy which includes the sharing of ideas and thought (Rationality). The second level is intimate actions, in which the sharing of activities and time together takes place (Activity). Finally, emotional intimacy consists of the sharing of positive and negative feelings, such as hurt, anger, joy, etc. (Emotionality). The important permeating thrust of this definition is the notion of reciprocity. It is impossible to achieve intimacy at any of these levels if there does not exist a feeling of reciprocal sharing.

MARITAL DEPRESSION

Although depression has historically been viewed as a phenomenologically intrapersonal problem there is increasing evidence that it contains an interpersonal component that is of primary importance (Coyne, 1976; Feldman, 1976; Hinchliffe, Hogan, and Roberts, 1978; Rubinstein & Timmins, 1978) Depression is an experience felt by one person, but only understood within the context of the depressed person's relationship with an intimate other.

Marriage poses developmental life cycle tasks that require individuals to address issues of intimacy. In adolescence the individual ideally achieves a separate identity from his/her parents and begins to relate to others, such as peers and members of the opposite sex, from a position of tested autonomy. Mating and marriage necessitate that the individual learn interdependence versus dependence or independence (Minuchin, 1974). Only through an interdependent relationship in which both members are able to mutually rely on and support each other can intimacy be achieved. Hooper and Sheldon (1969), for instance, found that newly married couples who encounter difficulty are those who

139

demonstrate little capacity for empathy or understanding with each other and little capacity for decisionmaking. Therefore, to find a clue to the understanding of the relationship between depression and intimacy it is important to examine the marital relationship, where and when intimacy is a focal issue.

Numerous researchers have found that depression and marital difficulties seem to be intricately and intrinsically related. Paykel, Myers, Dienfelt, and Klerman (1969) demonstrated that marital difficulties are the events most often reported by depressed women prior to the onset of depression. Rounsaville, Weissman, Pursoff, and Hercey-Baron (1979) discovered that depressed women involved in active marital disputes have a poorer prognosis in individual therapy than those without partners or with stable marriages. Also, women who were able to improve their troubled marriages in treatment were more likely to become less depressed. Overall (1971) examined the relation between symptom patterns and marital status in over 2,000 subjects and found that depressive mood and guilt were much more likely to be found in the married and once-divorced group. Overall concluded that this occurrence must be related to pathological dependency relationships. Schless (1974) found that depressed patients feel expecially vulnerable to marriage-related stresses, and that the vulnerability did not disappear when the patient had recovered. Hinchliffe, Hooper, Roberts, and Vaughn (1977) investigated depressed couples and discovered that long-term marital conflict was a poor prognostic sign in recovering from depression.

These studies do not explain the relationship between marriage and depression, but rather merely point to the existence of a relationship between the two. We submit that to understand this relationship the additional concept of intimacy must be included.

MARITAL DEPRESSION AND INTIMACY

Historically, depression has often been limited to the concept of psychological loss — physical, emotional, or imagined. However, as Paykel, Weissman, Prusoff, and Tonks (1971) observed, such a loss does not seem to be present in 15 to 20% of depressed women. Thus, loss alone cannot be a sufficient precondition for depression to occur. Every person experiences numerous losses within the course of a lifetime and responds with a bereavement experience. In effect, the loss of something or someone important precipitates the need for contact with others in terms of support and comforting. If the support of the bereavement of the individual by another is seen as comprising an intimate interaction, then it follows that loss precipitates a need for intimacy in relationships. The question of whether the loss is followed by normal bereavement or a chronic depressive reaction can be related to the presence or absence of intimacy in the afflicted person's primary social relationships (Brown & Harris, 1978). The presence of a stable, intimate relationship appears to be an insulating factor for many of life's crises (Brown, Bhrolchian & Harrris, 1975; Hinchliffe et al., 1977; Kreitman, Collins, Nelson & Troop, 1970; Ovenstone, 1973).

For depressed persons this insulating factor is of primary importance. Brown and Harris (1978) found that women without an intimate relationship with a husband or confidante were four times as likely to become depressed when faced with severe life event stress. The existence of intimacy in depressed individuals has rarely been cited. Brown and colleagues (1975), for instance, found only 4% of a sample of depressed women had a good intimate relationship. The stereotypical depressed housewife is a person placed in a situation demanding emotional reciprocity, yet she is unable to achieve it. Instead, she feels alone and eventually achieves aloneness by alienating others through her excessive demands and controlling interactions. Feldman (1979) commented on such an occurrence in terms of a marital-conflict cycle that appears to limit the degree of intimacy between a couple. According to Feldman, conflict is often stimulated by an actual or anticipated increase in intimacy. The interpersonal function of the conflict is to reduce the level of intimacy. However, once intimacy is decreased, a wish for intimacy reemerges. A similar relationship pattern appears to exist with depression and intimacy. Depression serves to reduce the level of intimacy in order to preserve the marital system. Marital systems prone to depression consequently are unions in which a high level of intimacy can be tolerated.

In order to understand this self-regulating, protective relationship between depression and intimacy the underlying paradoxical nature of depression in marriage will be examined.

PARADOXES OF MARITAL DEPRESSION

For centuries clinicians have marveled at the seemingly contradictory nature of the depressive experience. Beck (1967) wrote, "Depression may someday be understood in terms of its paradoxes" (p. 3). In our clinical work we have identified numerous paradoxes of depression that seem to be related to the previously cited paradoxes of intimacy.

The first paradox of intimacy states one has to be a separate, autonomous individual in order to share closeness with another without losing his own identity. The depressed individual lacks this initial solid basis of differentiation and becomes entrapped in his own interactional paradox because of it. The paradox is that depressed persons seek reassurances from others in order to feel better about themselves, but cannot accept the reassurances as genuine because of their inability to value themselves. To accept the reassurances of others would be to discount their own feelings of hurt, which paradoxically is the only way these individuals have of getting in touch with themselves. Depressed individuals feel guilty for not feeling the way their significant others want them to feel. The guilt then leads to increased feelings of worthlessness, hopelessness, and helplessness — i.e., depression. If the depressed individual attempts to accept the reassurance of another, then he is faced with the disjointed experience of unresolved pain masked by contradictory verbal statements of health. In short, verbal reassurances from significant others usually negate the presence of hurt and provide at best a short-term remedy. Interestingly, the well-intentioned, "nondepressed" spouse often is emotionally inexpressive (L'Abate, 1980). Thus, the reassurances offered are designed not only to help the depressed person, but also to help the nondepressed spouse to avoid dealing with intense emotion that may well be an issue for himself.

A second paradox of intimacy is that we must obtain comfort and be comforted by those we hurt and who have hurt us the most. This is an impossible task for the depressed individual. Depressive behavior can be seen as an attempt to elicit support from others but studies have demonstrated that opposite results have been achieved. For example, Liberman and Raskin (1971) found that the depressed individual alienates his family members to the point that the withdrawn depressive individual initiates more inter-actions with the family than the family members initiate with him/her. Thus, when intimacy is strived for by increasing the depressive behavior, the net result is alienation from others—which perpetuates the escalation of the depression. The more the depressed individual tries the more he experiences failure and powerlessness to change the situation. Consequently, the depressive learns hopelessness and helplessness in interactions in addition to discovering that support from others cannot be gained directly.

In a similar vein the intimacy paradox that states "the ones we love have the greatest power to hurt us" is central to another paradox of depression. This third paradox of intimacy is based on the depressed individual's ambivalence toward loved ones. When a person feels depressed there is a desire to be alone on one hand but a pressing need to be intimate with others on the other hand. In other words, there is a need to share hurtful feelings and receive support from an intimate other, but a fear that doing so will only lead to more hurt. Thus, the depressed peson attempts to withdraw, because of a distorted view of reality (Beck, 1967), whereby negative consequences are expected.

Finally, the last paradox of depression observes that it is a natural reaction for an individual to withdraw briefly from the environment to integrate experience in order to function more effectively; yet such a withdrawal in depression leads to dysfunction rather than improvement. This apparent paradox is likely due to the fact that the depressed person does not have a solid base (intimate relationships) from which to withdraw. Experience cannot be integrated without a firm sense of self, and the self is formulated from interactions with others. Therefore, to expect the depressed person with a negative self-concept to benefit from withdrawing from the ones he needs is an impossible expectation.

From these paradoxes it is clear that depression and intimacy cannot coexist. The depressive experience prohibits the existence of intimacy, yet desperately attempts to achieve it. Depression is the modulating homeostatic regulator for a marital system that cannot tolerate intimacy.

CLINICAL IMPLICATIONS

Because the therapist is also part of the therapeutic system composed of clients and therapist, he is subject to the same paradoxes of depression as the spouse of the depressed client. Unfortunately, our view is that therapists have too frequently failed in the same manner as the well-intentioned spouse. In view of the previously cited paradoxes, one can easily see how difficult it is to respond in a helpful manner to a depressed person. Rubinstein & Timmins (1978) Described two possible courses of action for the "caretaker" of the depressed person. He may either try to talk some sense into the client, or he may give false reassurances. Neither of these approaches allows the depressed individual to deal intimately with his pain with another. Consequently, the depression continues and the caretaker eventually distances himself or herself from the depressed person out of a sense of helplessness and frustration, which accelerates the depressive behavior of the client and confirms the cycle of depression. Rubinstein and Timmins referred to this process in marital couples as "microcycling." In fact, in some couples the helplessness felt by the caretaker precipitates his own depressive episode, and the couple takes turns being depressed. As long as one member remains depressed there is no hope of developing an intimate relationship.

The primary clinical question then becomes one of how to intervene to establish intimacy in a depressed relationship. The intervention can be done in a number of ways depending upon theoretical persuasion. The crucial variable is to instill only as much intimacy in the relationship as it can assimilate at any one time. The relationship must be pushed to reorganize on a higher level in a new way; but a way that is feasible. The dance of therapy is to push the couple into new interactional spheres until the system can tolerate no more, then back off, and then push some more. We have found a good rule of thumb in this regard is to try to help recreate the premorbid level of intimacy that existed in the relationship, and then to proceed from there until the system is stabilized at a satisfactory level. The premorbid level of intimacy must be considered carefully. A common mistake is for clinicians to attempt to prematurely force couples into sharing intense feelings, and the end result is that the relationship cannot stand the strain and opts out of treatment. As Minuchin (1974) stated, the first rule of therapy is to get the clients to come back. Cognitive and physical intimacy are much easier achieved initially, as we have noted previously, and seem to provide necessary steps in desensitizing the couple to tolerate increased emotional intimacy.

The common problem that presents itself in increasing the emotional intimacy of a couple is the imbalance of shared feelings. Often the depressed individual will attempt to "dump" all the negative feelings on the spouse. In other words, the depressed

144

individual becomes the pursuer and the spouse responds by distancing. This interactional sequence can usually be modified by having the nondepressed spouse begin first by discussing his own hidden depression, specifically feelings of helplessness. Such a maneuver requires that the therapist be very supportive and/or confrontive of the spouse and relabel the expression of hurt as a strength rather than a weakness. In the event that the depressed spouse attempts to reestablish the old pathological homeostasis in which he is the "sick" one, relabeling his behavior as protective of the other spouse's depression has been found to be very effective. In essence, each spouse is helped to verbalize intentional meta-communications that have previously gone unspoken, and often produced the fear of intimacy.

Tasks, behavioral contracts, paradoxical injunctions, etc., may be used to achieve these ends. The common denominator appears to be the reciprocal sharing induced, regardless of how it is accomplished. As Gottman (1979) concluded, the reciprocal element seems to be the glue of a successful relationship. Ultimately, the reciprocity proves to be the positive feedback that changes the depressive cycle.

The following is a case presentation that illustrates the inter-relatedness of intimacy and depression, and suggests a possible treatment approach.

CASE STUDY

A 32-year-old married woman with four children who had been depressed for four years and hospitalized once a year for her severe depression was seen in consultation with her primary nonmedical psychotherapist. In addition to four years of psychotherapy, she had also seen concurrently a psychiatrist who prescribed three different antidepressant drugs to be taken at the same time.

When first seen by the junior author she had indicated to her therapist that she was tired of her therapy and wanted to terminate in spite of her depression. It was at this time that her therapist asked for consultation. At the end of the visit she was given a letter to give to her husband. In spite of her protestations that her husband "would get mad at her" she was told to go ahead and give it to him. Helen was told that if he got mad she should not take any blame for the letter or for its delivery. If there was anyone to blame for the letter, that was me. One way to eliminate this problem is to preface the letter with the introductory statement "Very likely this letter is going to get you mad. However, I feel that etc., etc." This is an approximation of the letter given.

Dear Mr. X:

We want to compliment you for your wife's depression. We feel strongly that Helen has, through her continued depression, protected and isolated you from changing. It is very clear to us that your wife's love is so strong that she cannot bear to bring about any change in your marriage for fear of losing you. We hope that you will appreciate her loyalty and devotion that spares you from having to change and become more involved in confronting your marriage and yourself. We hope that your wife will continue protecting you by remaining depressed.

Respectfully yours,

The letter succeeded in unbalancing the individual nature of the depression by prompting the husband to call for an appointment for the two of them as a couple. In the next three sessions the wife became incensed at the husband and berated his passivity, indolence, and lack of involvement with the children. The wife's newfound anger was encouraged in an attempt to unbalance the marital system. Paradoxical maneuvers, such as restraining prescriptions — "you are giving up your depression too fast; you need to slow down," were utilized to aid in the unbalancing. By the fourth session, the wife had given up two of the three drugs and wanted to give up the third altogether. The issue in therapy evolved into dealing with the wife's anger and resentment and the husband's passivity, i.e., lack of interactional intimacy in their relationship. After the fifth session the wife's anger was so extreme that she walked out slamming the door off the hinges stating, "you should do therapy with him." Consequently the husband was given the assignment of asking the wife twice a week to "tell me what I have done wrong." The purpose of the assignment was to push the new intensity in the relationship beyond the normal limits in a way that avoided the normal self-regulation. The husband was quite resistant to the assignment because he did not understand its purpose. He was told that since he was already being told what to do he may as well ask for it. Furthermore, he was informed that if he could not fulfill the assignment there appeared to be little hope for his marriage.

The immediate effect of the assignment was as follows: (a) the wife no longer ordered and criticized her husband; (b) the husband's reaction was changed from that of distancing in reaction to his wife's criticism to actively pursing her derogatory remarks; and (c) the relationship was put in a state of crisis that was accompanied by intense emotionality that could not be resolved according to the old relationship rules. At this point, the couple

146

was ripe for change, and accordingly was ready to deal with intimacy unveiled by anger and depression. The turning point in therapy occurred when the husband was able to respond and share the pain with his wife both physically and emotionally. Unlike previous interactional sequences, the wife's plea for closeness was given in a genuine, congruent manner and the husband's response was not seen as one of false reassurance, but rather as a real effort to be intimate. By the seventh and final session, she had given up the last medicine (lithium) and was ready to confront the psychiatrist about what she felt was an overuse of drugs. A follow-up three weeks later revealed the following: (1) the couple was talking more with each other; (2) various issues of responsibility had been settled; (3) the couple was involved in leisure activities with the three older children as well as with each other; (4) they admitted that all issues were not resolved, but that they both felt able to deal with them, especially the issue of sharing hurt. Six months later, on Christmas day, the consultant received a call from Helen, wishing him and his family the best, and thanking him for his efforts.

In this case it happens that the husband was a rather passive man who liked to be thought of as being "a nice guy." Another husband may have reacted perhaps more belligerently. However, in our experience with husbands (and letters) a great deal of upset can be defused by starting the letter by predicting the anger and by mentioning (as some husbands do) that: "You may think that this letter is sarcastic: Nothing is further from that. This is a very serious letter. . .etc., etc." Thus the risks are lessened if they are talked about and predicted beforehand.

DISCUSSION

The depressive cycle in this couple was very similar to numerous other cases we have treated. Any movement toward increased intimacy or individual competence in a new area was met with homeostatic opposition from the undifferentiated marital system in the form of a depressive resistance. Previous attempts at encouraging individual differentiation within the marital system only served to activate the depressive cycle and maintain distance in the marriage. Therapy intervened in this process by (a) reframing the depression in interactional terms; (b) promoting intensity and open conflict within the couple; and (c)

147

creating a new interactional scenario in which resolution occurred through a reciprocal sharing of emotional pain and hurt. This new interactional pattern obviated the need for the previous depressive cycle and created a new homeostasis built on a sharing of hurt and freedom to express individuality through conflict. The treatment in this case was predominantly strategic and paradoxical in nature. Obviously the treatment goals could have been approached through other treatment philosophies and/or techniques. However, it has been our experience that paradoxical techniques with chronic depression are especially helpful in unblocking the impasses created by the aforementioned inherent experiential paradoxes.

The work of Waring (1980, 1981) in this regard is crucial to our thesis. As he has demonstrated repeatedly, intimacy, or lack of it, is a crucial factor in psychosomatic and psychiatric disturbances. Waring and Russell (1980) demonstrated how the marriages of patients with chronic physical symptoms of obscure etiology were characterized by specific incompatibilities in intimacy, socializing, and initiative. The family structure of these patients also demonstrated a preoccupation wth relationships within the family, with resulting isolation from extrafamilial social contacts and a lack of problem-solving ability. As Waring and Russell summarized the implications of their study:

> The study suggests that the level of intimacy in a marriage may be a predisposing vulnerability risk factor and an influence on ilness behavior, or a perpetuating factor in the sick role assumed by at least some hospitalized patients (p. 1981).

In a second study of 30 young married couples randomly selected from the general population, Waring, McElroth, Lefcoe and Weisz (1981) administered the following scales: (a) NIMH Courtship and Marriage and Study Questionnaire, (b) the Barron Ego Strength Scale; (c) the Locke-Wallace Marital Adjustment Scale; (d) the Family Environment Scale; and (e) the Fundamentals of Interpersonal Relations Orientation Scale. These authors found that personal identify and accurate perception of the spouse were significant correlates of intimacy. A factor analysis of all 17 variables measured by the questionnaires and scales yielded four dimensions of marital relationships: (a) compatibility, (b) structure;

148

(c) intimacy, and (d) problem solving. Furthermore, marital adjustment was significantly correlated with expressiveness, commitment, organization, expressed affection, and the absence of conflict.

In a third study, Waring, Tillman, Frelick, Russell, and Weisz (1981) interviewed 50 adults randomly selected from the general population on the topic of intimacy. In addition, 24 clinical and 24 control couples received a standardized interview where concepts of intimacy were systematically rated to help develop an operational definition of dimensions of intimacy were: self-disclosure considered as fundamental to the process, followed by expression of affection, compatability, cohension, identify, and the ability to resolve conflict. Sexual satisfaction was not found to be as important as previously thought, while perceptions of one's parents' level of intimacy were possible influences on the respondents' level of intimacy. Clinical couples were "less aware" of aspects of their marriage that influence intimacy.

In a fourth study Waring, McElroth, Mitchell, and Derry (1981) interviewed and administered self-report questionnaires to 90 married couples drawn from the general population to assess their level of intimacy. They found that high levels of intimacy were significantly associated with nonpsychotic emotional illness and psychiatric helpseeking. These results supported their other findings that the lack of marital intimacy may well be a vulnerability factor. In considering the therapeutic implications, Waring (1980, 1981) has suggested cognitive methods to facilitate self-disclosure in couples.

CONCLUSION

The time has come to begin dealing with the seeming individual experience of depression in interactional terms. The conceptual step we are proposing is the realization of the inherent connection between depression and intimacy in relationships, specifically marriage. This move provides a systemic frame for depression in a language that individual and family therapists alike can understand. Although more study is required to delineate the empirical relationship between intimacy and depression, the proposed transactional conceptualization offers a new clinical reality with a variety of resulting therapeutic options for treatment.

149

REFERENCE NOTE

1. Even though in this article we are discussing relatively unstructured modes of intervention like therapy, we are also using more linear approaches like an enrichment program dealing with depression (L'Abate & Sloan, 1981), and as a workshop format to help groups of couples learn to become more intimate.

REFERENCES

Beck, A. T. *Depression: Clinical, experimental and theoretical aspects.* New York: Harbor, 1967.

Brown, G. W., Bhrolchian, M. N., & Harris, T. Social class and psychiatric disturbance among women in an urban population. *Sociology,* 1975, *9,* 225-254.

Brown, G. W., & Harris, T. *Social origins of depression.* New York: Macmillan Publishing Co., 1978.

Coutts, R. L. *Love and intimacy: A psychological inquiry.* San Ramon, Ca: Consensus Publishers, 1973.

Coyne, J. C. Toward an interactional description of depression. *Psychiatry,* 1976, *39,* 28-40.

Dahms, A. H. Intimate hierarchy. In E. A. Powers & M. W. Lees (Eds.), *Process in relationship: Marriage and family.* St. Paul, MN: West Publishing House, 1974, pp. 73-92.

Derlega, V. J. & Chaikin, A. L. *Sharing intimacy: What we reveal to others and why.* Englewood Cliffs, N.J.: Prentice-Hall, 1975.

Davis, M. S. *Intimate revelations.* New York: The Free Press, 1973.

Feldman, L. B. Depression and marital interaction. *Family Process,* 1976, *15,* 389-395.

Feldman, L. B. Marital conflict and marital intimacy: An integrative psychodynamic-behavioral-systemic model. *Family Process,* 1979, *18,* 69-78.

Gottman, J. M. *Marital intervention.* New York: Academic Press, 1979.

Hinchliffe, M., Hogan, D., & Roberts, F.J. *The melancholy marriage.* New York: Wiley, 1978.

Hinchliffe, M., Hooper, D., Roberts, F.J., & Vaughn, P.W. The melancholy marriage: An inquiry into the interaction of depression, Part II, Expectiveness. *British Journal of Medical Psychology,* 1977, *50,* 125-142.

Hooper, D., & Sheldon, A. Evaluating newly married couples. *British Journal of Social and Clinical Psychology,* 1969, *8,* 169-182.

Jessee, E., & L'Abate, L. The paradoxes of marital depression: Theoretical and clinical implications. *International Journal of Family Psychiatry* (in press).

Kreitman, N., Collins, J., Nelson, B., & Troop, J. Neurosis and marital interaction. I. Personality and symptoms. *British Journal of Psychiatry,* 1970, *117,* 33-46.

L'Abate, L. Intimacy is sharing hurt feelings: A reply to David Mace. *Journal of Marriage and Family Counseling,* 1977, *3,* 13-16.

L'Abate, L. Inexpressive males or overexpressive females? A reply to Balswick. *Family Relations,* 1980, *29,* 229-230.

L'Abate, L. & Frey, J. The E-R-A model: The role of feelings in family therapy reconsidered: Implications for a classification of theories of family therapy. *Journal of Marital and Family Therapy,* 1981, *7,* 143-150.

L'Abate, L. & L'Abate, B. L. The paradoxes of intimacy. *Family Therapy,* 1979, *3,* 175-184.

L'Abate, L., & Sloan, S. Z. (Eds.), *Workbook for family enrichment: developmental and structural dimensions.* Atlanta, GA: Georgia State University, 1981.

Liberman, R.P., & Raskin, E. Depression: A behavioral formulation. *Archives of General Psychiatry.* 1971, *24,* 515-523

Minuchin, S. *Families and family therapy.* Cambridge, Mass: Harvard University Press, 1974.

Ovenstone, I.M.E. The development of neurosis in the wives of neurotic men. Part 2. Marital role function and marital tensions. *British Journal of Psychiatry,* 1973, *122,* 711-717.

Overall, J. Association between marital history and the nature of manifest psychopathology. *Journal of Abnormal Psychology,* 1971, *78,* 213-221.

Paykel, E. S., Myers, J.K., Dienfelt, M.N., & Klerman, G.L. Life events and depression: A controlled study. *Archives of General Psychiatry,* 1969, *21,* 753-760.

Paykel, E., Weissman, M., Prusoff, B.A., & Tonks, C. Dimensions of social adjustment on depressed women. *Journal of Nervous and Mental Disease,* 1971, *152,* 158-172.

Perlmutter, M.S., & Hatfield, E. Intimacy, intentional and metacommunication and second order change. *American Journal of Family Therapy,* 1980, *18,* 17-23.

Rounsaville, B.J., Weissman, M.M., Prusoff, B.A., & Hercey-Baron, R. L. The process of psychotherapy among depressed women with marital disputes. *American Journal of Orthopsychiatry,* 1979, *49,* 505-510.

Rubinstein, & D., Timmins, J.F. Depressive dyadic and triadic relationships. Journal of Marriage and Family Counseling, 1978, *4,* 13-23.

Schless, A.P. How depressives view the significance of life events. British Journal of Psychiatry, 1974, *125,* 406-410.

Waring, E. M. Marital intimacy, psychosomatic symptoms, and cognitive therapy. *Psychosomatics,* 1980, *21,* 595-601.

Waring, E. M. Facilitating marital intimacy through self-disclosure. *American Journal of Family Therapy,* 1981, *9,* 33-42.

Waring, E. M., & Russell, L. Family structure, marital adjustment, and intimacy in patients referred to a consultation-liaison service. *General Hospital Psychiatry,* 1980, *3,* 198-207.

Waring, E. M., McElroth, D., Lefcoe, D., & Weisz, G. Dimensions of intimacy in marriage. *The Journal of Psychiatry,* 1981, *44,* 169-175.

Waring, E. M., Tillman, M.P., Frelick, L., Russell, L., & Weisz, G. Concept of intimacy in the general population. *The Journal of Nervous and Marital Diseases,* 1981, *168,* 471-474.

Chapter 13

The Denial of Depression and Its Consequences

Luciano L'Abate

Abstract

The denial of depression produces many different consequences. Among the many possibilities are (a) addictions, (b) perpetuation of the drama triangle in the family, (c) distance regulation (inconsistency in approach-avoidance tendencies), and (d) the sabotage of treatment. The possible origins of this denial are discussed and therapeutic implications considered.

One of the most difficult and resistant individual and family patterns to work with is not depression. Once an individual admits the presence and power of depression in his or her life and family, it is relatively easy to find a variety of ways and means to deal with it successfully. A much more difficult pattern to deal with in family therapy is the denial of depression. For every individual or family who admits depression, as many as four to eight individuals or families may deny it.

Along the spectrum of the recognized forms of depression, at least four manifestations stand out: (a) depression with physical and physiological reactions, such as psychomotor retardation, vague physical symptoms without physical causes, mania, hypochondriacal preoccupations, as in low back pain, sleeplessness, inability to eat or lack of interest in food, fatigue, decreased sexual desire and potency, apathy, suicidal ideations and suicide attempts (Paykel, 1982); (b) depression with somewhat less obvious but identifiable psychological reactions, such as helplessness, hopelessness, sadness, feelings of inadequacy (Beck & Young, 1985); (c) a continuum of symptomatic behaviors stemming from or at least related to denial of depression; and (d) normal depressive reactions to life events.

The various categories of disorders stemming from the denial of depression (c) have been given a great deal of attention because of their almost epidemic qualities and their effect on our society as a whole. These categories include the various compulsive addictions, such as alcoholism, drug use, extramarital affairs, workaholism, compulsive shopping beyond one's financial means, gambling, compulsive sports and sport activities, overeating, and excessive TV watching. In my experience, however, less obvious but just as destructive consequences of this denial also manifest themselves. These less obvious outcomes of the denial of depression can be seen in at least three destructive patterns in the family: (a) the drama triangle (victim, rescuer, persecutor); (b) distance regulation (inconsistencies and contradictions in approach-avoidance tendencies), and (c) indirect and oftentimes subtle sabotage of treatment. The purpose of this paper is to elaborate on these three less obvious manifestations of the denial of depression in the family.

Denial of Depression in the Literature

The coverage of the denial of depression in the literature is sporadic and certainly less than systematic (Ban, Gonzalez, Jablensky, Sartorius, & Vartamian, 1981; Beckham & Leber, 1985; Rutter, Izard, & Read, 1986). To go into the literature on the origins and causes of depression and its derivatives, however, would take me away from the main purpose of this paper. Some authors have alluded to the denial of depression as "masked depression" (Hamilton, 1982), but they have usually neither followed up nor elaborated on the implications of this masking.

Since Freud's pioneering overall discussion of defense mechanisms against the upsurge of overwhelming results of breakthroughs or breakdowns of affect, especially painful affect (Coyne, 1986), most of the discussions on this topic can be found in the psychoanalytic literature (Geller, 1984). This pattern was mentioned earlier by Brill (1929), then by Deutsch (1937), who wrote the original article in German in 1933. The original formulation of denial was to see it as one of the mechanisms of defense used to avoid reality and decrease inner pain.

Other psychoanalytic writers, such as Linn (1953) and Rubinfine (1953, 1962), essentially maintained the same formulation until Strachey (1961) drew a sharp and necessary distinction between repression, which is directed against internal pressures, and denial per se, which is directed more toward a disavowal of external pressure. Dorpat (1985) did consider the defense of denial in its many and theoretical aspects. Unfortunately, he did not relate it directly or specifically to the denial of depression. He proposed, however, a theory of cognitive arrest that would retard the development of thinking according to age-appropriate stages. Haynal (1985), in a chapter on defenses against depression (pp. 121-127), listed a schizoid organization with paranoid or autistic features, in which "distance vis-a-vis the depressive affect is maintained at a cost of a distance in object relations," possibly due to "an early disappointment," or in Bowlby's terminology, "object loss, . . . allowing no more than 'shadow' object relations, scattered and of feeble intensity (part-object relations)" (p. 122). More to the point, Haynal wrote, "Denial is the defense mechanism specifically mobilized against reality, and is associated with idealization and omnipotence" (p. 125). Idealization is "another defense against narcissistic wounds and is sometimes a component of the denial of reality. . . . All such defensive solutions serve to forestall depression and the working through of mourning" (p. 127).

Haynal, of course, is not the only psychoanalytic writer to discuss this topic. Much earlier, Jacobson (1957), among many other early psychoanalytic writers (Coyne, 1986), viewed denial as a mechanism necessary to harness "dedifferentiation" and hide the original source(s) of the initial loss or painful experience. More recently, Fink (1977) mentioned denial fleetingly in relation to EST treatment. Denial was mentioned twice in case histories by Rounsaville & Chevron (1982, p. 118, 125) and in a more up-to-date version of what is known as the interpersonal psychotherapy of depression (Klerman, Weissman, Rounsaville, & Chevron (1984).

In their classic study of defense mechanisms, Miller and Swanson (1960) divided defense mechanisms into two "families." In the first family the defenses share

> simplicity, maximal distortion, generality, and the creation of social difficulties. Denial is representative of such mechanisms. Almost anything can be denied, be it observable fact or motivational state, since the mechanism results in a blotting out or reinterpreting of the event. The defense is as easy as dreaming, and requires little previous practice. . . . The man who denies his difficulties cannot take active steps to help himself. In fact, if he is frequently unable to estimate what is happening about him, he may not even be capable of carrying on normal social relationships. (p. 100)

Miller and Swanson characterized the second family of defenses as more complex (e.g., displaced aggression), with a smaller distortion of the perceptual field and applicable only to specific kinds of conflict, such as turning against the self. These authors observed that the second family of defenses "creates fewer social problems than the first" (p. 200). Thus, according to them (and I concur), denial would create more social problems than would most other defenses.

Outside the psychoanalytic school, Rogers (1959) also discriminated between two defensive processes: one distorts the meaning of the experience; the other denies the existence of the experience. Denial, then, helps preserve the integrity of the self from threat by not allowing the conscious expression of denial. Distortion, which Rogers considered a much more common defense, allows a threatening experience into awareness but in a way that makes it more congruent with self-perception (p. 205). Implicit in Rogers' formulation is a differentiation of emotions and feelings that has been stressed only recently (L'Abate, 1985); that is, how feelings and emotions are experienced receptively (i.e., inside an individual) needs to be sharply separated from how these same feelings and emotions are expressed outwardly. One may feel very bad inside but deny this experience to anyone, including oneself. One may feel very angry at somebody. Given the same feelings of anger, one person may walk away from the individual who is the source of anger; another person may take a gun and shoot the one who is the source of anger. This may well

155

be true of many addicts, especially alcoholics, who score as nondepressed on most self-report measures of depression but who do feel depressed inside. However, they are not about to admit these "bad" feelings because the admission would increase their feelings of vulnerability, helplessness, and inadequacy. Only after society or the family puts restraints or consequences on their destructive behavior can some of these people come to terms with the underlying experience. For example, many addicts become extremely depressed, even suicidal, only after they are admitted to a psychiatric ward or to a jail.

This further differentiation of internal, receptive emotional experience and external expressive admission of the emotional experience would produce a two-by-two model of defenses, including denial, which could take place receptively but not outwardly. For example, many addicts may pay lip service to being depressed but still avoid experiencing the depression; other addicts may experience the depression deeply but be unwilling to admit it outwardly. By the same token, distortions in reaction to emotionally threatening stimuli and situations could take place at the receptive or at the expressive level or at both levels. Of course, more work needs to be done to test the validity and usefulness of this framework.

As a defense mechanism, denial is associated either with repression or with the isolation of affect. Rosenhan and Seligman (1984) defined it within repression: "If repression obliterates facts, denial does away with distressing external ones. Denial commonly occurs when our sense of security and of being loved is threatened. The fact that people generally find it difficult to accurately perceive negative feelings directed toward themselves suggests that the denial process is widespread" (p. 72). Although I agree that denial is perhaps even more widespread than may be commonly thought, I do not agree that denial applies only to external rather than to internal situations. Further, there may be situations in which this denial may produce helpful outcomes, either externally or internally. Here, however, I am using denial specifically as an avoidance, a negation, or a refusal to consider that anything may be amiss in one's personality makeup. Depression, seen as a negative characteristic (especially by men), as a weakness, fault, or deficit in one's self, is denied as existing as a felt, internal, personal state.

Millon (1969), in this vein, considered a whole class of denial mechanisms under which he classified repression, isolation of affect, projection, reaction-formation, doing and undoing, fixation, and regression. For him, denial mechanisms represent "the banishing from consciousness of intolerable memories, impulses, and conflicts. By various maneuvers, the patient disavows these feelings and thoughts, and thereby avoids acknowledging their painful nature" (p. 88). I tend to agree more with Millon than with Rosenhan and Seligman that denial may be the outcome or by-product of a variety of defensive manuevers, including the two basic processes of defense--repression and isolation of affect.

156

The denial of depression may have some very deleterious effects on family functionality, especially when externalizations and projections occur. The depressed person, instead of looking inside himself or herself, tends to find external targets, culprits, or scapegoats nearest to the self, such as mate and children, who can then become the external focus of symptoms and conflicts. They distract, by irrelevant behaviors, the person from dealing with the depression, thus prolonging it (L'Abate, Weeks, & Weeks, 1977; L'Abate, Weeks, & Weeks, 1979).

Destructive Patterns

The Drama Triangle

The drama triangle has been discussed in detail (L'Abate, 1986) as a family model of dysfunctionality. When this triangle is evident in the reports or interactions of family members, it usually hides the denial of depression in one or more family members. This triangle is expressed through (a) a great deal of arguing or downright fighting between marital partners (both partners play all three parts--victim, persecutor, and rescuer); (b) sibling rivalry, in which siblings, perhaps as a metaphor of parental behavior, victimize each other, forcing the parent to rescue them; and (c) temper tantrums, in which the child plays the victim. However, through the tantrum the child is able to persecute the caretaker, who then acts as a rescuer by trying to find ways, usually ineffective, to terminate the tantrum.

In my experience, these three patterns indicate a breakdown of the parental coalition and inadequate parenting skills. Because of the intense strength of these resistant patterns, it may be necessary to use written, paradoxical procedures to decrease their influence on the family (chapters 10 and 11). More often than not, after the family has been helped to diminish the effects of these three patterns, the therapist needs to check for the presence of depression.

Distance Regulation

Another way of finding the presence of depression is to check whether the partners have developed a strong pattern of approach (pursuer) or avoidance (distancer). Usually a pattern of inconsistency between these two possibilities (i.e., inconsistencies and contradictions in approach or avoidance--"Come here, I need your help. Go away-- what you are offering me is no good") hides depression. For a more detailed description of this form of denial, see L'Abate (1986).

When the pattern of approach-avoidance is very strong, depression may be admitted readily. In fact, of the three patterns considered here, distance regulation allows a freer admission of depression than does the drama triangle or the sabotage of treatment.

Sabotage of Treatment

The sabotage of treatment is a much more subtle pattern than the two preceding ones. It may take up to a year of futile treatment to see that no progress has taken place, no matter what therapeutic changes or strategies may have been implemented. This pattern can only be detected over time; in most instances, the person refuses to deal with the depression directly. This is especially true of former cocaine addicts and the children of alcoholics. They present an outwardly cooperative stance, establish a strong pattern of dependency on the therapist, regale the therapist with juicy details of past painful family experiences, but, (and this is a major diagnostic sign) they cannot cry and mourn these painful experiences with their mates. Many of these people are middle- to upper-level managers or the equivalent, successful in their jobs, but unable to fulfill their responsibilities as partners and parents (L'Abate & L'Abate, 1981). They have superficial social skills in terms of relating well to prospective business clients but show a persistent pattern of continuous discounting of their wives and have no lasting friendships on their own. Usually, they are married to competent women, who become more and more dissatisfied with their lot and ultimately ask for therapy, which is typically refused by these men.

Men who deny depression come to therapy only after their wives threaten divorce or start divorce proceedings. If they are involved in an affair, many of them prefer to go on with the divorce rather than agree to therapy. Their priorities are focused on job achievement and status; they resist self-definition by personal and familial roles (person, partner, parent). Their self-definitions accord strictly with occupational status. Their language is one of activity and businesslike rationality (performance, problem solving). They cannot relate to their wives' stress on the importance of subjective feelings and closeness. Outwardly and socially they play the nice guy, the hail-fellow-well-met, the glad-hander. At home (when they are there) they tend to isolate themselves from everyday routines and responsibilities, leaving their wives to raise the children and to take responsibility for financial and social matters.

In therapy, therefore, these men tend to maintain the facade they have learned to use in public—being nice, accommodating, and cooperative. The lack of real involvement in the treatment process, however, is seen in how they deal with the written homework assignments, which are an important aspect of my therapeutic practice. They may perform the assignments without any real involvement, fail to complete them, or refuse to do them on the grounds that they "don't help" (L'Abate & Baggett, 1985). Sometimes they are joined in this refusal by their wives, who feel that they have gotten enough out of the treatment and collude with their husbands in not wanting to go any further. These difficulties in completing homework assignments have also been reported by Beck and Young (1985), who discussed therapeutic maneuvers for dealing with these difficulties that are very similar to my experience with written homework assignments.

The main characteristics of the denial of depression are (a) the presence of an addiction or addictive pattern, going from blatant drug usage to less blatant and sometimes more socially acceptable patterns of compulsiveness in eating, working, or shopping; (b) drivenness to the point that the person is bent on doing (working) and having (money, possessions) and has no interest in being with oneself (i.e., reflecting, meditating, resting) and with loved ones, not listening to their feedback and reactions about how hurtful this pattern is to them; (c) emotional withdrawal and isolation of affect, as a by-product of either stress on impulsive and persistent action or early childhood practices (e.g., "Strong men don't cry") or both, producing an inability, possibly alexithemia (Sifneos, 1973), to deal with feelings and emotions in oneself and others.

More indirect but still indicative patterns that may also be present are (a) reactive fights and arguments or equivalent uproars, accidents, and explosive fits of anger or rage; (b) overemphasis on a facade of "normality," at the expense of being oneself and allowing others in the family to be themselves; (c) insomnia or the inability to relax and to let go of everyday pressures and stresses, with overreliance on an addictive pattern to avoid confronting the painful consequences of one's behavior.

The Measurement of Denial of Depression

In addition to the patterns discussed, which are discernible from careful interviews or from subsequent therapy sessions, the therapist can assess the denial of depression by using the validity scales of the Minnesota Multiphasic Personality Inventory (e.g., high scores on the Lie, F, and K scales coupled with a low Depression scale score in spite of the fact that the person has experienced many depressive episodes).[1] Usually this kind of person has confused priorities about the self, marriage, children, parents/in-laws/siblings, work, friends, and leisure time (L'Abate, 1986) and shows a constellation made up of a strong and entrenched occupational identity ("I am what I do in my work"), few friends or shallow and short-lived friendships, and no hobbies or interests outside work.

Discussion

At least two sets of issues are relevant to the denial of depression. One set deals with possible theoretical explanations for the denial of depression. The second set deals with whether this denial is the outcome of the depressed person's inability or unwillingness to admit depression.

159

Theoretical Explanations

Most theoretical explanations that are relevant to an understanding of depression, which are contained in the phenomenological, experiential literature (Fann, Karacan, Pokorny, & Williams, 1977) of the cognitive and psychoanalytic schools (Coyne, 1986) or the behavioral school (Paykel, 1982), are of little use in trying to understand the denial of depression, especially in borderline cases of depression. These theories are of course useful in understanding the origin of the denied depression, but they are not sufficient to explain the denial. We need alternative explanations for the overuse of denial.

First, the therapist needs to consider whether the denial is the by-product of the depression or whether the depression is an outcome of denial. Does one deny because one is depressed, or is one depressed because one is denying? This, of course, is the old chicken-egg argument, which is difficult to resolve unless empirical evidence, at this moment nonexistent, can be mustered to answer this riddle. The therapeutic and theoretical implications go beyond the scope of this paper, but whether one comes before or "causes" the other, the therapist needs to concentrate on the outcome of the process of denial.

The two most helpful sources, in a beginning theoretical understanding of the denial process, are Friedman, Harris, and Hall (1984) and Geller (1984). Friedman et al. explained how the circuiting of feelings in general may lead persons to exhibit either Type A or Type B behavior and how Type A behavior relates to proneness to a heart attack. Type A persons express emotions nonverbally, through motoric discharge, rather than verbally. Geller elaborated on the same proposition, using the concept of intensity in lifestyle and emotional expression: "Characterologically intense individuals tend to interpret their feelings on the basis of the actions and responses of other people, rather than on the basis of internally generated clues, sensations, and thoughts. This externalizing orientation, if overgeneralized, can interfere with the differentiation of one feeling from another, and limits the capacity to spontaneously express feelings or fantasies in words" (p. 179).

Three models (L'Abate, 1986) have been found useful in understanding the outcomes of the denial of depression. One model deals with apathetic-abusive, reactive-repetitive, and conductive-creative styles. The second model deals with competence in the family on the basis of a balance of emotionality, rationality, activity, awareness, and context. The third model includes six classes of resources: services, information, money, possessions, love, and status, which are grouped into three areas of competence--doing (information and services), having (money and possessions), and being (love and status). Persons who typically deny depression have a strong propensity toward activity, or their language indicates a strong activity orientation. At best and secondarily, they may also rely on rationality (i.e., over-

160

intellectualization), but they cannot deal with emotionality and words relating to feelings and emotions. As a result, their emphasis is on doing and having, not on being. A key question is "What do you do when you do nothing?" or "Can you do nothing?" The answer is invariably that they cannot stop, reflect, introspect, and meditate. They are unable to be themselves without the help of activities and possessions.

Inability vs. Unwillingness?

The denial of depression results from an inability to deal with depression rather than a personal unwillingness or resistance. What may appear externally and superficially as unwillingness is really an inability. This conclusion is based on the work of Sifneos (1973), who described the "alexithymic" pattern, or the inability to deal with feelings and emotions. This pattern has been cross-validated on an Italian sample (Trabucco, Pasqualini, & Malesani, 1985), in whom this characteristic was found in a "normal" cross section of the population. Could it be that the denial of depression is the outcome of painful experiences that have produced a verbal inhibition to dealing with emotions and feelings in general that has then resulted in hyperactivity? In most cases, this hyperactivity and impulsivity (Geller's "intensity"?) is directed toward socially accepted pursuits, such as overreliance on work and activities as distractors and as means of avoiding unpleasant and painful feelings. Unfortunately, the result is that these people do not get close to anybody, especially their spouses.

Therapeutic Implications

The main therapeutic implication of this discussion is really diagnostic. The therapist needs to identify persons who deny depression as soon as possible, before they are allowed to sabotage treatment. Denial needs to be explored from the outset of therapy, along with the possible costs implied by that denial. How can a therapist help somebody deal with depression if it is denied all along?

One way to deal with denial is to talk about overinvolvement with work, compulsive behaviors, inability to relax, distance from the mate, problems in raising children, failure to make a commitment to the family, as manifestations of a denied depression. A second step is to assert that if no one is depressed, the family should be able to complete the assigned homework. If homework assignments are not done, a denied depression is still present. The assignment of the drama triangle homework (L'Abate, 1986) or of homework to describe, positively reframe, and prescribe arguments, sibling rivalry, or temper tantrums (chapters 10 and 11) helps to flush out the denial, especially when the mate admits depression.

It is therapeutically crucial to avoid concentrating on the denier as the identified patient. It is always important to balance any confrontation of the denying member with equal attention to other family members who admit depression or who genuinely are not depressed. If the denier is the husband, it is very important to confront the depression as "marital" or "familial," rather than individual ("It affects everybody in the family").

Conclusion

The denial of depression may well be a more pervasive and important process than it has been thought. It may be responsible for a great many family conflicts and symptoms; it may even be the basis of many divorces, suicides, and homicides. It needs to be dealt with therapeutically from the very beginning, lest it prolong therapy to an ultimate failure.

Theoretically, this paper goes back to an early formulation (L'Abate, 1975) about the pathogenic role of fathers and their contribution to an avoidance of intimacy (L'Abate & L'Abate, 1981). This formulation raises the question whether (a) I have unexplored issues of countertransference toward males, or whether (b) this formulation is in line with the results of longitudinal research on the father's influence in the genesis of psychopathology in children (Robins, 1966) and in line with possible discrepancies in emotional expressiveness between males and females (L'Abate, 1980).

Footnote

[1]An experimental scale to measure denial of depression is available for research purposes only from Social Training, P. O. Box 450843, Atlanta, GA 30345.

References

Ban, T. A., Gonzalez, R., Jablensky, A. S., Sartorius, N. A., & Vartamian, F. E. (1981). Prevention and treatment of depression. Baltimore: University Park Press.

Beck, A. T., & Young, J. E. (1985). Depression. In D. H. Barlow (Ed.), Clinical handbook of psychological disorders (pp. 206–244). New York: Guilford.

Beckham, E. E., & Leber, W. R. (Eds.). (1985). Handbook of depression: Treatment, assessment, and research. Homewood, IL: Dorsey Press.

Brill, A. A. (1929). Unconscious insight: Some of its manifestations. International Journal of Psychoanalysis, 10, 145–161,

Coyne, J. C. (Ed.). (1986). Essential papers on depression. New York: New York University Press.

Deutsch, H. (1937). Psychoanalysis of the neuroses. London,

England: Hogarth Press.

Dorpat, T. L. (1985). Denial and defense in the therapeutic situation. New York: Jason Aronson.

Fann, W. E., Karacan, I., Pokorny, A. D., & Williams, R. L. (Eds.). (1977). Phenomenology and treatment of depression. New York: Spectrum.

Fink, M. (1977). EST: A special case in pharmacotherapy. In W. E. Fann, I. Karacan, A. D. Pokorny, & R. L. Williams (Eds.), Phenomenology and treatment of depression (pp. 285-294). New York: Spectrum.

Friedman, H. S. Harris, M. J., & Hall, J. A. (1984). Nonverbal expression of emotion: Healthy charisma or coronary-prone behavior? In V. Van Dyke, L. Temoshok, & L. S. Zegans (Eds.), Emotions in health and illness: Applications to clinical practice (pp. 151-165). Orlando, FL: Grune & Stratton.

Geller, J. D. (1984). Moods, feelings, and the process of affect formation. In C. Van Dyke, L. Temoshok, & L. S. Zegans (Eds.), Emotions in health and illness: Applications to clinical practice (pp. 171-186). Orlando, FL: Grune & Stratton.

Hamilton, M. (1982). Symptoms and assessment of depression. In E. S. Paykel (Ed.), Handbook of affective disorders (pp. 3-11). New York: Guilford

Haynal, A. (1985). Depression and creativity. New York: International Universities Press.

Jacobson, E. (1957). On normal and pathological moods. In R. S. Eissler, A. Freud, H. Hartmann, & E. Kris (Eds.), The psychoanalytic study of the child (vol. 12, pp. 74-113). New York: International Universities Press.

Klerman, G. L., Weissman, M. M., Rounsaville, B. J., & Chevron, E. S. (1984). Interpersonal psychotherapy of depression. New York: Basic Books.

L'Abate, L. (1975). Pathogenic role rigidity in fathers: Some observations. Journal of Marriage and Family Counseling, 1, 69-79.

L'Abate, L. (1980). Inexpressive males or overexpressive females: A reply to Balswick. Family Relations, 29, 229-230.

L'Abate, L. (1985). The status and future of family psychology and therapy. In L. L'Abate (Ed.), Handbook of family psychology and therapy (vol. 2, pp. 1417-1435). Homewood, IL: Dorsey Press.

L'Abate, L. (1986). Systematic family therapy. New York: Brunner/Mazel.

L'Abate, L., & Baggett, M. S. (1985). A failure to keep the father in family therapy. In S. B. Coleman (Ed.), Failures in family therapy (pp. 222-240). New York: Guilford.

L'Abate, L., & L'Abate, B. L. (1981). Marriage: The dream and the reality. Family Relations, 30, 131-136.

L'Abate, L., Weeks, G. R., & Weeks, K. G. (1979). Of scapegoats, strawmen, and scarecrows. International Journal of Family Therapy, 1, 86-96.

L'Abate, L., Weeks, G. R., & Weeks, K. G. (1977). Protectiveness, persecution, and powerlessness. International Journal of Family Counseling, 5, 72-76.

Linn, L. (1953). The role of perception in the mechanism of denial. Journal of the American Psychoanalytic Association, 1, 690-705.

Miller, D. R., & Swanson, G. E. (1960). Inner conflict and defense. New York: Henry Holt & Co.

Millon, T. (1969). Modern psychopathology: A biosocial approach to maladaptive learning and functioning. Philadelphia: W. B. Saunders.

Paykel, E. S. (Ed.). (1982). Handbook of affective disorders. New York: Guilford.

Robins, L. N. (1966). Deviant children grown up: A sociological and psychiatric study of sociopathic personality. Baltimore, MD: Williams & Wilkins.

Rogers, C. R. (1959). a theory of therapy, personality, and interpersonal relationships as developed in the client-centered framework. In S. Koch (Ed.), Psychology: A study of a science (pp. 185-256). New York: McGraw-Hill.

Rosenhan, D. L., & Seligman, M. E. P. (1984). Abnormal psychology. New York: W. W. Norton.

Rounsaville, B. J., & Chevron, E. (1982). Interpersonal psychotherapy: Clinical applications. In A. J. Rush (Ed.), Short-term psychotherapies of depression (pp. 107-142). New York: Guilford.

Rubinfine, D. L. (1953). On denial of objective sources of anxiety and pain. In S. Lorand (Ed.), Yearbook of psychoanalysis: Vol. 9 (pp. 543-544). New York: International Universities Press.

Rubinfine, D. L. (1962). Maternal stimulation, psychic structure, and early object relations: With reference to aggression and denial. In D. L. Rubinfine (Ed.), Psychoanalytic study of the child (Vol. 17, pp. 265-282). New York: International Universities Press.

Rutter, M., Izard, C. E., & Read, P. B. (Eds.). (1986). Depression in young people: Developmental and clinical perspectives. New York: Guilford.

Sifneos, P. E. (1973). The prevalence of "alexithymic" characteristics in psychosomatic patients. Psychotherapy and Psychosomatics, 22, 255-262.

Strachey, J. (Ed.). (1961). The standard edition of the complete works of Sigmund Freud. London: Hogarth.

Trabucco, G., Pasqualini, A., & Malesani, P. G. (1985). Valutazione del fenomeno alessitimico in un campione di 220 soggetti normali. Psicologia Clinica, 2, 217-229.

CHAPTER 14

Treatment of Depression in a Couple With Systematic Homework Assignments

Trudi B. Johnston
Michael Levis
Luciano L'Abate

ABSTRACT. To increase the process of generalization from the therapy office to the home, theory-derived and theory testing Systematic Homework Assignments (SHWAs) have been developed to deal with marital depression, negotiation, and intimacy. The background and rationale of the first application of the depression SHWAs with some preliminary results are given. In addition, an illustrative case study is presented to suggest how to apply these SHWAs in clinical work with marital depression, to supplement and possibly improve therapeutic outcome.

The clinical literature is replete with examples of various theories and treatments for depression (Akisadal & McKinney, 1975; Paykel, 1982). These theories have tended to focus on the psychoanalytic (Arieti, 1978), behavioral (Lewinsohn, Sullivan & Grossup, 1982), biochemical (Baldessarini, 1975), and cognitive (Beck, 1976) aspects of the disorder. Despite the impressive array of possible interventions now available for the treatment of depression, it is only recently that clinicians have attempted to understand and treat depression from a social and interpersonal perspective (Brown & Harris, 1978; Hinchliffe, Hooper, & Roberts, 1978; Weissman & Paykel, 1974).

There is evidence to suggest that the marriages of depressed women are often characterized by "interpersonal friction" and poor communication, while their close relationships often involve marked levels of resentment, and inhibited communication (Weissman & Paykel, 1974). However, an intimate relationship may serve to "protect" anyone from becoming depressed (Jessee & L'Abate, 1985). As Brown and Harris (1978) have noted, the lack of a boyfriend or husband with whom to confide in increases a woman's chances for being at risk for depression. In addition, the depressed person's behavior can induce negative moods, feelings of guilt and inhibition in others (for a comprehensive review of the interpersonal aspects of depression, see Coyne, Kahn & Gotlib, 1984).

Regardless of how the depression was originally developed, numerous sources have suggested that the depressed person's close interpersonal relationships serve to maintain the depressive symptomatology (Feldman, 1976; Coyne, 1984). Feldman (1976) described "patterns of reciprocal stimulation and reinforcement" which allow the depressed person to feel helpless, guilty and self-deprecating, while the spouse maintains the role of the "omnipotent" and "overprotective" one. Similarly, Rubenstein and Timmins (1978) contend that depressed persons involve themselves with caretaking partners. The caretaker may be "compliant" by offering explanations, reassurance and support. They may also take an "aggressive" role and attempt to "talk sense" to the depressed partner. Regardless of the caretaking role, the interaction tends to focus on the complaints and demands of the depressed partner, thereby reinforcing the depressive behavior. It has been suggested that one way of altering the entrenched, interactional depressive patterns between partners is through the application of paradoxical interventions (Coyne, 1984; Jessee & L'Abate, 1985; Madanes, 1981).

The effectiveness of paradoxical interventions for the treatment of depression in couples has been documented in several case and experimental studies (reviewed by Jessee & L'Abate, 1985). At a minimum, these interventions usually involve: (1) reframing of the depressive behavior in positive terms; (2) prescribing of the depressive behavior; and (3) predicting a relapse. Often the caretaker is directed to remind the spouse to be depressed during the week. This approach, of course, serves to undermine the traditional "compliant" or "aggressive" roles of the caretaking spouse, thus leading to an alteration in the patterns of interaction which help to maintain the depression.

The purpose of this paper is to present preliminary clinical research in the use of initially paradoxical Systematic Homework Assignments (SHWAs) for the treatment of depression. A brief description of a pilot study on the use of SHWAs will be presented. This introduction will be followed by a full case-study which illustrates the use of SHWAs in treating a depressed couple case. Finally, specific suggestions for the appropriate use of SHWAs will be discussed.

PRELIMINARY RESEARCH

Recently, attempts have been made to assess the effectiveness of a "package" of paradoxical homework assignments which are designed to reduce depression in a partner or spouse (Levis & L'Abate, research in progress). Rather than treating the client in the office, the homework assignments are designed to be completed in writing by the client at home. These assignments are elaborations on the three main paradoxical interventions described above. These Systematic Homework Assignments (SHWAs) are part of a whole series of written modules developed by L'Abate (1986) to increase the process of generalization and the efficiency of marital and family therapy. Each couple or family that is accepted for therapy is required to spend one hour together at home for every hour of therapy in order to work *on their own* on these assignments. These written modules were derived from models developed to test a theory of personality development and competence in the family (L'Abate, 1986; L'Abate & Wagner, submitted for publication) and, therefore, become a new way of testing the validity and usefulness of the theory underlying the models.

One preliminary study on the effectiveness of these assignments has been completed with individual undergraduates (only some of whom were involved in long-term relationships). These subjects were volunteers who received credit toward a research participation requirement for an undergraduate psychology course. Two treatment conditions were investigated. Under the "massed" condition, subjects were asked to complete the series of six homework assignments within the period of a week. Under the "spaced" condition, subjects were to complete the six assignments within six to seven weeks. Subjects' pre- and post-treatment levels of depression were assessed for both conditions using the Beck Depression Inventory (Beck, Ward, Mendelson, Mock & Erbaugh, 1961).

The results indicated that there was no significant difference between the pre- and post-treatment Beck scores in the "spaced" condition. It was determined, however, that the pre- and post-scores in both the "spaced" and "massed" conditions were statistically comparable. As such, they were combined into one treatment condition of 27 subjects. There was, in fact, a significant difference between pre- and post-Beck Depression Inventory (BDI) scores for the combined group of 27 subjects.

In order to assess the possible effect of the treatment on the more and less severely depressed subjects, the scores of the 27 subjects were separated into three groups. Group 1 consisted of 10 subjects who had pretest BDI scores of less than 5. Group 2 consisted of 10 subjects with BDI pre-test scores from 5 to 9. Group 3 consisted of the remaining 7 subjects with BDI pre-test scores ranging from 10 to 25. (Thus, only group 3 could be considered to be "clinically" depressed.)

While it was determined that there was no significant difference between the pre- and post-BDI scores in Group 1, a significant difference was found between pre- and post-scores in Group 2 and in the clinically depressed, Group 3. These preliminary results suggest that the paradoxical depression homework assignments may have had an effect in reducing depression in "clinically" depressed individuals. However, at this

169

point, the absence of a control group requires that these results be interpreted as merely suggestive. Further controlled research in this area with the application to depressed couples is in progress to substantiate the effectiveness of the homework assignments. These SHWAs have already been applied to the treatment of depression (Levis, research in progress), negotiation (Lutz, 1985), and intimacy in married couples (L'Abate, Young, and Lutz, research in progress). In fact, Jessee and L'Abate (1985) suggest that intimacy is an antidote for depression. However, in therapy, usually intimacy in marital couples cannot be reached until and unless, depression has been successfully dealt with first within the marriage, and then the couple can learn to negotiate most conflictual issues (L'Abate, 1986). Intimacy may well be the antidote for depression, but negotiation is the bridge between the two! Many of these points will be illustrated by the following case-study.

BACKGROUND AND TREATMENT

This couple had been married 12 years when family therapy was initiated. Each is a child of an alcoholic parent. The husband is the oldest of eight and the wife the younger of two. The wife had been in therapy for severe depression and was hospitalized at one point about 5 years ago. She could be described as highly emotional, sensitive and verbal. The husband grew up as the parental child, highly responsible, controlled to the point of rigidity and not verbal but rather quiet and withdrawn.

The mother scheduled the first session for herself and her 7 year old boy and 9 year old girl. The presenting complaint was her concern for the emotional and social development of the children. She explained that both of them were having some behavior problems at school, and she thought they needed to learn how to express anger and other feelings. After seeing the children and talking with their school teachers, the therapist determined that the children's difficulties stemmed from the parents' disagreements about how they should be managed at home and with the school. The father was distant and maintained a punitive and cold attitude toward the children and their homework. The mother was obviously overinvolved with the children's learning and was also mostly responsible for their parenting, their management and school work. The father was asked to attend the sessions with his wife in order to better help the children. After several sessions in which the children and their behavior was the focus, it became clear that the tensions between the parents and the school and between the parents and the children were directly tied to the tension between husband and wife. She needed her husband's emotional support, and because this support had not been and was not forthcoming, she spent most of her energy on the children rather than herself or the marriage.

The situation reached crisis proportion as the mother became increasingly helpless and the father became increasingly distant and angry. The intensity of the situation and the rigidity of the entrenchment in the family patterns required that a written summary be made of the situation and that a positive reframing be made *in writing,* to join the family and to clear the decks of past recriminations, gunny-sacking, etc. in the marriage. A paradoxical letter was written and read to the couple by the therapists (L'Abate, Ganahl, & Hansen, 1986, p. 122).

This letter had much impact. For the first time in therapy the couple held hands and cried. Both admitted that the letter was correct and that they needed help for their relationship. At this point the couple's relationship became the focus of therapy. Parenting issues were discussed occasionally, but the couple had now become convinced that things would go much better with the children if they focused on resolving some of their relationship difficulties. During this phase of treatment, the therapist continued working on developing a therapeutic relationship with each of them, being careful to congratulate and confront each person on an equal basis. The spouses' inability to discuss issues openly with each other was apparent. The husband often gave short, one-word answers to his wife. She often compensated for his silence with many words which often were tangential. Most of their discussions with each other did not lead to sharing feelings or thoughts, but rather led to further avoidance of important issues. The avoidance usually led to more distance. The husband would withdraw into his work, friends or alcohol, and the wife would get busy with the household or sometimes would spend money. After days or weeks of maintaining distance, the husband would "explode," threatening to leave his wife, change jobs, get a divorce or make other equally drastic changes. The "explosion" usually led to extreme silence and distance, which later led to the return to quieter conditions.

This cycle was reinterpreted to the couple by the therapist as great passion in their marriage. It was explained that only people who care about each other bother to fight and "explode," and that although this cycle indicates their love and need for each other and usually resulted in some eventual closeness, it was a painful cycle which could be changed for the better. Some attempts were made to institute change toward intimacy but these therapeutic attempts failed.

In a therapy session following such an explosion, the wife complained that the husband withdrew from her by staying at work, visiting his parents and drinking. He complained about her overspending and her unwillingness to talk with him about important matters. Both seemed extremely discouraged with themselves and their marriage. The wife readily admitted that she still suffers from bouts of depression and low self-esteem. The husband's withdrawal, apathy and other clinical symptoms also pointed to depression. Although it was clear that the couple's level of inti-

171

macy was low and needed to be addressed in therapy, the depression was seen as fundamentally important and necessary to manage prior to intimacy issues. Marital depression may be a desperate attempt to achieve intimacy but actually prevents it. It was decided that the Systematic Homework Assignments (SHWAs) with depression would be administered over a period of six sessions in order to facilitate each partner's management of his or her depression.

The husband was confronted with the opinion that he was depressed. He responded by saying that he knew he was. His revealing this information about himself in front of the therapist and his wife was interpreted as a major step for him, because in the past he seldom expressed emotions or admitted to being vulnerable.

One session was devoted to preparing the couple for the depression SHWAs. They were asked to work on the assignments independently at first. It was explained that there are ways to control depression which are very effective. They were challenged to give the necessary time to the assignments during the week. Session time was devoted to discussing the concept of homework and whether they were willing to begin the process. The first assignment was given to them and some time spent explaining the directions. They were told that in the next session they could discuss important issues which were introduced by the homework.

The paradoxical approach to the treatment of depression assumes that depression is good and can be helpful to the individual (Jessee & L'Abate, 1985; L'Abate, 1986). Therefore, the *first* homework assignment challenges the client to define depression and to look for the positive elements in the depression.[2] The husband defined depression as "a feeling of lost control, unable to overcome problems with reasonable approaches, large frustration buildup." The wife reported, "Depression for me has many stages. It can be anything from a feeling of tiredness or sadness to a 'big black cloud' that completely engulfs you and drains you of all energy, joy or other emotions. At its worst, the simplest tasks are almost impossible to accomplish, and you don't care about anything, even living or dying."

The above definitions of depression illustrate the typical negative connotation of depression. The couple admitted that their usual way of dealing with depression was to avoid it, stay busy and not openly confront it. This approach they also admitted, usually did not help. Perhaps it should be noted that the written homework assignments seemed to be an important technique in encouraging the husband to communicate his thoughts and feelings. Openly discussing them was difficult for him prior to his experience with writing them down. The act of writing down his thoughts and feelings facilitated his expressing them verbally later to the therapist and to his wife.

The next homework assignment for each spouse was to rank order nine positive definitions of depression. Although each of the definitions is dif-

172

ferent in some way, they all include some positive description of depression. For example, one definition states, "Depression can be a useful feeling and one which, eventually if you can use it correctly, may lead you to understand and appreciate its importance." Others include ideas that depression is common to all humans, can be a friend, is a choice and is an indicator that you know your true feelings.

The *second* homework assignment suggests that each spouse allow himself or herself to be depressed on three separate occasions. They are to notice the benefits of the experience and write them down. After this exercise the husband wrote: "My depression builds to an overwhelming size in a short period of time. This is followed by an abandonment of hope which is varying in length depending on the problem. I found that if I sit down and start to look at the problem rather than hoping it will go away, then I can deal with it and not sit and worry about it any more. This also breaks it into little pieces rather than one large doom cloud."

Because of the wife's history with severe depression, she had difficulty seeing depression as having positive attributes. She expressed her overwhelming fear of the "black cloud" and could not imagine intentionally trying to make herself depressed or "inviting the cloud." In her opinion this was to be avoided at all times. However, she did agree to try the assignment which instructed her to make herself depressed and later reported, "The more I *thought* about my feelings rather than giving in to them, I didn't feel as exhausted as usual when I am depressed."

The *third* and *fourth* assignments are to aid in controlling depression. The couple is asked to think of methods which they can use to start a depression. They are informed that if they want to learn to stop a depression they must begin by starting it. This allows them to control their own depression. Ways to elicit depression often involve thinking negatively about ourselves, the world or our future. The spouses are to select the method which works best for them. They are asked to describe the time and place where they usually are depressed, and the homework assignment asks them to select a time, place and method to intentionally start up a depression during the next week. A time limit of 15 minutes for the first and 25 minutes for the second episode are to be set. They are to concentrate on the feelings of depression and to write them in detail as they come up. This procedure gives the couple control of the depression. During the following week the wife wrote, "I managed to control the depression rather than let it control me. There were moments when it threatened to overwhelm me but I *chose* to work on things instead of giving up." Later she wrote that she was now able to control the depression and no longer was as afraid that it will overwhelm her. In the last exercise she reported that learning to start and stop the depression was the most helpful element of the treatment.

The husband reported that making a list of things that were on his mind

173

helped him to look at the realities rather than worrying about possible disasters, and that this look allowed him to consider solutions for the real problems. He noted that setting time limits for the depression episode was helpful.

Assignment *five* is on "Letting Others Help." The idea is that when depressed it is often helpful to share feelings with others and ask for their help. After this assignment the husband wrote, "It unburdens me to share my problems with my wife and it brings up aspects I do not readily see." This statement summarizes one of the major break-throughs in the case which indicated his willingness to confront and discuss his feelings of depression with his wife. Because of her own feelings of depression she had been afraid of his feelings, due to her fear that their combined depression would overwhelm them. Thus, she and her husband had become excellent avoiders. They had chosen to withdraw, avoiding themselves and their marriage. In spite of the risk involved, they now could admit their common feelings openly and share them with each other. Due to many years of avoiding their feelings, new ways of communicating were needed. The next treatment strategy was for the example to learn new ways of expressing feelings and negotiating solutions to their conflicts. The last stage in therapy involved dealing with intimacy (L'Abate, 1986).

These SHWAs proved to be a structure that many couples and families need for a step-wise, gradual learning to express oneself non-judgementally, taking chances in expressing feelings helpfully, and talking face-to-face like adults, negotiating and problem-solving under controlled condition (L'Abate, 1986; L'Abate, Ganahl, & Hanse, 1986). In fact, upon the completion of the depression homework, the negotiation homework assignments were begun with this couple, followed by systematic homework assignments dealing with intimacy. Negotiation consists of SHWAs dealing with: (a) practicing the "I" position; (b) learning to discriminate apathetic and abusive responses from repetitive, reactive reactions, and assuming more of a coductive stance in emotional situations; (c) discriminating emotional from rational, actional, awareness, and contextual answers; (d) dealing with intrafamilial, interpersonal, and resource priorities, and eventually (e) all of these lessons culminate in practicing to negotiate on conflictual issues according to the structure learned in the process.

The intimacy SHWAs start with a definition of love that requires: (a) physical caring; (b) seeing the good; (c) forgiving oneself and loved ones for past mistakes, and finally (d) sharing of past and present hurts. This stage of therapy is considered by L'Abate (1986) the most difficult but also the most important task of life.

It should be mentioned that the only paradoxical aspect of these SHWAs lies in the positive reframing of the initial lesson on depression. All of the other SHWAs follow strictly linear models. Since these models derive from theory, it is important that this theory be testable (L'Abate & Wagner, submitted for publication). One way of testing the usefulness of the models on which these SHWAs are based is to evaluate couples and families on a pre-post treatment basis. Of course, there are other ways to test a theory (L'Abate & Wagner, submitted for publication), but this is the way most often used in this field.

Consequently, this couple was administered parts of the Marital Evaluation Battery consisting of: (a) Holmes and Rahe's (1967) Schedule of Events to measure the amount of recent situational stress undergone by the couple. This scale is usually administered only once because it has been shown to be insensitive to therapeutic changes, but it does reflect the amount of subjectively felt stress reported by each partner; (b) the Beck Depression Inventory (Beck et al., 1961), which is considered the standard instrument to evaluate depression; (c) Spanier's (1976) Dyadic Adjustment Scale, which is considered the most popular of many paper-and-pencil tests to evaluate degree of marital quality, and (d) Stevens' Sharing of Hurts Scale, which is still an experimental paper and pencil test developed to measure marital intimacy according to L'Abate's (1986) definition of intimacy as the sharing of hurts.

Currently, the couple is trying to face the fact that the husband may be an alcoholic. He is facing this issue now, when previously he would not. The couple now is able to deal with this issue because of the progress made in their relationship; namely their new ability to manage the onset and duration of depression and to share those feelings with each other.

EVALUATION

At the time the couple completed the pre-test measures, the focus of therapy was on the children and the couple as parents. Because the therapist had not yet been invited into the marriage, it is possible that the test scores do not accurately represent the true status of the marriage. There may have been an effort made to present a positive picture of the marriage on the pre-test, whereas the post-test may be a more accurate picture of the marriage.

On the Schedule of Events, the husband's score of 77 is rather low and was interpreted as his initial denial and downplay about the seriousness of the problems his children were facing, and a direct contradiction of the amount of stress felt, reported, and expressed by his wife.

In contrast, the wife's extremely high score of 605 seems to reflect her overdramatization of many life events. The exaggeration is characteristic of her highly emotional and expressive style, perhaps in reaction to her husband's denials. Again the objective measure correlated with the therapist's subjective observation. The extreme difference between the spouses' scores also reflected their wide differences in perception and interpretation of events. The same kind of discrepancy between the two spouses was found on the Beck Inventory, where the husband admitted to only 12 points while his wife admitted to 25. On the Dyadic Adjustment Scale, their scores were very similar (95 for the husband and 89 for the wife) and showed no change as a result of therapy. On the Sharing of Hurts Scale, on the other hand, there was a significant reversal. While the husband initially admitted to much greater hurt than his wife (118 versus 96), at the end of therapy his score decreased to 99 and hers increased from 96 to 111, suggesting that perhaps there were shifts in the awareness and willingness to admit to vulnerability, fallability, and neediness (L'Abate, 1986).

DISCUSSION

Therapy is continuing with this couple. Overall the depression SHWAs have proven very helpful and laid the necessary ground-work for additional therapy focusing on the relationship. The couple can now share their feelings of depression more openly. The prognosis is much more hopeful than earlier on in treatment. On the basis of this case-study as well as additional experience with the use of SHWAs with couples, some suggestions about their use may be relevant.

The client must be able to admit that he or she has indeed been experiencing depression. Other words for depression, such as discouragement and "being down" much of the time, can be used because many people either use different descriptors or have a negative view of the term. All clients must understand the meaning of depression and realize the need to deal with it.

The therapist must convincingly present the concept that depression can be a positive experience. This statement may mean that the therapist needs to believe this positively to be true and not simply a good "paradoxical" technique. Often clients challenge this positive position and it is important for the therapist to be prepared. L'Abate (1986) suggests that negativity is one of the hallmarks, among many others, of family dysfunctionality. Consequently, the therapist needs to contradict this position directly and indirectly, postulating a positivity not only about depression but about most symptomatic behavior. Hence, it may be necessary for therapists who want to use these SHWAs to experience them directly themselves, as we do in our training program.

The therapist must begin each session by collecting the homework assignments and focusing some time on the written work. After some discussion of the past week's assignment the next one can be given. If the previous week's assignment has not been completed, it should be returned to the couple to complete before going on to the next assignment. Preferably, discussion would be devoted to the reasons for the delay. Perhaps this person would prefer not to continue the SHWAs. Perhaps more time should be spent during the session prior to the discussion of homework assignments.

There is no question that SHWAs can elicit resistance in some couples, necessitating their doing these assignments in the therapist's office, and making them more expensive than they could be if done at home. Or, more importantly, if and when these SHWAs are not done, it means that the couple is still at the initial stage of treatment and that depression has not been successfully dealt with (L'Abate, 1986). These SHWAs are only an adjunct to therapy. How powerful this adjunct can be depends on the nature of the problem, the commitment of the therapist to obtain change as effectively and expeditiously as possible, and on the couple's motivation to change.

CONCLUSION

Through this case-study we have attempted to show how SHWAs can be used as complementary and supplementary to the process of therapy with depression in couples. They, of course, are not a panacea that will supplant the therapist. They are just another tool in our continuous and unrelenting search for more effective ways to deal with depression and to help marriages and families. Like any tool, SHWAs can be used for the distinct advantage of both therapists and couples, provided that they are applied properly.

FOOTNOTES

1. This couple has given informed written consent to publish this case study provided their anonymity is fully guaranteed.
2. The published (L'Abate, 1986) version introduces the Depression Program with Variations on the Drama Triangle (Victim-Rescuer-Persecutor), followed by the Distance Regulation Triangle (Distance-Regular-Pursuer). This definition of depression, then, becomes the third assignment in a series of *eight* assignments.

REFERENCES

Aksikal, H., McKinney, W. (1975). Overview of recent research in depression: Integration of ten conceptual models into a comprehensive clinical frame. *Archives of General Psychiatry, 32,* 285-303.
Arieti, S., & Bemporad, J. (1978). *Severe and mild depressions.* New York: Basic Books.
Baldessarini, R. (1975). The basis for the amine hypothesis in affective disorders. *Archives of General Psychiatry, 32,* 46-58.

Beck, A. (1976). *Cognitive therapy and the emotional disorders.* New York: International Press.

Beck, A., Ward, C., Mendelson, M., Mock, J., & Erbaugh, J. (1961). An inventory for measuring depression. *Archives of General Psychiatry, 4,* 561-571.

Brown, G., & Harris, T. (1978). *Social origins of depression.* New York: Free Press.

Coyne, J. (1984). Strategic therapy with depressed married persons: Initial agenda, themes, and interventions. *Journal of Marital and Family Therapy, 10,* 53-62.

Coyne, J., Kahn, J., & Gotlieb, I. (1984). Depression. In T. Jacobs (Ed.), *Family interaction and psychopathology.* New York: Pergamon.

Feldman, L. (1976). Depression and marital interaction. *Family Process, 15,* 389-395.

Hinchliffe, M., Hooper, D., & Roberts, F. (1978). *The melancholy marriage.* New York: John Wiley.

Holmes, T. H., & Rahe, R. H. (1967). The social readjustment rating scale. *Psychosomatic Medicine, 11,* 213-218.

Jessee, E. H., & L'Abate, L. (1985). Paradoxical treatment of depression in married couples. In L. L'Abate (Ed.), *Handbook of family psychology and therapy* (pp. 1128-1151). Homewood, IL: Dorsey Press.

L'Abate, L. (1986). *Systematic family therapy.* New York: Brunner/Mazel.

L'Abate, L., Ganahl, G., & Hansen, J. C. (1986). *Methods of family therapy.* Englewood Cliffs, NJ: Prentice-Hall.

L'Abate, L., & Wagner, V. (submitted for publication). Testing a theory of personality development in the family.

L'Abate, L., Young, L., & Lutz, J. (research in progress). The usefulness of systematic homework assignments to teach couples negotiation and intimacy skills.

Levis, M. (research in progress). A comparison of cognitive versus paradoxical treatments for depression. Ph.D. dissertation.

Lewinsohn, P., Sullivan, J., & Grossup, S. (1982). Behavioral therapy: Clinical implications. In A. J. Rush (Ed.), *Short-term psychotherapies for depression.* New York: Guilford Press.

Lutz, J. (1985). *Empirical evaluation of a set of structured communication tasks with couples: Homework assignments-practice versus traditional workshop format.* Unpublished Master's thesis, Georgia State University, Atlanta, Ga.

Madanes, C. (1981). *Strategic family therapy.* San Francisco: Jossey Bass.

Paykel, E. (Ed.) (1982). *Handbook of affective disorders.* New York: Guilford Press.

Rubensetin, D., & Timmins, J. (1978). Depressive dyadic and triadic relationships. *Journal of Marriage and Family Counseling, 4,* 13-23.

Spanier, G. B. (1976). Measuring dyadic adjustment: New scales for assessing the quality of marriage and similar dyads. *Journal of Marriage and the Family, 38,* 15-28.

Weeks, G., & L'Abate, L. (1982). *Paradoxical psychotherapy: Theory and practice with individuals, couples, and families.* New York: Brunner/Mazel.

Weissman, M., & Paykel, E. (1974). *The depressed woman.* Chicago: University of Chicago.

SECTION III.   ENRICHMENT AND PREVENTION

Chapter 15

The Evolution of Family Life Education

A Historical Perspective

Luciano L'Abate

Abstract

The thesis of this perspective is that traditional family life education, which began as a uniform, didactic, educationally informative approach to family living, has evolved into myriad interpersonally interactive, applied programs for couples as partners before, during, and after marriage, for couples as parents, and for parent-child relationships. Hence, one needs to differentiate between these two approaches, appreciating what each can offer in its own right and acknowledging that most applied family programs need the information base available from traditional family life education.

Family life education (FLE), which traditionally was based on a didactic classroom approach, has proliferated into myriad applied programs that deserve view and review within a historical perspective. FLE has evolved from an educationally informative, relatively inert impartation of factual knowledge (DeSpelder & Prettyman, 1980; Figley, 1977; Fisher & Kerckhoff, 1981; Hoover & Hoover, 1979; Somerville, 1972) into an excitingly active, interactively experiential diversity of approaches that, whether they like or not, owe a debt of gratitude to FLE. Furthermore, most applied programs need to rely on FLE for a knowledge base of factual information that complements direct applications (see chapter 16; L'Abate, 1986a; Levant, 1986).

Historical Background

The development of FLE is summarized in Table 1. (Although I have attempted to distinguish the didactic and applied programs, I found it very difficult and would appreciate suggestions on how to achieve a clearer distinction.)

The beginning was slow and humble. The Child Study Association of America, founded in 1888, was instrumental in arousing interest in the plight of immigrant foundlings working in sweatshops (Croake & Glover, 1977). The Lake Placid Conference (McFadden, 1981) was responsible for establishing home economics as a formal academic discipline. From these humble roots, the momentum for development grew faster after the beginning of the 20th century. The formation of early parent groups, the creation of parent education (PE) curricula, and the creation of a decennial White House Conference on Child Welfare during the first decade (Alexander, 1981) were probably

Table 1
A Chronology of Family Life Education and Applied Programs

Didactic FLE		Applied programs
Child Study Association of America	1888	
Lake Placid Conference	1901	
Parents groups started	1908	White House Conference on Child Welfare
American Home Economics Association founded	1909	
Curricula for PE created	1911	
	1912	Children's Bureau founded
	1917	Smith Hughes Act
E. R. Groves starts classes	1923–1925	
National Council for Parent Education	1929	
Paul Papanoe FLE classes	1930	
Conference on Education for Marriage & Family Relations	1934	
	1935	Social Security Act
NCFR founded	1938	
E. C. Brown Foundation	1939	
World War II starts	1940	
National Training Laboratories	1947	Department of Health, Education & Welfare created
	1949	National Institute of Mental Health established
Human potentials movement	1959	

Table 1 (continued)

Didactic FLE		Applied programs
	1962	National Institute of Child Health & Human Development; Aid for Dependent Children Act
R. K. Kerckhoff's review	1964	M. W. Brown's review
Marital enrichment movement	1965	
Parent Effectiveness Training & Social Skills Training started	1970	
Association of Couples for Marital Enrichment founded	1973	
Family growth programs reviewed	1974	
	1979	Nebraska Family Strengths Conference started
Family Relations issue dedicated to FLE	1981	
	1983	Family Wellness (Prevention
L'Abate's & Levant's reviews of progress to date	1986	

instrumental in the creation of the Children's Bureau in 1912. The Smith Hughes Act, passed at the outbreak of World War I, solidified the importance of FLE in home economics curricula in colleges and universities. After the war, E. R. Groves and Paul Papanoe (Broderick & Schrader, 1981) became the pioneers of the first college classes in FLE. The number of FLE classes expanded rapidly before World War II and culminated in the founding of the National Council for Family Relations and the commitment of the E. C. Brown Foundation to support family life in the United States (Womble, 1983). In addition, a variety of organizations and institutions started to work directly with families (Brown, 1964).

The number of FLE classes in colleges and universities continued to expand after World War II (Broderick & Schrader, 1981). However, the founding of the National Training Laboratories in Bethel, Maine, by Kurt Lewin's students, plus, no doubt, other professional and practical needs, added impetus to active group work that began to filter into more active approaches to FLE, both inside and outside the classroom (Luckey, 1974, 1978). Toward the end of the 1950s, humanistic psychology was introduced to this country, the human potentials movement reaching its peak in the late 1960s. This movement emphasized direct disclosure of feelings, active confrontation in a group setting, and role playing as the main form of experiential learning. It started to produce approaches that made immediate and directly affective (rather than cognitive, which had been as stressed until then) change a prerequisite of most structured interventions.

During the 1960s, the marital enrichment movement started to take hold in the United States (Otto, 1976), culminating two decades later in a great variety of secular, saintly, and semitherapeutic marital approaches, such as the encounter movement and communication training for couples (L'Abate & McHenry, 1983; Levant, 1986). In addition to the human potential movement and the many derivatives in FLE, behavioral psychology and its derivatives relevant to FLE (e.g., parenting programs) started to take hold. Both movements, the humanistic and the behavioral, plus increasing cultural and societal concerns about the importance of the family, and, of course, the booming family therapy movement (Broderick & Schrader, 1981), culminated in the 1970s with Alberti and Emmons's (1970) work on assertiveness training and Gordon's (1970) Parent Effectiveness Training (PET). Increased emphasis on assertiveness was instrumental in developing, together of course with the upswing of behavior modification, the social skills training movement (L'Abate, 1981; L'Abate & Milan, 1985; Phillips, 1985). PET stressed a much more active approach and increased involvement in parent education (PE), aided by the popularity of Heim Ginott (1965), who in turn had been influenced by more active human potentials approaches to PE.

In the 1970s, family clusters (Sawin, 1982), enrichment (L'Abate, 1981), growth (Anderson, 1974), facilitation (Hoopes, Fisher, & Barlow, 1984; Wright & L'Abate, 1977), and enhancement (Guerney & Guerney, 1981), among a plethora of approaches, became differentiated from one another. Applied FLE then became practically institutionalized, though it has yet to fulfill its potential and has not been able to reach as many families as it would like.

Current Status

There are at least five areas in which didactic FLE, as commonly understood and traditionally practiced, and applied FLE need to concern themselves: (a) increase in applied emphases, (b) delivery system, (c) need for research, (d) materials, and (e) training.

Applied Emphases

The applied emphases are of course of direct concern to didactic FLE (Bowman, 1981; Burr, Jasen, & Brady, 1977; Cromwell & Thomas, 1976; Daly & Reeves, 1973; Goodwin, 1972; Guerney & Guerney 1981; Hoopes et al., 1984; Mace, 1981; Spoon & Southwick, 1972). Luckey (1974) acknowledged at least two main drawbacks in didactic FLE: the impersonality of the classroom and the inadequacy of mutual trust, which is necessary for the teacher-student relationship. When one adds the fear of self-disclosure and apathy about trying to change seemingly hopeless family situations, one wonders whether didactic FLE may even produce negative outcomes by implicitly asking the student to change less than ideal conditions in the family. More active approaches can be implemented, but not in the classroom, because of the limitations mentioned. The best a teacher can do is make appropriate referrals to clinical facilities. Thus, didactic FLE can remain a source of information and referral, but probably not much else.

As concluded in most of the recent reviews of premarital, marital, and postmarital programs (see chapter 16; L'Abate, 1986a; L'Abate & McHenry, 1983; Levant, 1986) the embarrassment of riches in terms of a multiple, variegated technology is stymied by two main drawbacks: (a) the lack of specialized trainers (Mace, 1983) and (b) the inadequacy of delivery systems. (Both drawbacks are discussed later.)

If parent education (PE) is to make an impact, the needs of single-parent families, families with teenagers, stepfamilies, and foster families (Croake & Glover, 1977; Hicks & Williams, 1981; Jensen & Kingston, 1986) need to be considered. Like FLE in general, PE in particular needs to develop a corps of specialized trainers working in a variety of delivery systems and using a variety of different programs.

PE is critically important at all stages of the family life cycle, including parent-child interactions. However, under what conditions should the parent-child interaction be dealt with directly (see chapter 16; L'Abate, 1986a, Levant, 1986)? Unless we are able to distinguish the family interactions on which PE can be used alone and the family interactions on which the whole family needs to work together, how can we effectively change them? Intuitively, one might suggest that PE should be the training modality of choice with preschool children and that parent-child interactions should be the focus of training with children of school age and above. If this is true, which approach is the one to use? Behavior modification? Clusters? Enrichment? Enhancement? These questions can be answered only when further research investigates the issues raised by these questions.

Even though sex education (SE) may still be alive and well (Benjamin, 1971; Kirby & Scales, 1981; Scales, 1981, 1983), the criticisms by Gaylin (1981) and by Shornack & Shornack (1982) indicate that not all is well in this field. It may have failed to make a significant dent in a society in which teenage pregnancy has reached epidemic proportions and in which the parents of teenagers, who need this training most of all, are resistant to any form of external intervention (Scales & Kirby, 1981). How can one implement a substantial and substantive course of SE training when those who are given responsibility for this training (e.g., physical education teachers) are poorly selected and trained (Gaylin, 1981)? It is doubtful that SE will ever make a significant contribution unless it becomes mandated from the highest levels of political power.

Delivery Systems

One of the most critical issues in FLE and all its subspecialties is delivery systems. Whether they are in community settings (Bowman, 1981; Fisher, 1982), extension services (Daly, 1981; Frasier, 1971), mental health centers, schools, colleges, universities (Kennedy & Southwick, 1975; McFadden, 1981), or churches (Sawin, 1981), none of these settings seems established as the setting of choice for FLE programs. Churches could become one of these choices because Sunday school rooms are empty and available most of the time. Unfortunately, this connection is still haphazard and tenuous. FLE will need to content itself with whatever delivery system it can find. TV and commercial entrepreneurial efforts remain unexplored, yet they could become the main sources for expansion and outreach, replacing the traditional settings that have provided unsatisfactory and incomplete solutions.

Need for Research

More than two decades ago, Kerckhoff (1964) concluded his seminal historical review of FLE with words that, unfortunately, remain valid today:

> At present, it seems impossible to say that there is proof that family life education improves family life, and, if it does not, or if there is a suspicion that it does not, then critics may ask: "What is it for?"
>
> Attempts at evaluation have not been lacking, however; they have simply been inadequate. Some are rather impressionistic statements by people who have been engaged in the work of family education. Numerous testimonials to the value individual teachers, students, or administrators, place on this kind of education abound in the literature. (p. 908)

This conclusion has been echoed throughout the past two

186

decades (Luckey, 1974, 1978; Mace, 1981; McFadden, 1981; Miller, Schvaneveldt, & Jenson, 1981; Olson, 1971; Wright & L'Abate, 1977). However, most of these pleas will continue to fall on deaf ears as long as the evaluation of applications is not an integral part of training and of credentialing requirements (Mace, 1983). Then and only then will evaluation receive its due as a standard operating procedure of any form of intervention, be it FLE and its various derivatives, counseling, or therapy. As long as requirements for accreditation and certification do not require evaluation and accounting, it is very doubtful that they will be respected.

Materials

There is no question that a veritable armamentarium of multimedia technology is available to the active FLE trainer (DeSpelder & Prettyman, 1980; Griggs, 1981; Hoover & Hoover, 1979; Somerville, 1972; Wilson & Benson, 1981). The chief issue is whether this formidable array of materials aids substantially in improving family life. How can we generalize from what happens in the classroom (or in the office, for that matter) to the home? To increase the effectiveness of office interventions, L'Abate (1986b) has developed three series of systematic homework assignments dealing with depression, the learning of negotiation skills, and finally, learning how to settle issues of intimacy in the family.

Training

Many authors (e.g., Kerckhoff, Hancock, & panel, 1971; Whatley, 1973; Womble & Yeakley, 1980; Wright & L'Abate, 1977) have mentioned various components as desirable in the training and the personality traits of FLE trainers. There is no question that the complexity and variety of this field is crying out for a more concerted effort to improve standards of training and certification. Wright and L'Abate (1977), for instance, suggested the following sequence: (a) an undergraduate curriculum in didactic FLE, (b) followed by graduate training and experience in a variety of applied FLE programs with theses at the master's degree level, and (c) topped by additional research training, with doctoral dissertations focused on comparing the effectiveness of these applied programs.

Future Directions

The explosion of applied programs in the past decade makes one's crystal ball a little cloudy. There is no doubt, though, that the next decade will belong to applied FLE. Family therapy has reached its peak and, like all the movements that preceded it (psychoanalysis, human potentials, behaviorism), will tend to descend into institutionalized absorption among the many established modalities of intervention. The following are a few of the many exciting possibilities.

During the past decade, divorce mediation has become a full-fledged movement (L'Abate & McHenry, 1983; Lemmon, 1985) and deserves separate review. As a specialty, it has set its own standards of training and certification, even though it has failed, like most applied fields, to support its claims of effectiveness with empirical evidence.

The annual Nebraska conference on family strengths has generated a remarkable number of reports (Rowe et al., 1984; Stinnett, Chessar, & DeFrain, 1979; Stinnett, Chessar, DeFrain, & Knaub, 1980; Stinnett, DeFrain, King, Knaub, & Rowe, 1981; and Stinnett et al., 1982). Unfortunately, they, like similar recent efforts (Hoopes et al., 1984), have failed to demand that their participants produce short- and long-term evidence for the results they claim. Unless this becomes a standard requirement for participation at a national conference, the field of family strengths will only perpetuate all the shortcomings of FLE and then some! Where do issues of sheer advocacy begin and issues of intervention end? Thus far, family strengths seem to have meant that any well-intentioned, albeit methodologically weak, effort is better than no effort. FLE and family strengths may have reached the point at which efforts without evidence may be tantamount to advocacy. Ultimately, empirical results will count more than advocacy.

According to the guide compiled by Sell, Shoffner, Farris, and Hill (1980), enrichment and social skills training will grow, provided they continue to follow up, routinely and empirically, their interventions (see chapter 16; L'Abate, 1980; L'Abate & Milan, 1985). One of its main problems will be to find its own system of delivery in institutional settings.

As reiterated in many publications (see chapter 16; L'Abate, 1986a) the effectiveness of prevention in mental health and family life (Mace, 1983) is difficult to prove unless a few years have elapsed since the initial intervention. Thus, the term prevention remains a promissory note without supporting evidence that it has indeed delivered what it promised. Consequently, it would be more modest and realistic to call the programs that promise prevention psychoeducation programs (see chapter 16; L'Abate, 1981; L'Abate, 1986a; Levant, 1986). With this proviso, applied FLE can make a distinct contribution to a variety of populations in dire need of help. Among the many possibilities, at least four priority populations could use specialized FLE programs: (a) people who practice alternative lifestyles (Macklin, 1981), (b) single-parent families (Porter & Chatelain, 1981), (c) abusive families (Marion, 1982), and (d) chemically dependent families (Rose, Battjes, & Leukefeld, 1984). A fifth, usually overlooked, population is families in bankruptcy; in my experience, they are quite resistant to any kind of intervention.

Health promotion is an upcoming and important area where applied FLE could make a significant contribution, if--and only if--it supports its claims with evidence (Springer & Woody, 1985).

Conclusions

FLE has evolved from an informative classroom approach to myriad active and interactive applied approaches that need to acknowledge their historical debt and knowledge base to didactic FLE. There is no question that traditionally cognitive FLE has given place to more active, interactive experiential approaches that attempt to include as many family members as possible. Two main problems will continue to plague future applications of FLE: (a) the increasing need for its own delivery system, perhaps separate from established public and mental health institutions, and (b) the need for more outcome and long-term follow-up research.

There is no better way to conclude this historical review than by quoting what Olson (1971) wrote more than a generation ago: "In order to learn how best to serve families, there is need for more and improved research and theory about families. After completing a rather comprehensive review of the fields of marital and family therapy, it was discouraging to discover the lack of rigorous and relevant research and theory. There seems to be a barrier between family researchers and family practitioners" (p. 292).

One could reframe this conclusion by stating that despite the tremendous strides made in family sociology and psychology in the past decade, both in theory and in research, practitioners (whether in FLE, mental health, prevention, or promotion) are and will be mostly separated, conceptually and practically, from researchers. This gap, or separation, is as it has been in the past. Unfortunately, there is no evidence to suggest that it will not continue this way in the future. The sooner we accept this separation as a fact of life, the better off we will be. Whether the families we want to serve will be better off remains to be seen.

References

Alberti, R. E., & Emmons, M. L. (1970). Your perfect right: A guide to assertive behavior. San Luis Obispo, CA: Impact.

Alexander, S. J. (1981). Implications of the White House Conference on Families for family life education. Family Relations, 30, 643-650.

Anderson, D. A. (1974). The family growth group: Guidelines for an emerging means of strengthening families. The Family Coordinator, 23, 7-13.

Benjamin, R. R. (1971). Programs in sex education: Use of clinics in a community hospital for training graduate students. The Family Coordinator, 20, 341-347.

Bowman, T. W. (1981). A dream taking form: Family life education in community settings. <u>Family Relations,</u> <u>30</u>, 543-548.

Broderick, C. B., & Schrader, S. S. (1981). The history of professional marriage and family therapy. In A. S. Gurman & D. P. Kniskern (Eds.), <u>Handbook of family therapy</u> (pp. 5-35). New York: Brunner/Mazel.

Brown, M. W. (1964). Organizational programs to strengthen the family. In H. T. Christensen (Ed.), <u>Handbook of marriage and the family.</u> Chicago: Rand McNally.

Burr, W. R., Jasen, M. R., & Brady, L. G. (1977). A principles approach to family life education. <u>The Family Coordinator,</u> <u>26</u>, 225-234.

Croake, J. W., & Glover, K. E. (1977). A history and evaluation of parent education. <u>The Family Coordinator,</u> <u>26</u>, 151-158.

Cromwell, R. E., & Thomas, V. L. (1976). Developing resources for family potential: A family action model. <u>The Family Coordinator,</u> <u>26</u>, 13-20.

Daly, R. T. (1981). A forward look: Family life education in the cooperative extension service. <u>Family Relations,</u> <u>30</u>, 537-542.

Daly, R. T., & Reeves, J. P. (1973). The use of human interaction laboratories in family life courses. <u>The Family Coordinator,</u> <u>23</u>, 413-417.

DeSpelder, L. A., & Prettyman, N. (1980). <u>A guidebook for teaching family living.</u> Boston: Allyn & Bacon.

Figley, C. R. (1977). Family life education: Teacher selection, education, and training issues: A selected bibliography. <u>The Family Coordinator,</u> <u>26</u>, 160-165.

Fisher, B. L., & Kerckhoff, R. K. (1981). Family life education: Generating cohesion out of chaos. <u>Family Relations,</u> <u>30</u>, 505-510.

Fisher, C. D. (1982). Community-based family life education: The Family Life Council of Greater Greensboro, Inc. <u>Family Relations,</u> <u>31</u>, 179-183.

Frasier, R. C. (1971). Meeting the problems of today's families through extension programs. <u>The Family Coordinator,</u> <u>20</u>, 337-340.

Gaylin, N. L. (1981). Family life education: Behavioral science wonderbread? <u>Family Relations,</u> <u>30</u>, 511-516.

Ginott, H. (1965). <u>Between parent and child.</u> New York: Macmillan.

Goodwin, R. H. (1972). The family life educator as change agent: A participant in problems and solutions. The Family Coordinator, 21, 303-311.

Gordon, T. (1970). Parent effectiveness training. New York: Peter H. Wyden.

Griggs, M. B. (1981). Criteria for the evaluation of family life education materials. Family Relations, 30, 549-555.

Guerney, B., Jr., & Guerney, L. F. (1981). Family life education as intervention. Family Relations, 30, 591-598.

Hicks, M. W., & Williams, J. W. (1981). Current challenges in educating for parenthood. Family Relations, 30, 579-584.

Hoopes, M. H., Fisher, B. L., & Barlow, S. H. (1984). Structured family facilitation programs: Enrichment, education, and treatment. Rockville, MD: Aspen Systems.

Hoover, H., & Hoover, K. H. (1979). Concepts and methodologies in the family: An instructor's manual. Boston: Allyn & Bacon.

Jensen, L. C., & Kingston, M. (1986). Parenting. New York: Holt, Rinhart & Winston.

Kerckhoff, R. K. (1964). Family life education in America. In H. T. Christensen (Ed.), Handbook of marriage and the family (pp. 881-911). Chicago: Rand McNally.

Kerckhoff, R. K., Hancock, T. W., & panel. (1971). The family life educator of the future. The Family Coordinator, 20, 315-324.

Kennedy, C. E., & Southwick, J. (1975). Inservice program for family life educators: Cooperative program with mental health centers and university. The Family Coordinator, 25, 75-79.

Kirby, D., & Scales, P. (1981). An analysis of state guidelines for sex education instruction in public schools. Family Relations, 30, 229-237.

L'Abate, L. (1980). Toward a theory and technology for social skills training: Suggestions for curriculum development. Academic Psychology Bulletin, 2, 207-228.

L'Abate, L. (1981). Skill training programs for couples and families. In A. S. Gurman & D. P. Kniskern (Eds.), Handbook of family therapy (pp. 631-661). New York: Brunner/Mazel.

L'Abate, L. (1986a). Preventive programs for marital and family problems. In B. Edelstein & L. Michelson (Eds.), Handbook of prevention (pp. 177-193). New York: Plenum.

L'Abate, L. (1986b). Systematic family therapy. New York: Brunner/Mazel.

L'Abate, L., & McHenry, S. (1983). Handbook of marital interventions. New York: Grune & Stratton.

L'Abate, L., & Milan, M. (Eds.). (1985). Handbook of social skills training and research. New York: Wiley.

Lemmon, J. (1985). Family mediation practice. New York: Free Press.

Levant, R. F. (Ed.). (1986). Psychoeducational approaches to family therapy and counseling. New York: Springer.

Luckey, E. B. (1974). What I have learned about family life. The Family Coordinator, 24, 307-313.

Luckey, E. B. (1978). Family life education revisited. Family Relations, 27, 69-74.

Mace, D. (1981). The long, long trail from information-giving to behavioral change. Family Relations, 30, 599-606.

Mace, D. R. (Ed.). (1983). Prevention in family services: Approaches to family wellness. Beverly Hills, CA: Sage.

Macklin, E. D. (1981). Education for choice: Implications of alternatives in lifestyles for family life education. Family Relations, 30, 567-577.

Marion, M. (1982). Primary prevention of child abuse: The role of the family life educator. Family Relations, 31, 575-582.

McFadden, J. R. (1981). Family life education and university outreach. Family Relations, 30, 637-642.

Miller, B. C., Schvaneveldt, J. D., & Jenson, G. D. (1981). Reciprocity between family life research and education. Family Relations, 30, 625-630.

Olson, D. H. (1971). The family specialist--Past, present, and future: The younger generation speaks. The Family Coordinator, 20, 293-294.

Otto, H. A. (1976). Marriage and family enrichment programs: An overview of a movement. In H. A. Otto (Ed.), Marriage and family enrichment: New prospective and programs (pp. 11-27).

Nashville, TN: Abingdon.

Phillips, E. L. (1985). Social skills: History and prospect. In L. L'Abate & M. Milan (Eds.), Social skills training and research (pp. 3-21). New York: Wiley.

Porter, B. L., & Chatelain, R. S. (1981). Family life education for single parent families. Family Relations, 30, 515-525.

Rose, M., Battjes, R., & Leukefeld, C. (1984). Family life skills: Training for drug abuse prevention. Rockville, MD: National Institute on Drug Abuse.

Rowe, G., DeFrain, J., Lingren, H., MacDonald, R. Stinnett, N., Van Zandt, S., & Williams, R. (Eds.). (1984). Family strengths. 5: Continuity and diversity. Newton, MA: Education Development Center.

Sawin, M. M. (1981). Family life education in religious institutions: Catholic, Jewish, and Protestant. Family Relations, 30, 527-535.

Sawin, M. M. (Ed.). (1982). Hope for families: Stories of family clusters in diverse settings. New York: Sadler.

Scales, P. (1981). Sex education in the '70s and '80s: Accomplishments, obstacles and emerging issues. Family Relations, 30, 557-566.

Scales, P. (1983). Sense and nonsense about sexuality education: A rejoinder to the Shornacks' critical view. Family Relations, 32, 287-295.

Scales, P., & Kirby, D. (1981). A review of exemplary sex education programs for teenagers offered by nonschool organizations. Family Relations, 30, 238-245.

Sell, K. D., Shoffner, S. M., Farris, M. C., & Hill, E. W. (1980). Enriching relationships: A guide to marriage and family enrichment literature. Greensboro: University of North Carolina, Department of Child Development and Family Relations.

Shornack, L. L., & Shornack, E. M. (1982). The new sex education and the sexual revolution. Family Relations, 31, 531-544.

Somerville, R. (1972). Introduction to family life and sex education. Englewood Cliffs, NJ: Prentice-Hall.

Spoon, D., & Southwick, J. (1972). Promoting mental health through family life education. The Family Coordinator, 21, 279-286.

Springer, J. R., & Woody, R. H. (Eds.). (1985). Health promotion and family therapy. Rockville, MD: Aspen Systems.

Stinnett, N., Chessar, B., & DeFrain, J. (Eds.). (1979). Building family strengths: Blueprints for action. Lincoln: University of Nebraska Press.

Stinnett, N., Chessar, B., DeFrain, J., & Knaub, P. (Eds.). (1980). Family strengths: Positive models for family life. Lincoln: University of Nebraska Press.

Stinnett, N. DeFrain, J., King, K., Knaub, P., & Rowe, R. (Eds.). (1981). Family strengths. 3: Roots of well-going. Lincoln: University of Nebraska Press.

Stinnett, N., DeFrain, J., King, K., Lingren, H., Rowe, G., Van Zandt, S., & Williams, R. (Eds.). (1982). Family strengths. 4: Positive support systems. Lincoln: University of Nebraska Press.

Whatley, A. E. (1973). Graduate students' perceptions of needed personal characteristics for family life educators. The Family Coordinator, 23, 193-198.

Wilson, D., & Benson, R. (1981). Audio-visual materials for family life education. Family Relations, 30, 651-660.

Womble, D. L. (1983). The E. C. Brown Foundation: A Pioneering enterprise in family life and sex education. Family Relations, 32, 173-178.

Womble, D. L., & Yeakley, E. B. (1980). A review of the academic preparation of some Indiana secondary school family life educators and the state's new certification requirements. Family Relations, 29, 151-153.

Wright, L., & L'Abate, L. (1977). Four approaches to family facilitation: Some issues and implications. The Family Coordinator, 26, 176-181.

Chapter 16

Recent Developments in Psychoeducational Skills Programs for Families: A Review of Reviews

Luciano L'Abate

Abstract

The purpose of this review is to survey and bring up to date the literature on psychoeducational skill-oriented programs for marriages and families. The continuous growth of these programs bodes well for the future of preventive work with families. In addition to the need for long-term follow-up and comparative testing, three main issues remain unresolved: delivery and marketing of services, high attrition rates, and need for specialized personnel.

This paper updates, and I hope upgrades, a recent review of preventive programs for families (L'Abate, 1986a), that is, programs allegedly designed to alleviate stress and improve the quality of life for functional as well as semifunctional families. The growth of the literature in this field is so phenomenal that the 1986 review was out of date by the time it saw the light of publication. Therefore, this is essentially a review of reviews, an attempt to put together what has been gathered thus far about programs designed to improve family living since the earlier review was written. I have tried to avoid duplicating the 1986 review and to include any sources that may have been omitted from it.

In the literature reviewed earlier (L'Abate, 1986a) five main conclusions stood out in terms of needs: (a) long-term follow-ups, (b) comparative testing of diverse programs focusing on similar family processes, (c) improvement in the delivery and marketing of preventive programs, (d) lowering of high attrition rates, and (e) specialized training for personnel in this area. Most of the reviews included here have contributed to meeting these five needs.

The term psychoeducational includes programs called preventive, interpersonal, psychosocial, enrichment, and social skills--all terms that describe programs whose emphasis is on improving interpersonal skills according to an established series of topics and methods, following a linear and gradual acquisition of these skills through active participation, role playing, homework assignments, some lectures, and audiovisual training aids. These programs supplant what has been called family life education (FLE). They differ from traditional FLE primarily because they rely on more active modalities than lecturing and passive listening (L'Abate, Kearns, Richardson, & Dow, 1985).

The term preventive seems inappropriate because, as I observed in the 1986 paper, it is a presumptuous promissory note. We cannot really know whether prevention has taken place unless a 5- to 10-year follow-up has been done. In the pervasive absence of such follow-ups in most of the programs reviewed here and earlier, it would be more realistic and less presumptuous to use the general title psychoeducational (Levant, 1986a), with the qualifying phrase interpersonal skills to designate the connection with family living. All these programs stress interpersonal competence as their common denominator (Curran, Wallander, & Farrell, 1985; Hatfield, 1985; Rathjen, 1980; Schlundt & McFall, 1985; Shure, 1980; Wine & Smye, 1981).

The chief advantage that these programs have over family therapy lies in their stress on pre- and postevaluation. This stress should pay off in the long run if, but only if, long-term follow-ups become standard operating procedures. Once this deficit has been taken care of, the field of psychoeducational, interpersonal skills training programs will be able to complement and supplement--not supplant--family therapy. Each approach would perform different functions. Initially, family therapy would take care of critical and clinical families. Because these families are at risk for relapse (Leff & Vaughn, 1985), most of these families would benefit from additional skill training to help them for the long haul (L'Abate, 1986b), after the referring symptom has been dealt with.

This review is organized according to a life-stage progression: (a) premarital, (b) marital, (c) postmarital, including divorce, (d) parental, and (e) the family in general or parent-child relationships. This review cannot compete with what Levant and his collaborators (1986a) have done in covering this field thoroughly, critically, and competently. I can only point to their extremely important contributions as being much needed and welcome and to cite them, albeit briefly, along with other reviews, as the standard reference for the future.

I cannot begin this review without mentioning other meritorious work, namely, the meta-analysis of 85 premarital, marital, and family enrichment programs that will remain a model in the field of evaluation for some time to come (Giblin, 1986). As is true of Levant's (1986a) contribution, space limitations preclude a detailed summary of their results. Suffice it to say that their conclusions support their continued efforts in these endeavors.

Premarital Programs

According to Levant (1986a) premarital programs can be divided into three substages: pre-, neo-, and meso-premarital in terms of temporal propinquity to the marriage. One aspect of pre-premarital programs that has been cornered by behavioral approaches is heterosexual skills, mostly related to dating anxiety (Curran, et al., 1985; Kolko & Milan, 1985; Spence, 1983). Typically, training takes place in groups (mostly undergraduates), which practice a variety of behavioral rehearsals, role playing, incremental skills. Although the short-term results, according to all three reviews, are still questionable, all of them skirt the critical issue with this class of skills; that is, if long-term effects (after marriage) cannot be shown, the lasting benefit of this type of program is questionable; however, futility can no more be assumed than can effectiveness.

Fournier and Olson (1986) classified neo-premarital programs into family life education courses, instructional counseling, enrichment (Giblin, 1986), and counseling. They concluded that specific issues of compatibility in religious, ethnic, socioeconomic, and educational background need to be addressed directly. They also listed recommended policies concerning premarital services.

Marital Programs

Following Levant's classification of pre-, neo, meso-, and postmarital programs, one needs to pay attention to sexuality (D'Augelli & D'Augelli, 1985) and increased preparation for childbirth (Bruce & Kiladis, 1986).

Critical consideration must be given to all marital programs in terms of outcome. Chartier (1986) especially recommended that methodological shortcomings in research be improved with a greater coordination among theory, research, and evaluation. One of the greatest needs of these programs lies in adding direct observations to the self-report evidence that currently represents the bulk of outcome data. On the basis of methodological improvements, more frequent comparative testing of competing programs can then take place (Epstein, 1985; Fournier & Olson, 1986; Giblin, 1986; Guerney & Guerney, 1985; Guerney, Guerney, & Cooney, 1985; Wackman & Wampler, 1985.)

Postmarital Programs

Most postmarital (divorce) programs (Joanning, 1985; Levant, 1986a; Storm, Sprenkle, & Williamson, 1986) have recommended that, at least with mixed-gender groups, leaders of both genders should present clear goals and procedures from the beginning. Considering the pain being experienced at the time, divorced persons should be encouraged to express their feelings without shame, using the leaders and the group as an initial support group until an external support group is available. Most of these reviews have stressed the need for communication skills training.

Parental Programs

As Levant (1986a) stressed repeatedly, psychoeducational programming should be based on existing research, and parental programs are no exception (Belsky & Vondra, 1985; Moss, Abramowitz, & Racusin, 1985; Roosa, Fitzgerald, & Crawford, 1985). Unfortunately, this is not true of most parenting manuals (Carkhuff, 1985) and of most parenting programs bordering on advocacy. A strong exception is the work of Andrews, et al., (1982); Mischley, Stacy, Mischley, and Dush (1985); and Tableman and Hess (1985). Becoming a parent is the third important responsibility after becoming a person and a partner (Entwistle, 1985; L'Abate, 1986b; Pollack & Grossman, 1985).

Among the many nonbehavioral parenting programs available (Levant, 1986b), the Guerneys' relationship enhancement programs for parent-child, parent-adolescent, and marital relationships (Brock & Coufal, 1985) deserve special mention for their untiring emphasis on continual pre- and postevaluation (Guerney & Guerney, 1985; Guerney, et al., 1985).

Among the behaviorally oriented programs (Budd, 1985; Lamb, 1986) is an almost evangelistic fervor that tends to make their advocates blind to the obvious deficiencies in the programs, one of which is differential effectiveness with parents at different socioeconomic and educational levels and stages of the family life cycle (Levant, 1986b). As Lamb (1986) concluded in his review, even though parental education is "alive and flourishing . . . it is suffering from the same ailments as other modes of intervention" (p. 193).

Family and Parent-Child Relationships

Although most of the reviews in this section use the term family, most of them focus on parent-child relationships (Graziano, 1986; Henderson, 1981; Weiss & Jacobs, 1984) and on issues of parenting (Hatfield, 1985; Robin, 1980; Shure, 1980; Wandersman & Hess, 1985).

A few of the programs are devoted to the family as a whole, and they have also been reviewed by Levant (1986a). Most of them suffer from inadequacies concerning the complexities of research with families. One solution is the use of single-subject methodology (Coleman, 1986; M. A. Milan and I are preparing an article on this topic).

Conclusion

In addition to the five needs mentioned at the outset--(a) long-term follow-ups, (b) increase in the comparative testing of competing programs, (c) improvement in delivery and marketing of services, (d) lowering of high attrition rates, and (e) specialized training for personnel--the main challenge for psychoeducational programs lies in their future application to minority families (Coleman, 1986; Irvine & Stevens, 1985), to families of handicapped children (Foster & Berger, 1985), gifted children (Frey & Wendorf, 1985), so-called nontraditional families (Eiduson & Zimmerman, 1985), dual-earner families (Walker & Walston, 1985), and single-parent families

(Hanson & Sporakowski, 1986). Fortunately the publication of a casebook and a manual of structured enrichment (L'Abate & Weinstein, 1987; L'Abate & Young, 1987), which contains 50 programs for the kinds of families just mentioned, will allow us to meet this challenge head-on. The next decade will tell the story.

References

Andrews, S. R., Blumenthal, J. B., Johnson, D. L., Ferguson, C. J., Lasater, T. M., Malone, P. E., & Wallace, D. B. (1982). The skills of mothering: A study of parent-child development centers. Monographs of the Society for Research in Child Development, 47 (Serial No. 198).

Belsky, J., & Vondra, J. (1985). Characteristics, consequences, and determinants of parenting. In L. L'Abate (Ed.), Handbook of family psychology and therapy (Vol. 1, pp. 523-556). Homewood, IL: Dorsey Press.

Brock, G., & Coufal, J. D. (1985). Parent education as skill training. In L. L'Abate & M. Milan (Eds.), Handbook of social skills training and research (pp. 263-283). New York: Wiley.

Bruce, S. J., & Kiladis, P. A. (1986). Childbirth education. In R. F. Levant (Ed.), Psychoeducational approaches to family therapy and counseling (pp. 146-159). New York: Springer.

Budd, K. S. (1985). Parents as mediators in the social skills training of children. In L. L'Abate & M. Milan (Eds.), Handbook of social skills training and research (pp. 245-262). New York: Wiley.

Carkhuff, R. R. (1985). Productive parenting skills. Amherst, MA: Human Resource Development Press.

Chartier, M. R. (1986). Marriage enrichment. In R. F. Levant (Ed.), Psychoeducational approaches to family therapy and counseling (pp. 233-265). New York: Springer.

Coleman, D. (1986). Structured enrichment with black families. Unpublished master's thesis, Georgia State University.

Curran, J. P., Wallander, J. L., & Farrell, A. (1985). Heterosocial skills training. In L. L'Abate & M. Milan (Eds.), Handbook of social skills training and research (pp. 136-169). New York: Wiley.

D'Augelli, A., & D'Augelli, J. F. (1985). The enhancement of sexual skills and competence: Promoting lifelong sexual unfolding. In L. L'Abate & M. Milan (Eds.), Handbook of social skills training and research (pp. 170-191). New York: Wiley.

Eiduson, B. T., & Zimmerman, I. L. (1985). Nontraditional families.

In L. L'Abate (Ed.), Handbook of family psychology and therapy (Vol. 2, pp. 810-844). Homewood, IL: Dorsey Press.

Entwisle, D. R. (1985). Becoming a parent. In L. L'Abate (Ed.), Handbook of family psychology and therapy (Vol. 1, pp. 557-585). Homewood, IL: Dorsey Press.

Epstein, N. (1985). Structured approaches to couples' adjustment. In L. L'Abate & M. Milan (Eds.), Handbook of social skills training and research (pp. 477-505). New York: Wiley.

Foster, M., & Berger, M. (1985). Research with families with handicapped children: A multilevel systemic perspective. In L. L'Abate (Ed.), Handbook of family psychology and therapy (Vol 2, pp. 741-780). Homewood, IL: Dorsey Press.

Fournier, D. G., & Olson, D. H. (1986). Programs for premarital and newlywed couples. In R. F. Levant (Ed.), Psychoeducational approaches to family therapy and counseling (pp. 194-231). New York: Springer.

Frey, J., III, & Wendorf, D. J. (1985). Families of gifted children. In L. L'Abate (Ed.), Handbook of family psychology and therapy (Vol. 2, pp. 781-809). Homewood, IL: Dorsey Press.

Giblin, P. (1986). Research and assessment in marriage and family enrichment: A meta-analysis study of premarital, marital and family interventions. Journal of Marital and Family Therapy, 11, 257-271.

Graziano, A. M. (1986). Behavioral approaches to child and family systems. In R. F. Levant (Ed.), Psychoeducational approaches to family therapy and counseling (pp. 98-130). New York: Springer.

Guerney, L., & Guerney, B., Jr. (1985). The relationship enhancement family of family therapies. In L. L'Abate & M. Milan (Eds.), Handbook of social skills training and research (pp. 506-524). New York: Wiley.

Guerney, B. G., Jr., Guerney, L., & Cooney, T. (1985). Marital and family problem prevention and enrichment programs. In L. L'Abate (Ed.), Handbook of family psychology and therapy (Vol. 2, pp. 1179-1217). Homewood, IL: Dorsey Press.

Hanson, M. H., & Sporakowski, M. J. (Eds.). (1986). Single- parent families. Family Relations, 35 (Whole No. 1).

Hatfield, A. B. (1985). Family education: A competence model. In H. A. Marlowe, Jr., & R. B. Weinberg (Eds.), Competence development: Theory and practice in special populations (pp. 177-202). Springfield, IL: C. C. Thomas.

200

Henderson, R. W. (Ed.). (1981). <u>Parent-child interactions: Theory,</u> <u>research, and prospects.</u> New York: Academic Press.

Irvine, R. W., & Stevens, J. H., Jr. (1985). A historical perspective on black family research. In L. L'Abate (Ed.), <u>Handbook of</u> <u>family psychology and therapy</u> (Vol. 2, pp. 663-697). Homewood, IL: Dorsey Press.

Joanning, H. (1985). Social skills training for divorced individuals. In L. L'Abate & M. Milan (Eds.), <u>Handbook of social skills training</u> <u>and research</u> (pp. 192-215). New York: Wiley.

Kolko, D. J., & Milan, M. A. (1985). Conceptual and methodological issues in the behavioral assessment of heterosexual skills. In L. L'Abate & M. Milan (Eds.), <u>Handbook of social skills training and</u> <u>research</u> (pp. 50-73). New York: Wiley.

L'Abate, L. (1986a). Preventive programs for marital and family problems. In B. Edelstein & L. Michelson (Eds.), <u>Handbook of</u> <u>prevention</u> (pp. 177-193). New York: Plenum.

L'Abate, L. (1986b). <u>Systematic family therapy.</u> New York: Brunner/Mazel.

L'Abate, L., Kearns, D., Richardson, W., & Dow, W. (1985). Enrichment, structured enrichment, social skills training, and psychotherapy: Comparisons and contrasts. In L. L'Abate & M. Milan (Eds.), <u>Handbook of social skills training and research</u> (pp. 581-603). New York: Wiley.

L'Abate, L., & Weinstein, S. (1987). <u>Structured enrichment programs</u> <u>for couples and families.</u> New York: Brunner/Mazel.

L'Abate, L., & Young, L. (1987). <u>Casebook: Structured enrichment</u> <u>programs for couples and families.</u> New York: Brunner/Mazel.

Lamb, W. (1986). Parent education. In R. F. Levant (Ed.), <u>Psycho-</u> <u>educational approaches to family therapy and counseling</u> (pp. 160-193). New York: Springer.

Leff, J., & Vaughn, C. (1985). <u>Expressed emotion in families.</u> New York: Guilford.

Levant, R. F. (1986a). An overview of psychoeducational family programs. In R. F. Levant (Ed.), <u>Psychoeducational approaches to</u> <u>family therapy and counseling</u> (pp. 1-51). New York: Springer.

Levant, R. F. (1986b). Client-centered skills training programs for the family. In R. F. Levant (Ed.), <u>Psychoeducational approaches</u> <u>to family therapy and counseling</u> (pp. 52-97). New York: Springer.

Mischley, M., Stacy, E. W., Jr., Mischley, L., & Dush, D. (1985). A parent education project for low-income families. In B. Tableman & R. Hess (Eds.), Prevention: The Michigan experience (pp. 45-57). New York: Haworth.

Moss, N. E., Abramowitz, S. I., & Racusin, G. R. (1985). Parental heritage: Progress and prospect. In L. L'Abate (Ed.), Handbook of family psychology and therapy (Vol. 1, pp. 499-522). Homewood, IL: Dorsey Press.

Pollack, W. S., & Grossman, F. K. (1985). Parent-child interaction. In L. L'Abate (Ed.), Handbook of family psychology and therapy (Vol. 2, pp. 586-622). Homewood, IL: Dorsey Press.

Rathjen, D. P. (1980). An overview of social competence. In D. P. Rathjen & J. P. Foreyt (Eds.), Social competence: Interventions for children and adults. New York: Pergamon.

Robin, A. (1980). Parent-adolescent conflict: A skill-training approach. In D. P. Rathjen & J. P. Foreyt (Eds.), Social competence: Interventions for children and adults. New York: Pergamon.

Roosa, M. W., Fitzgerald, H. E., & Crawford, M. (1985). Teenage parenting, delayed parenting, and childlessness. In L. L'Abate (Ed.), Handbook of family psychology and therapy (Vol. 2, pp. 623-659). Homewood, IL: Dorsey Press.

Schlundt, P. G., & McFall, R. M. (1985). New directions in the assessment of social competence and social skills. In L. L'Abate & M. Milan (Eds.), Handbook of social skills training and research (pp. 22-49). New York: Wiley.

Shure, M. (1980). Real-life problem-solving for parents and children: An approach to social competence. In D. P. Rathjen & J. P. Foreyt (Eds.), Social competence: Interventions for children and adults. New York: Pergamon.

Spence, S. (1983). The training of heterosexual social skills. In S. Spence & G. Shepherd (Eds.), Developments in social skills training (pp. 275-303). New York: Academic Press.

Storm, C. L., Sprenkle, D. H., & Williamson, W. (1986). Innovative divorce approaches developed by counselors, conciliators, mediators, and educators. In R. F. Levant (Ed.), Psychoeducational approaches to family therapy and counseling (pp. 266-309). New York: Springer.

Tableman, B., & Hess, R. (Eds.) (1985). Prevention: The Michigan experience. New York: Haworth.

Wackman, D. D., & Wampler, K. S. (1985). The couple communication program. In L. L'Abate & M. Milan (Eds.), Handbook of social skills training and research (pp. 457-476). New York: Wiley.

Walker, L. S., & Strudler Wallston, B. (1985). Social adaptation: A review of dual-earner family literature. In L. L'Abate (Ed.), Handbook of family psychology and therapy (Vol. 2, pp. 698-740). Homewood, IL: Dorsey Press.

Wandersman, A., & Hess, R. (Eds.). (1985). Beyond the individual: Environmental approaches and prevention. New York: Haworth.

Weiss, H., & Jacobs, F. (1984). The effectiveness and evaluation of family support and education programs. Cambridge, MA: Harvard Family Research Project, Harvard Graduate School of Education.

Wine, J. D., & Smye, M. D. (Eds.). (1981). Social competence. New York: Guilford.

CHAPTER 17

Structured Enrichment (SE) with Couples and Families*

LUCIANO L'ABATE*

The historical background of Structured Enrichment (SE) with couples and families is linked to the need for educational, preventive intervention models that are ethical, realistically relevant, cost-efficient, useful, versatile, and easily tested. The nature and process of SE are also related to its diagnostic, preventive, paratherapeutic, propaedeutic/didactic, and research functions. Four major representative functions are summarized briefly to indicate the testability of SE. The future of SE is considered in terms of further research on comparative usefulness, expansion to clinical populations, and the testing of component skills.

This paper summarizes and reviews the past decade of work to develop Structured Enrichment (SE) programs (L'Abate, 1975a, 1975b, 1977; L'Abate & Rupp, 1981; L'Abate & Sloan, 1981). The SE programs have been used to train students to work with families—first, in a very structured format (Jessee & L'Abate, 1981), and, later, under less structured conditions (Kochalka & L'Abate, 1983).

Historical Background

The remarkable growth of the family therapy movement in the past decade has resulted in a need to deal with less dysfunctional families at a preventive/educational rather than a therapeutic/crisis level. Furthermore, most families, no matter how functional, need skill training in all facets of family life. For each family in therapy, we can assume that 4 to 10 families could benefit from educationally based skill training. As Alexander and Parsons (1982) contended, helping families involves crisis intervention through therapy and skill building through education. This model is the corner-stone of SE: Education can help more families than therapy can ever reach. O'Leary and Turkewitz (1978), writing about methodological errors in marital and child treatment research, stated:

> Failure to specify therapeutic procedures in detail is one of the most common and yet most serious problems in psychotherapy research. To rectify the problem some journal editors . . . have recently required . . . treatment manuals. Without such manuals . . . , replication of treatment studies is almost impossible. (p. 254)

Psychotherapy outcome is also difficult to assess because the number of sessions varies. Hence, controlling all possible variables, including what is asked and said during intervention, requires that instructions be followed verbatim.

How can therapists control service delivery? A therapist cannot, or should not, control people; however, therapists can control services through careful programming of what is delivered and how they deliver it. Therapists cannot calibrate, modulate, limit or control human beings; however, therapists can calibrate, modulate, limit and control what is delivered to couples and families, and can debug, edit, and improve written instructions for them. This position is the heart of SE. An individual's behavior cannot be controlled. A program can be controlled and, if necessary, changed. Programs, not individuals, must bear the burden of change in couples and families. Psychotherapy puts a premium on the individual helper's influence; skill training and SE put the premium on the program as a testable, repeatable event (Guerney, 1977).

*An earlier version of this paper was an address to the Prevention Branch of the National Institute of Drug Abuse, Rockville, MD, on March 16, 1982. This version was a keynote address to the Third Annual Family Enrichment Conference at Weber State College, Ogden, Utah, on September 17, 1982.
**Luciano L'Abate is Professor of Psychology and Director, Family Study Center, Georgia State University, Atlanta, GA 30303.

Key Words: family life education, family therapy, intervention, prevention, psychotherapy, structured enrichment.

(Family Relations, 1985, 34, 169-175.)

The Goals of SE

The goal of SE is to provide a process by which family members can come together to increase and to improve the frequency and quality of their interactions through face-to-face, novel experiences. This process may lead toward certain secondary goals: (a) the opportunity for family members to experience alternative ways of relating to each other and (b) the training of graduate students to work with families (Jessee & L'Abate, 1981) under structured conditions that should minimize anxiety (L'Abate & Rupp, 1981).

Assuming that social support, especially family support, moderates stress, increasing and improving family support through structured programs should decrease stress in families. SE programs were written to train couples and families, allowing them to come together and give and take in ways not usually available at home or elsewhere. Most couples and families, no matter how functional (Lewis, Beaver, Gossett & Phillips, 1976), do not usually know how to spend time together talking about relevant family topics. Consequently, a goal of SE is to help families develop greater awareness of each other and of themselves vis-à-vis other family members. Presumably, this awareness would then translate into greater differentiation within, between, and among themselves (L'Abate, 1976). In addition, the process of goal setting should determine the specific goals for each couple or family and how SE programs can best fulfill those goals by matching programs with the needs of each couple or family.

The Nature of SE

Although the process is the same for all programs (i.e., initial interview, evaluation, six sessions of SE, feedback after a week of posttesting, and a 3- to 6-month follow-up), the content of the various programs is deliberately eclectic so that as many situations as possible can be encompassed.

The first manual (L'Abate, 1975a) consists of 27 programs; each program comprises 3 to 10 lessons. Each lesson contains five to six exercises, which a family, with an enricher's help, can complete in about an hour. Detailed verbatim instructions are given for each exercise. Programs vary in degree of complexity (from simple to complex along the rational-experiential continuum) and in degree of specificity (from very specific, e.g., families of addicts, to very general).

In contrast to the first manual, which was based on structural characteristics (simple-complex, general-specific, affective-cognitive), the programs in the second manual (L'Abate, 1975b) deal with the developmental span of the family life cycle, thus expanding and making the preceding manual more complex. This manual contains 27 different programs in 10

chapters, ranging from courtship and premarital problem solving to sexuality and sensuality, man-woman relationships, becoming parents, the family as a whole, family breakdowns, widow- and widowerhood, and death. The manual can be used by professionals and middle-level professionals interested in working with couples, parents, groups of divorced persons, widows and widowers, and families who have faced or are facing the death of a loved one.

The third manual (L'Abate & Sloan, 1981) consists of 16 programs. After two introductory chapters (Section One), "The Social Skills Training Movement" and "How to Write an Enrichment Program," the 16 programs are divided into three sections: Section Two—family development, starting with newlyweds and continuing through a new baby in the family, the middle years, adaptational tasks of the elderly, senile relatives, and widow- widowerhood; Section Three—special family needs (i.e., the marital journey, resources in the family, interpersonal problem solving, closeness-distance, health needs, and depression); Section Four—special families (i.e., divorcing, blended, dual employment, and over-advantaged).

Guidelines for SE

At least six distinct guidelines have influenced the origin and development of SE. Although these guidelines have taken time to develop, they have now emerged explicitly to define better what SE is all about.

Ease of Testability

For a program of intervention to be effective, it must be testable. To be maximally testable, the program needs to be maximally structured, hence the reliance on written instructions that trainers read verbatim. The characteristic of written instructions that are read verbatim makes each program repeatable and thus testable. The possibility that the outcome of a program may well be due to effects of the trainers brings us back to the field of psychotherapy rather than to social skills training. The more structured the program, the clearer the function and process of intervention will be.

Of course, the extreme degree of structure may disincline many creative and autonomous individuals. Graduate students with therapy experience find it very difficult to follow the constraints of written, planned programs. They are somewhat mollified to learn that they will be able to supervise less experienced individuals in the delivery of such programs. Undoubtedly, SE is the most structured form of skill training for couples and families (L'Abate, 1981). By the same token, it is also more easily tested, efficient, and cost effective than are most skill training approaches.

Usefulness

The whole issue of usefulness, or effectiveness, will be dealt with in greater detail in the section on research. Suffice it to say here that the standard operating procedures of SE consist of pre/post evaluations with 3- to 6-month follow-ups. For too long, we have had to evaluate individuals for other professionals who had been treating those individuals without the benefit of retesting at the end of the treatment. If there cannot be a reevaluation, neither should there be evaluation. Only through retesting can we evaluate how each couple or family has benefited from SE and whether there should be further interventions.

Realistic Relevance

Family roles are learned, in part, from our families of origin. In this context, we build up restricted, oftentimes irrelevant, ideas of what ideal family roles are. Yet, these roles, which most of us take for granted, are the most difficult ones to learn, and there is no one to teach us except our parents and our siblings. No one has safe situations in which roles can be tried. One need, then, is to provide couples and families with true-to-life experiences, through roles concocted from admittedly preconceived notions and through relevant situations that do not force them to become what they are not.

Efficiency and Cost Effectiveness

To be applicable to large numbers of families, a program of enrichment needs to be inexpensive. To meet this requirement, a program should have at least three ingredients: (a) ease of training, (b) ease of application, and (c) reliance on paraprofessional personnel. In SE, training is extremely easy because the requirement is the ability to read instructions. That seems easy, but there is, of course, more to SE than simply reading instructions. Because learning, for most families, can occur immediately through role playing, learning is experiential, direct, and immediate. A trainee does not have to wait until a course of instruction has been finished before working with families but can start right away and get immediate satisfaction, knowing that a contact has been made.

When general principles of interviewing, reaching rapport, and making contact have been learned, a trainee needs to learn about process, which in SE is pretty well reduced to written instructions and note-taking. The most difficult aspect of SE that trainees face is the matching of a program with a specific family, a process that usually takes place under supervision. The trainee does need to ask what the family wants to work on and, taking this information at face value, add possible alternative programs that may include needs of which the

family is unaware. Once the choice of a program has been made from the two or three presented to a family, the rest requires observation of and note-taking about how a family works or fails to work. All of these procedures can be applied by reasonably mature, fairly sensitive individuals with a bachelor's degree or the equivalent, thus reducing the cost of application and leaving the professional to supervise, advise, and support the trainees (L'Abate, 1977).

Ethical and Professional Considerations

The foremost principle of intervention is that a program must be ethically acceptable and professionally sound. It must meet whatever criteria of moral and socially accepted practices are required by the professional community as well as the community at large. In this sense, the contents and processes of SE programs have been distilled from published literature that has been shown to possess a certain degree of professional acceptance and that has already been accepted as part of the lore of family life, both theoretical and practical. For instance, each program is based on a review of literature on the topic at hand, a distillation of points and issues that defines the topic and that have been reduced to lessons and exercises. The lessons are then presented sequentially, from the most fundamental, or simplest, to more complex, or secondary, concepts.

One ethical issue relevant to SE is that of *indoctrination*. How much does the therapist influence families to think as the therapist does? Is not what the therapist thinks better than what the family thinks? Where is the line between education and indoctrination, or brainwashing? With SE, this problem has been limited by raising questions that families can answer for themselves—in whatever way works for them, not for the enricher(s). Admittedly, in the course of raising questions, the enricher may transmit to families some biases that are socially acceptable and culturally sanctioned!

Prescriptive Specificity, Flexibility, and Versatility

Meeting the criteria of prescriptive specificity, flexibility, and versatility means providing a better match between the family and the program desired for that family, or an optimal match between the family and the program. Most programs for parents or between parents and children (L'Abate, 1981) are not systemic, in the sense that they do not include other children (to the best of my knowledge) and in that the family must fit the program. The reverse is true of SE: The program has to fit the family. Thus, the match between the family and the program is much more specific and systemic than in other skill training programs for families (Guerney, 1977) because the whole family is involved (with the exception of children younger than 6 years of age or children who are uncontrollable or uncooperative).

The major shortcoming of prescriptive specificity lies in its tailor-matching one program with one family, thus precluding application to a variety of families at the same time. The variability of family functioning makes it difficult to conceive a single program to fit all families. Any program, no matter how eclectic or encompassing (e.g., PET, Gordon, 1976; Relationship Enhancement, Guerney, 1977; clusters, Savin, 1979) would be too general to meet the specific needs of most families. One important issue here is parental versus family models. Most of the family models, with the exception of Guerney's and Savin's (L'Abate, 1981), are really not systemic and do not involve the whole family. They may focus on the parents or on the parent-child relationships but do not involve the family as a whole.

The Functions of SE

SE has four kinds of functions: (a) didactic-propaedeutic, (b) diagnostic-evaluative, (c) preventive-paratherapeutic, and (d) research. As for the first function, Broffenbrenner's (1977) dictum—if you want to know how a system works, try to change it—holds very well for SE. During SE with families, the therapist can see them directly rather than through the distractions and deviations of standard test batteries, which are still used for evaluations of the family and of the program's effectiveness. Equal importance, however, needs to be given to the subjective impressions and observations of trainees. How a family functions in the therapist's presence over a period of time is just as important (more important, some would argue) than what family members write on a piece of paper or how they sort a batch of test cards. Trainees learn to deal with families under protective conditions.

The paratherapeutic nature of SE makes the preventive function paramount. Unfortunately, to show preventive effects, one has to wait quite a few years. Thus far, we have been able to show only consumer satisfaction: 80% of couples and families indicated satisfaction with the experience (L'Abate & Rupp, 1981). In a few years, however, the pool of couples and families will be sufficient to allow comparison of the pool with couples and families who have not received SE and comparison of the two groups by a variety of indices of family disruption (e.g., divorce, hospitalization, job stability).

The research function of SE is especially important in proving effectiveness and versatility. Four studies indicate how researchable SE really is. One study (Frey, Holley & L'Abate, 1979) was aimed at testing the validity of three conflict-reducing approaches—Ellis's rational-emotive, Bach's fair fighting, and the sharing of hurt feelings (L'Abate, 1983). In a total of three sessions, each couple received all three approaches, administered in random order. Each lesson was a summary (in SE terms) of the approach advocated by each of the three theorists. Regardless of the outcome, the study did demonstrate SE's potential for the comparative testing of competing and contrasting viewpoints.

A second study (L'Abate, 1983) considered the validity of using letters in family therapy, a procedure advocated by the Milano associates (Selvini-Palazzoli, Boscolo, Cecchin & Prata, 1978). A control group of 12 couples received no intervention but was evaluated pre- and postintervention. A second group of 12 couples received SE only. A third group received SE plus a straightforward feedback letter at the end of the fourth SE lesson. The three groups that received SE did significantly better than did the control group. This study indicates SE's usefulness in comparative testing of contrasting and competing viewpoints.

The third study, by L'Abate and Smith (L'Abate, 1977) evaluated the usefulness of SE with 55 families (a total of 217 people). The evaluation of families is not, however, a simple matter. How can a therapist evaluate the way a 6-year-old child views the family or the way the child's college graduate parents view it? To evaluate a theory of personality development in the family (L'Abate, 1983), a battery of four picture tests, not requiring reading ability or other education, was constructed and validated, originally by Golden (1974) and, more recently, by Gallope (1979). The pictures are made up of symbols correlated in previous studies with affective states: human figures showing various intensities of emotions (anger, sadness, acting out, and controlled intellectualizing), situations (blaming, placating, distracting, and computing), and animal pictures to deal with unspoken feelings within the family under two conditions of administration—actual and ideal. Because each family member is asked to select cards to represent self and others in the family, each test yields individual as well as dyadic and family scores (L'Abate & Wagner, in press). The battery has been used by Stanton and colleagues to evaluate the outcome of family therapy with heroin addicts (Stanton, Todd, Heier, Van Deusen & Skibinuski, 1979).

The 55 families composed two groups—clinical and nonclinical. The first group was defined by having one member identified as patient and by having asked for help. The second was defined by not having an identified patient, not needing professional help, and having been asked to participate in the project. The groups were then split into test/retest, with or without enrichment, which yielded four groups of families: clinical enriched ($n = 10$), clinical not enriched ($n = 20$), nonclinical enriched ($n = 7$), and nonclinical not enriched ($n = 18$). The results of pre-/posttests were analyzed for individual family members (father, mother, child) by ANOVA, with main effects for before, after, or no intervention for clinical/nonclinical status. Because a major issue in the statistical analysis of families is the different number of family members in each family, all of the analyses were conducted on individuals. (For a detailed description of the statistical analyses of test scores, see the original study, L'Abate, 1977, pp. 95–101). Suffice it to say that families who received SE (regardless of clinical or nonclinical status), when compared with families who had not received SE, showed significant changes in card selection.

A fourth study, Ganahl (1981), dealt specifically with the effectiveness of SE in changing couples' marital adjustment, satisfaction, and communication. The effects of enrichment program type, sex and number of therapists, and clients' level of adjustment were also assessed. Subjects, 126 married couples and 1 cohabiting couple, were either clients of the Family Study Center at Georgia State University or university students who volunteered for research credit as part of the introductory psychology course. Subjects were, in general, in their late 20s, well educated, of diverse occupational backgrounds, and had been married for an average of 5 years, with an average of one child. The population was predominantly composed of Caucasian couples, either Protestants or of no religious preference.

The nonclinical enrichment group results were compared with results of (a) a no-treatment control group, (b) a group receiving written homework instructions in communication, (c) an enrichment group with homework assignments, and (d) a clinical enrichment group composed of couples presenting with marital difficulties, which was contrasted with (e) a clinical sample receiving marital therapy.

Results were analyzed by one-factor analyses of variance, with analysis of covariance applied to positive results of groups whose pretest scores were significantly different from each other. Improvement was assessed by the Locke-Wallace (1959) Short Marital Adjustment Test (MAT), the Primary Communication Inventory (PCI; Navran, 1967), the Marital Happiness Scale (MHS; Azrin, Naster & Jones, 1973), and a composite test battery composed of questions about marital satisfaction in a variety of areas of functioning. Pre- and posttests were administered, with 6–7 weeks intervening between pre- and posttesting.

Results indicated that SE prorams were improving self-reported marital satisfaction and adjustment. Results were mixed for communication. The enrichment group showed positive changes on the MAT, the composite battery, and the communication item of the MHS. The enrichment and the homework groups produced positive results on the battery and on the PCI. The homework group showed positive results only on the battery score.

Clinical groups, because of insufficient data, were not evaluated on the MAT or the PCI. The clinical enrichment group improved significantly on the battery, the MHS, and the communication item of the MHS. Differences between the clinical and the nonclinical groups were nonsignificant. The clinical enrichment group was found to be inferior to the therapy group on the battery and on the communication item of the MHS.

No sex differences were found in response to treatments, program types, or therapist sex and number. Minimal differences were found among programs. Ganahl (1981) discussed the results in terms of their implications for extending enrichment to clinical populations and to nonclinical settings with paraprofessionals.

The Future of SE

Structured Enrichment is now confronting five distinct directions: (a) more testing of programs, (b) wider applications to clinical populations, (c) segmentation of components that make up enrichment programs, (d) expansion to multicouples and multifamilies, and (e) computer designed SE.

More Testing of Programs

With 70+ programs already written, the task of testing all of them is well-nigh impossible. We can only test some of them, at least those we use, and avoid experimenter effects by leaving the testing to those who use the programs outside our laboratory. In further testing, we need to emphasize the need for comparative testing within and outside various SE programs (i.e., comparing SE programs with programs by authors such as Gordon, 1976, or Guerney, 1977).

Wider Applications to Clinical Populations

Until now, most SE has been done with couples and families from the undergraduate student body; they furnished most of the research data for work by O'Shea, (research in progress), with families of terminally or chronically ill patients; Caiella (1982), with families of drug-abusive adolescents; Stevens (1982), with divorcees; Sloan (1983), on increasing intimacy with married couples; Dow and L'Abate (research in progress), on creating an SE play program for families; Kochalka (1983), on application of a sexual attitudes program with groups of individuals; and Schulte (1984), on an art enrichment program for families.

Segmentation of Components

Segmenting components is probably the most difficult of all the future directions. As an example, Sloan (1983), in her dissertation research, evaluated the validity of a concept about intimacy (L'Abate, 1983) and its usefulness in applying an intimacy workshop format to groups of couples (L'Abate & Sloan, 1984). Her design had two groups: One group received all instructions in the program except the sharing of hurt, the heart of the theory about intimacy; the other group did receive exercises in hurt sharing. The results were to indicate whether the sharing of hurt does or does not increase intimacy (it did not!). Further testing of component skills needs to continue.

Expansion to Multicouples and Multifamily Groups

If SE is to fulfill the claim that it is a cost-effective procedure, it must deal with more than one family at a time. In addition to the intimacy workshops, two other projects have addressed this issue. Rupp (personal communication, 1981), who conducted an SE program with four families at a time in a Sunday school, got enthusiastic reports from all families. Yarborough (1983), using the Negotiation program (L'Abate, 1975b) with groups of couples, examined the effects of the structured marital enrichment program for negotiation training in a group format. The Negotiation program had not been investigated before in a group format, only in a dyadic format. The dependent variables examined were dyadic adjustment, assessed by the Spanier (1976) Dyadic Adjustment Scale (DAS); satisfaction, assessed by the Barrett-Lennard Relationship Inventory (RI; Wampler & Powell, 1982); and intimacy, assessed by the Interpersonal Relationship Inventory (IRS; Guerney, 1977). Also examined were differential effects of the program for men and women, durability of effects at 6- to 8-week follow-up, and the effects of group leader facilitation on levels of the dependent variables.

Subjects for the study were 24 couples from the Athens, Georgia, area. Two treatment groups ($n = 12, n = 16$) and a testing-only control group ($n = 20$) were used. Couples were recruited from the University of Georgia Counseling and Testing Center and a local church.

Participants in the treatment groups were randomly assigned to a 6-week training program that was neither (a) actively facilitated by the group leader, with group interaction after exercises, or (b) an aggregate group, with no interaction among couples. Instructions for the lessons were given by graduate student leaders.

A quasi-experimental design involving pre-, post-, and follow-up assessment was used. At posttesting there were no statistically significant effects as a result of negotiation training alone. The control group showed higher scores at pre- and posttesting than did either treatment group. At 6- to 8-week follow-up, the two treatment groups showed statistically significant changes on the Consensus and Satisfaction subscales of the DAS and the Empathy subscale of the RI. No control group data were available for follow-up comparisons. Some superiority of the facilitated group was noted; the treatment appeared to be durable at follow-up and equally effective for men and women. Anecdotal data revealed that participants considered the program somewhat effective.

Computer Designed SE

The library of 432 + lessons and more than 2,500 exercises (L'Abate, 1975a, 1975b; L'Abate & Sloan, 1981) allows the possibility of coding all of these exercises into various categories and entries (e.g., communication, emotion, problem solving). Placed in a computer bank for fast retrieval, the exercises could be used for even more detailed tailoring to the needs of various couples and families. The crucial issue here, of course, is a diagnostic one. Prescribing the matching, or best fitting, program of enrichment requires the identification of specific assets and liabilities in couples and families (L'Abate, 1981).[1]

Based on this summarization, it would appear that SE has the potential to enhance and enrich the functioning of a wide range of families.

REFERENCES

Alexander, J., & Parsons, M. (1982). *Functional family therapy.* Monterey, CA: Brooks/Cole.

Azrin, N. H., Naster, B. J., & Jones, B. (1973). Reciprocity counseling: A rapid learning-based procedure for marital counseling. *Behavior Therapy, 11,* 365–382.

Broffenbrenner, V. (1977). Toward an experimental ecology of human development. *American Psychologist, 32,* 513–531.

Caiella, C. (1982). *Structured enrichment with a family of an adolescent drug dependent.* Unpublished case study, Georgia State University, Family Study Center, Atlanta.

Frey, J. III, Holley, J., & L'Abate, L. (1979). Intimacy is sharing hurt feelings: Comparing three conflict resolution methods. *Journal of Family Therapy, 5,* 33–41.

Gallope, R. A. (1979). *Test profile variabilities within families and their relationship to family disturbance.* (Unpublished doctoral dissertation, Georgia State University, Atlanta, 1979.) *Dissertation Abstracts International, 40*(7), 3394B.

Ganahl, G. F. (1981). *Effects of client treatment and therapist variables on the outcome of structured marital enrichment.* (Unpublished doctoral dissertation, Georgia State University, Atlanta, 1981.) *Dissertation Abstracts International, 42*(11), 4576B.

Golden, R. P. (1974). *A validation study of family assessment battery.* (Unpublished doctoral dissertation, Georgia State University, Atlanta, 1974.) *Dissertation Abstracts International, 35*(8), 4171B.

[1]This possibility was suggested by Jim Kochalka, to whom I am grateful for continuous support and encouragement.

Gordon, T. (1976). *PET in action: Inside PET families, new problems, insights, and solutions.* New York: Wyden Books.

Guerney, B., Jr. (1977). *Relationship enhancement.* San Francisco: Jossey-Bass.

Jessee, E., & L'Abate, L. (1981). Enrichment role-playing as a step in training family therapists. *Journal of Marital and Family Therapy, 7,* 507-514.

Kochalka, J. (1983). *Structured enrichment of sexual attitudes.* Unpublished master's thesis, Georgia State University, Atlanta.

Kochalka, J., & L'Abate, L. (1983). Clinical training in family psychology. In L. L'Abate, *Family psychology: Theory, therapy, and training* (pp. 287-299). Washington, DC: University Press of America.

L'Abate, L., & Associates. (1975a). *Manual: Family enrichment programs.* Atlanta: Georgia State University.

L'Abate, L., & Associates. (1975b). *Manual: Enrichment programs for family life cycles.* Atlanta: Georgia State University.

L'Abate, L. (1976). *Understanding and helping the individual in the family.* New York: Grune & Stratton.

L'Abate, L. (1977). *Enrichment: Structured interventions for couples, families, and groups.* Washington, DC: University Press of America.

L'Abate, L. (1981). Skill training programs for couples and families. In A. S. Gurman & D. P. Kniskern (Eds.), *Handbook of family therapy* (pp. 631-661). New York: Brunner/Mazel.

L'Abate, L. (1983). *Family psychology: Theory, therapy, and training.* Washington, DC: University Press of America.

L'Abate, L., & Rupp, G. (1981). *Enrichment: Skill training for family life.* Washington, DC: University Press of America.

L'Abate, L., & Sloan, S. Z. (Eds.). (1981). *Workbook for family enrichment: Developmental and structural dimensions.* Atlanta: Georgia State University.

L'Abate, L., & Sloan, S. Z. (1984). A workshop format to increase intimacy in married couples. *Family Relations, 33,* 245-250.

L'Abate, L., & Wagner, V. (in press). Theory-derived, family-oriented test batteries. In L. L'Abate (Ed.), *Handbook of psychology and psychotherapy.* Homewood, IL: Dow Jones-Irwin.

Lewis, J. A., Beaver, W. R., Gossett, M. T., & Phillips, V. A.
(1976). *No single thread: Psychological health in family systems.* New York: Brunner/Mazel.

Locke, H. J., & Wallace, K. M. (1959). Short-form marital adjustment and prediction tests: Their reliability and validity. *Journal of Marriage and Family Living, 21,* 251-255.

Navran, L. (1967). Communication and adjustment in marriage. *Family Process, 6,* 173-184.

O'Leary, K. D., & Turkewitz, H. (1978). Methodological errors in marital and child treatment research. *Journal of Consulting and Clinical Psychology, 46,* 747-758.

Savin, M. (1979). *Family enrichment with family clusters.* Valley Forge, PA: Jackson Press.

Schulte, J. (1984). *An art enrichment program for families.* Central Michigan University, Mt. Pleasant. (Research in progress.)

Selvini-Palazzoli, M., Boscolo, L., Cecchin, P., & Prata, G. (1978). *Paradox and counterparadox.* New York: Jason Aronson.

Sloan, S. Z. (1983). *Assessing the differential effectiveness of two enrichment formats in facilitating marital intimacy and adjustment.* (Unpublished doctoral dissertation, Georgia State University, Atlanta, 1983.) *Dissertation Abstracts International,* 44(8), 2569B.

Spanier, G. B. (1976). Measuring dyadic adjustment: New scales for assessing the quality of marriage and similar dyads. *Journal of Marriage and the Family, 38,* 15-28.

Stanton, M. D., Todd, J. C., Heier, F., Van Deusen, J., & Skibinuski, E. (1979). *Family characteristics and family therapy of heroin addicts: Final report, 1974-1978.* Grant No. R01 DA 0119, submitted to the National Institute of Drug Abuse, Washington, DC, by the Philadelphia Child Guidance Clinic.

Stevens, F. (1982). *A structured enrichment program for young divorcees.* (Unpublished paper, Georgia State University, Family Study Center, Atlanta.

Wampler, K. S., & Powell, G. (1982). The Barrett-Lennard Relationship Inventory as a measure of marital satisfaction. *Family Relations, 31,* 139-145.

Yarborough, M. (1983). *Effects of structured negative training on dyadic adjustment, satisfaction, and intimacy.* (Unpublished doctoral dissertation, University of Georgia, Athens, 1983). *Dissertation Abstracts International,* 44(8), 2422A.

CHAPTER 18

A Workshop Format to Facilitate Intimacy in Married Couples

Luciano L'Abate and Sadell Sloan*

To sustain an intimate committed marriage, two differentiated individuals with well developed identities need to cultivate the skills of communicating, accommodating and negotiating within the partner dyad. This article presents a structured enrichment workshop designed to facilitate marital intimacy, featuring three modules: (a) self-hood and differentiation, (b) communication of emotions, and (c) negotiation. Theoretical bases of each module are outlined, with special attention given to the role of sharing of hurt feelings as a primary dimension of intimacy. Specific exercises in each module are also described.

The marriage enrichment movement attempts to foster individual growth and the ability to be intimate within the context of a committed marital relationship. With marriage enrichment programs reaching hundreds of thousands of couples (Gallagher, 1975; Otto, 1976), enrichment may contribute to the 1980's becoming the "We" decade. Paralleling the growing interest among married couples in enhancing emotional intimacy is a wider consideration of the issues of intimacy by scholars and clinicians, as well (Fisher & Stricker, 1982; Parelman, 1983; Sloan & L'Abate, in press).

Recently, a number of writers have attempted to develop models of intimacy. Spooner (1982) summarized a comprehensive model of intimacy originally proposed by Rytting (Note 1). It consists of two spheres, sexual and nonsexual and three modalities: physical, mental and emotional/spiritual. In the sexual sphere there is (a) sensuality (touch, giving/taking, pleasure/pain); (b) meaning (sexual stimulating, thoughts, fantasies, behaviors, arousal/nonarousal); and (c) transcendence (no control, that which cannot be told or described). In the nonsexual sphere there is: (a) continuality (proximics), privacy (sharing, comfort/discomfort, and closeness/distance); (b) sex role interaction (self-disclosure, open/closed, honest/phony, friendly/hostile and role taking vs. role playing); and (c) person-person interaction (eye contact, feelings, I/Thou, love/hate, joy/misery). The six categories listed above are facets of intimacy. The first term in each category is the dominant means of communication, while the other terms are content or basic polarities.

Schaefer and Olson (1981) derived a five factor model of intimacy including the following factors: emotional, social, sexual, intellectual and recreational. They used these factors to develop a questionnaire assessing real and ideal perceptions of a couple's intimacy. Dahms (1974) suggested a three tiered hierarchical model of intimacy including:

Level 1. Intellectual, based on superficial selling of one's self-ideal rather than the real self;

Level 2. Physical, which includes touching and sexuality; and

*Luciano L'Abate is Professor of Psychology and Director, Family Study Center, Department of Psychology, Georgia State University, Atlanta, GA 30303. Sadell Z. Sloan, is a graduate of the Department of Psychology, Georgia State University, and resides at 1266 Holly Lane NE, Atlanta, GA 30329.

Key Concepts: intimacy, marital communication, marriage, negotiation, personality differentiation, structured enrichment.

Level 3. Emotional, characterized by (a) mutual accessibility, (b) naturalness, (c) nonpossessiveness, (d) processed over time.

The work of Waring (1980a, 1980b) and his associates (Waring, McElrath, Mitchell & Derry, 1981; Waring, McElrath, Weisz, & Lefcoe, 1981; Waring & Russell, 1980; Waring, Tillman, Frelick, Russell, & Weisz, 1980) is a milestone in the area of research on intimacy and its important functions in marriage. Generally, the conclusion which may be drawn from the studies of Waring and his associates is that couples with higher levels of intimacy are less likely to present themselves for treatment of nonpsychotic emotional illness than those with lower levels of intimacy. Waring has developed a therapeutic approach designed to enhance intimacy which thereby alleviates the symptoms of the identified patient spouse.

In addition to our personal interest in the paradoxes of intimacy (L'Abate & L'Abate, 1979), based on the work of Waring and others, we have suggested that intimacy in marriage may be an antidote for depression (Jessee & L'Abate, in press-a, in press-b). The capacity to be a spouse in an intimate (close and enduring) marital relationship requires an individual who is, first of all, just that: an individual and not a Bobbsey twin who derives his/her identity and self-esteem only from the spouse status. But being one's own person is not enough to sustain an intimate, committed marriage. One also needs the skills to communicate oneself to one's partner, and the skills to receive communication from, accommodate to and negotiate with one's spouse.

This paper presents a workshop format used to facilitate intimacy in married couples. Thus far, we have been presenting the format as a 1 day, 6 hour workshop structured into modules: (1) Self-hood and differentiation, (2) Communication of Emotions, and (3) Rational Negotiation of Actions. These modules could conceivably be also presented within other time frames. For example, each 2 hour module could be presented on a weekly basis, to allow for greater practice by couples at home of the techniques presented. A short summary of the theoretical underpinnings of each module will be presented along with an outline of the exercises themselves.

Self-hood and Differentiation

A strong sense of personal identity is viewed as a prerequisite to the capacity for intimacy in the developmental theory of Erikson (1963). Describing the adolescent process of developing and solidifying a mature identity, Erikson noted that this developmental task involves "falling in love," i.e., "an attempt to arrive at a definition of one's identity by projecting one's diffused ego image on another and by seeing it, thus reflected and gradually clarified. This is why so much of young love is conversation" (Erikson, 1963, p. 162). Taken together, then, these statements of Erikson's suggest that individual personality development takes place within the context of a committed relationship and requires the ability to communicate and compromise (i.e., negotiate). Other writers (Gould, 1972; Levinson, Darrow, Klein, Levinson, & McKee, 1978; Sheehy, 1974; Vaillant, 1977) have amplified Erikson's initial work by providing a data base indicating that specific issues in identity development come to the fore throughout the adult life span which entail introspection, working through and resolution. Vaillant's (1977) study revealed that virtually all subjects judged to be best outcomes, (i.e., achieving successful adjustment) enjoyed at least 10 years of a stable, satisfying marriage.

Based on the Eriksonian principle that intimacy derives from a firm sense of identity, the workshop opens with a module on Self-hood and Differentiation designed to assist participants in clarifying their sense of self. In the first exercise, spouses separate and pair up with an opposite sex stranger to introduce themselves. Following this introduction, the group reconvenes and each participant introduces his/her partner to the group. Thus, the opening of the workshop is structured to increase couples' awareness that each is a separate individual, at the same time highlighting areas of similarity and difference between them. This exercise also serves as an "ice breaker" in generating a supportive group process (Guerney, 1977; Miller, Nunnally, & Wackman, 1976; Yalom, 1970).

The next exercise is designed to help participants examine the expectations they have of themselves as spouses, to become aware of their ideal role models and their actual role performance as spouses. Such a process involves their considering the resources they bring to their marriage and the priorities they place on different spheres of life. Participants are asked to categorize their own qualities in terms of Being, Doing, and Having (L'Abate, Sloan, Wagner, & Malone, 1980). Theoretically, the exercise derives from Foa and Foa's (1974) resource classes of Love, Status (Being); Information, Services (Doing); Money and Goods (Having). Partners are then asked to consider their own qualities of *Being*—the creative receptivity to one's existential meaning (Sartre, 1956), a nonjudgemental attitude essential for authentic sharing and caring (Daniels & Horowitz, 1976) and the establishment and maintenance of intimacy (L'Abate & L'Abate, 1979). An appraisal of their performance in familial, occupational and recreational areas of living, *Doing* is also encouraged, since, as Singer (1955) noted, authentic activity, *Doing*, is essential for achieving and maintaining psychological health. Self-examination of *Doing* is designed to help participants differentiate between those activities which facilitate a deeper sense of *Being*, from "pseudoactivity," driven actions, and *Doing* for the sake of *Doing*, which obscure the self. Finally, participants consider the importance they attach to *Having*, the acquisition of goods and money, exploring the extent to which *Having* enables them to own their needs and wants, valuing themselves enough to satisfy material needs and to what extent their pursuit of material goods obscures their sense of self and development of a satisfying marital relationship.

Once both partners have completed *Mate Available* Want Ads in which they advertise themselves as a spouse who *is*, *does* and *has*, couples are structured to discuss the extent of balance between *Being*, *Doing* and *Having* in their lives and to use their ads as a way of becoming aware of their priorities in the following life areas: self, marriage, children, extended family, work, friends and recreation. Similarities and differences in life priorities (L'Abate, 1976) may be used later in the workshop when negotiation skills are introduced.

Thus far in the workshop, participants have been structured to become aware of similarities and differences within themselves (between their real and ideal selves) and between

themselves and their spouses without attempting to make any judgement or negotiate these differences. As couples become aware of their similarities and differences, anxieties may be expected to develop. Feldman (1979) outlined five major types of fear of intimacy which exist side by side with the wish for intimacy. L'Abate and L'Abate (1979) condensed these fears into the fear of sharing past hurts and the fear of being hurt in the future. The possibility exists of couples dealing with these inner anxieties by engaging in externalizing behavior, and with it, the confusion of self and other. Therefore, at this point, they are asked to fill out a series of sentence completion items all beginning with "I," e.g., "I fear _____." They then read their "I statements" to their spouses, getting nonverbal feedback from their spouse (a nod indicating receipt of a true I statement which reveals self; a raised hand indicating a disguised "you statement" which blames other and avoids self). They then make modifications so that they learn how to express self without putting the spouse on the defensive. The I statements exercise closes the Self-hood and Differentiation module and provides a transition to the Communication of Feelings module by introducing couples to the concept that the way in which one communicates may enhance or confuse one's own sense of self.

Communication of Emotions

The Communication of Emotions module begins with a presentation of the ARC model and is designed to clarify interpersonal styles utilized in intimate relationships (L'Abate, 1983, in press). A (Apathy) refers to relationships characterized by autism, maximal distance from others, alienation, a lack of emotional investment (indifference), R (Reactivity) refers to relationships characterized by reaction, repetition of the same or opposite pattern and rebuttals (blaming and counterblaming). C (Conductivity) refers to relationships characterized by creativity, congruence and commitment to change. Group leaders model verbal and nonverbal exchanges characterizing apathy, reactivity and conductivity. Then couples practice the three types of exchanges and discuss how it felt to engage in the three styles.

In apathetic relationships, there is minimal motivation for change, and the lack of concern or caring between partners results in a denial of context (Satir, Stachowiak, & Taschman, 1975). In reactive relationships, partners engage in "recurring unproductive sequencies" (Haley, 1976), and examples are provided of reactive interchanges based on the Drama Triangle roles of Victim-Persecutor-Rescuer (L'Abate, Weeks & Weeks, 1979) and Satir's incongruent stances (L'Abate, 1976) of Blaming, Placating, Computing and Distracting. Examples of conductive interchanges illustrate that the greatest importance is placed on the relationship and cooperation, rather than on competition. Partners in a conductive relationship are aware of spatial and temporal contexts (L'Abate, 1976), and take initiative and responsibility in both problem solving and decision making. In conductive relationships, partners feel secure enough within themselves and with each other to risk breaking the rules of their relationship and thereby may achieve second order change (Perlmutter & Hatfield, 1980; Watzlawick, Weakland, & Fisch, 1974).

The final section of the Communication module teaches the participants the ERAAwC model: E—Emotions, R—Rationality, A—Activity, Aw—Awareness, and C—Context (L'Abate & Frey, 1981; L'Abate, Frey, & Wagner, 1982). This model separates the definition of a situation from the definition of the reaction to it. Participants are encouraged to recall how they have shortcircuited their emotional systems by equating emotionality either with rationality or with activity and jumping from feelings to acting without thinking. They are also asked to remember how they may have confused thinking with feeling. Through group discussion, they explore the misconceptions that there are "positive" and "negative" emotions or that rationality (thinking, analyzing) is "good" while irrationality (emotionality) is "bad." Couples then are encouraged to share angry feelings with their spouses first by writing them down, and then, using their written statement as a guide, sharing them verbally with their spouse.

Following the sharing of angry feelings, couples are asked to share hurt feelings which may underlie the anger. The progression of sharing angry feelings, and only then going on

to expressing feelings of hurt and vulnerability, is based on a hierarchical model of intimacy derived from two studies reported by Frey, Holly, and L'Abate (1979). According to this model, self-presentational intimacy involves superficial efforts at being intimate—efforts which enhance one's image, phenotypic intimacy involves attempts at conflict resolution and dealing with anger, while the deepest level, genotypic intimacy, involves the risk and vulnerability of sharing our hurts and fears. Brown (1979) presented a model of intimacy which similarly incorporated a hierarchical model of intellectual, physical and emotional intimacy, the latter involving a progression from sharing loves and hates to, last of all, humiliations.

In introducing the sharing of hurt exercise, group leaders discuss how people often confuse or hide their hurt with anger. Since hurt is thus often avoided, it may be helpful to become aware of two major ways to define or label hurt within ourselves. One is by focusing on our deficits—our foibles, fears, frailties and fallabilities. The other is by focusing on our hopelessness and helplessness in the face of death, sickness, our emptiness (which has nothing to do with our deficits), and our loneliness (which has nothing to do with physical pain). The former definition would very likely relate to how we think about ourselves, while the latter would relate very likely to how we feel about ourselves. Thus, hurt is both an emotional and a cognitive concept. It is at the very bottom line of our existence. How we deal with it influences how we relate to ourselves and to others, especially but not exclusively, intimate others (L'Abate, Weeks, & Weeks, 1979).

Rational Negotiation of Actions

The final module of the workshop, Negotiation, follows the exercises in emotion sharing. The ERAAwC (L'Abate, Frey & Wagner, 1982) model is used as the basis of our negotiation blueprint. Couples are told that we need to acknowledge and share our emotions so that we can then calmly reason together and work out a mutually acceptable plan of action. Couples then choose one of the conflictual issues in which they focused their awareness earlier in the workshop, and share feelings of anger and hurt, present alternative plans, and taking into account their feelings, develop a proposal for action.

The workshop ends with an invitation to evaluate the entire experience, to wind up any unfinished business and to compare expectations with realities.

Conclusion

Hof and Miller (1981), in presenting a detailed description of their Creative Marriage Enrichment Program, acknowledged that they had no presumptuous belief that their program is the best or most effective marriage enrichment program available. Likewise, we present our Intimacy Workshop as a format we are using to facilitate marital adjustment and intimacy between spouses. Research just completed will enable more objective assessments of success (Sloan, 1983). Finally, we would like to offer the definition of intimacy one husband gave prior to participating in our workshop, since we feel it captures the essence of our approach. He said, "To me, every man/woman is like a moon, i.e., has its own dark side that doesn't show to anybody. Intimacy, is, in my opinion, showing this side without being afraid of making a fool of yourself or being embarrassed."

In contrast to other approaches which emphasize coping with angry feelings (L'Abate & McHenry, 1983), our approach recognizes that while angry feelings need to be expressed, the underlying emotion of hurt must be acknowledged and shared as well, before couples can go on to a rational negotiation of a plan of action which constitutes complete resolution of an issue.

REFERENCES

Brown, E. (1979). Intimacy and anxiety in psychotherapy. Voices, 15, 21-23.

Dahms, A. (1974). Intimate hierarchy. In E. A. Powers & M. W. Lees (Eds.), Process in relationship: Marriage and family. St. Paul: West Publishing House.

Daniels, B., & Horowitz, L. (1976). Being and caring. Mayfield: Palmetto, CA.

Erikson, E. (1963). Childhood and society. New York: W. W. Norton & Co.

Feldman, L. (1979). Marital conflict and marital intimacy: An integrative psychodynamic behavioral systemic model. Family Process, 18, 69-78.

Fisher, M., & Stricker, G. (Eds.). (1982). Intimacy. New York: Plenum Press.

Foa, V., & Foa, E. (1974). Societal structure of the mind. Springfield, IL: C. C. Thomas.

Frey, J., Holley, J., & L'Abate, L. (1979). Intimacy is sharing hurt feelings: A comparison of three conflict resolution models. Journal of Marital and Family Therapy, 5, 35-41.

Gallagher, C. (1975). The marriage encounter: As I have loved you. Garden City, NY: Doubleday.

Gould, R. (1972). Faces of adult life: A study of developmental psychology. American Journal of Psychiatry, 126, 33-43.

Guerney, B. (Ed.). (1977). Relationship enhancement. San Francisco: Jossey-Bass.

Haley, J. (1976). Problem solving therapy: New strategies for effective family therapy. San Francisco: Jossey-Bass.

Hof, L., & Miller, W. (1981). Marriage enrichment: Philosophy, process, and program. Bowie, MD: Robert J. Brady Co.

Jessee, E., & L'Abate, L. (1984). Intimacy and marital depression: interactional partners. International Journal of Family Therapy, 5, 39-53.

Jessee, E., & L'Abate, L. (in press). The paradoxes of marital depression: Theoretical and clinical implications. International Journal of Family Psychiatry.

L'Abate, L. (1976). Understanding and helping the individual in the family. New York: Grune and Stratton.

L'Abate, L. (1983). Styles in intimate relationships: The A-R-C model. The Personnel and Guidance Journal, 63, 277-283.

L'Abate, L. (in press). Systematic family therapy. New York: Brunner/Mazel.

L'Abate, L., & Frey, J. (1981). The ERA model: The role of feelings in family therapy reconsidered: Implications for a classification of theories of family therapy. Journal of Marriage and Family Therapy, 7, 143-150.

L'Abate, L., Frey, J., & Wagner, V. (1982). Toward a classification of family therapy theories: Further elaborations and implication of the E-R-A-Aw-C Model, Family Therapy, 9, 251-262.

L'Abate, L., & L'Abate, B. (1979). The paradoxes of intimacy. Family Therapy, 6, 175-184.

L'Abate, L., & McHenry, S. (1983). Handbook of marital interventions. New York: Grune & Stratton.

L'Abate, L., Sloan, S., Wagner, V., & Malone, K. (1980). The differentiation of resources. Family Therapy, 7, 237-246.

L'Abate, L., Weeks, G., & Weeks, K. (1979). Of scapegoats, strawmen, and scarecrows. International Journal of Family Therapy, 7, 86-96.

Levinson, D., Darrow, L., Klein, B. E., Levinson, M., & McKee, B. (1978). Seasons of a man's life. New York: Alfred A. Knopf.

Miller, S., Nunnally, E., & Wackman, D. (1976). A communication training program for couples. Social Casework, 57, 9-18.

Otto, H. (Ed.). (1976). Marriage and family enrichment: New perspectives and programs. Nashville: Arlington.

Parelman, A. (1983). Emotional intimacy in marriage: A sex roles perspective. Ann Arbor: University of Michigan Research Press.

Perlmutter, M., & Hatfield, E. (1980). Intimacy: Intentional metacommunication and second order change. American Journal of Family Therapy, 8, 17-23.

Rytting, M. (1980, May). Creative limits: Exploring the paradoxes of intimacy. Paper presented at the Midwest Regional Conference of the Association for Humanistic Psychology, Chicago.

217

Sartre, J. (1956). *Being and nothingness.* New York: The Philosophical Library.

Satir, V., Stachowiak, J., & Taschman, H. A. (1975). *Helping families to change.* New York, Jason Aronson.

Schaefer, M., & Olson, D. (1981). Assessing intimacy: The PAIR inventory. *Journal of Marital and Family Therapy,* **7,** 47-60.

Sheehy, G. (1974). *Passages: Predictable crises of adult life.* New York: E. P. Dutton & Co.

Singer, J. L. (1955). Delayed gratification and ego development: Implications for clinical and experimental research, *Journal of Consulting Psychology,* **19,** 259-266.

Sloan, S. (1983). Assessing the effectiveness of an enrichment workshop in facilitating marital intimacy. Unpublished doctoral dissertation, Georgia State University, Atlanta.

Sloan, S., & L'Abate, L. (in press). Intimacy in marriage. In L. L'Abate (Ed.), *Handbook of family psychology and therapy.* Homewood, IL: Dow-Jones Irwin.

Spooner, S. E. (1982). Intimacy in adults: A developmental model for counselors and helpers. *The Personnel and Guidance Journal,* **61,** 168-171.

Vaillant, G. (1977). *Adaptation to life.* Boston: Little, Brown, & Co.

Waring, E. M. (1980a). Marital intimacy, psychosomatic symptoms and cognitive therapy. *Psychosomatics,* **21,** 595-601.

Waring, E. M. (1980b). Marital intimacy and non-psychotic emotional illness. *Psychiatric Forum,* **9,** 13-19.

Waring, E. M., McElrath, D., Mitchell, P., & Derry, M. E. (1981). Intimacy in the general population. *Canadian Psychiatric Association Journal,* 1981, **26,** 167-172.

Waring, E. M., McElrath, D., Weisz, G. M., & Lefcoe, D. (1981). Dimensions of intimacy in marriage. *Psychiatry,* **44,** 169-175.

Waring, E. M., & Russel, L. (1980). Family structure, marital adjustment, and intimacy in patients referred to a consultation-liaison service. *General Hospital Psychiatry,* **3,** 198-203.

Waring, E. M., Tillman, M. P., Frelick, L., Russell, L., & Weisz, G. M. (1980). Concepts of intimacy in the general population. *Journal of Nervous and Mental Disease,* **168,** 471-474.

Watzlawick, P., Weakland, J., & Fisch, R. (1974). *Change: Principles of problem formation and problem resolution.* New York: W. W. Norton & Co.

Yalom, I. D. (1970). *The theory and practice of group psychotherapy.* New York: Basic Books.

CHAPTER 19

Structured Enrichment (SE) of a Couple

Frederic E. Stevens
Luciano L'Abate

ABSTRACT. This case study illustrates the nature and process of structured enrichment with a couple.

STRUCTURED ENRICHMENT OF A COUPLE

The wide variety of social skills training programs which are currently available for couples (L'Abate & McHenry, 1983) attest to efforts to develop interventions that are effective and inexpensive. What makes these programs particularly useful is their concern for prevention rather than crisis intervention (Mace, 1983). In these programs, prevention is defined as oriented toward growth with ''couples who have what they perceive to be a fairly well functioning marriage and who wish to make their marriages even more naturally satisfying'' (Otto, 1976, p. 13). From this perspective (L'Abate, 1985) it is possible to intervene so that couples will not need psychotherapy. For many couples, enrichment may be more appropriate than therapy. Enrichment is also more cost-effective and may be delivered by paraprofessionals. As the delivery of these services relies on subprofessionals and paraprofessionals, it is possible to reach a larger number of couples who need some help but who are not so needy as to require the intervention of a fully trained therapist.

STRUCTURED ENRICHMENT (SE)

Among various preventive programs, structured enrichment (SE) attempts to impart knowledge in a linear and gradual fashion to improve the interpersonal dimensions of a marriage (L'Abate, 1985). At the base of SE is the belief that enrichment can help more couples than therapy. Thus, prevention, growth, and skill building are the various goals of SE.

Goals of Structured Enrichment

The aim of SE is to provide a way in which couples can join with one another to increase and to improve their interaction through novel face-to-face experiences. These experiences hopefully teach them alternative ways of relating to one another. These alternatives are administered in a standardized directly structured manner, such as teaching individual couples communication skills. In spite of the structured nature of SE, where trainers follow *verbatim* instructions through manuals, it provides space for couples to be both interactive and disclosing (L'Abate, 1985).

SE and Other Enrichment Programs

What distinguishes SE from other forms of enrichment is the wide variety of programs which are designed to be administered around selected relationship issues. The three manuals (L'Abate & associates, 1975a; L'Abate & associates, 1975b; L'Abate & Slone, 1981) contain a total of 71 different programs. With this wide range of choices an enrichment program may be custom-tailored to suit the interpersonal needs of a particular couple. By moving flexibly around specific relationship issues, SE is able to confront a wide spectrum of marital issues. For instance, following are examples of the most commonly used programs.

1. Confronting change
2. Sexual clarification and fulfillment
3. Cohabitation
4. Reciprocity
5. Communication
6. Assertiveness
7. Working through
8. Conflict resolution

The Process of SE

A standard SE program consists of six lessons requiring eight one-hour sessions which may take four to nine weeks to complete. The sessions follow a standard sequence of intake-pretest, six enrichment sessions, post-test, feedback and phone or questionnaire follow-up. The SE process begins with the initial intake interview to gain rapport with the couple. This rapport is gained through a simple questioning about how the couple met, etc. Also, at this point a couple is informed of what enrichment is about and what they may expect from it. A consent form is then signed which acts as a contract for enrichment.

With non-clinical, highly functioning couples, rapport is usually easily established. However, with some couples this initial interview may be indicative of future resistance to the enrichment process or the inappropriateness of enrichment. While some shyness and recalcitrance on the part of the couple is to be expected, continued ambivalence to gentle questioning about the marriage can be indicative of some underlying difficulties in the relationship. These difficulties may best be diagnosed in the second step of enrichment, the use of paper-and-pencil measures. Paper and pencil evaluation tools have included, in different combinations, a Family Information Sheet, Feelings About the Family Scale, a Marital Questionnaire, a Semantic Differential Sheet, the Azrin Marital Happiness Scale, the Spanier Dyadic Adjustment Scale, the Holmes-Rahe Schedule of Events, and the Family Adjustment Inventory (L'Abate & McHenry, 1983; L'Abate & Rupp, 1981).

The interview and paper and pencil evaluations serve as a way of tailor-making a specific course of SE as well as a measure of therapeutic change. This measurement is difficult to obtain since most couples are non-clinical and their scores may be above the norm in the pretest, which does not leave much room in the test scores for measureable positive change. However, the measures also serve a diagnostic function by pinpointing specific relationship issues to follow-up during SE.

From the subjective interview and the objective evaluation, a plan is made to offer to the couple a choice of three SE programs. Sometimes a couple will request attention in a particular interpersonal area. Most often, a couple is rather vague in specifying exactly why they want enrichment and what they want from it. In these instances, reliance on specific evaluation tools may indicate the specific area of enrichment for the couple.

In some cases, an individual will respond to a question about why they want enrichment by talking about what the spouse or partner needs to do. This individual may fault the partner or at least give some indications that it is the partner who needs enrichment. These situations plus poor scores on the various paper and pencil tests may be indicative of resistance on the part of at least one member and may suggest that the couple is at risk. Under these conditions, the enricher needs to explore whether the couple may need therapy rather than enrichment. Other indicators of a need for referral to therapy are far less subtle: (a) partners who seek enrichment when they are presently considering whether to end their relationship; (b) incidents of abuse, infidelity, and serious drug abuse are among the indicators of the need for more intensive interventions.

In the first enrichment session, the three possible programs are presented. There are few limits to the programs available to the couple.

221

If necessary, one may be designed for them. Following the selection of a program by the couple, the first session of SE begins as the enricher reads to the couple the sections that deal with the stated interests of the couple and the impression of the trainer from an SE manual.

During the course of SE, a program may be changed at any time. In some cases, a change will be planned contingent on the level of a couple's participation, or the level at which they perform in particular enrichment exercises. A couple may also request a change in the program saying the current one is too serious or does not suit them well.

Following the six enrichment sessions, a post-test feedback session is scheduled. The feedback seeks to discover the couple's impression of both the enricher and enrichment program. Then, the enricher shares his/her impressions with the couple. Invariably, these impressions are framed in a positive manner. Following this feedback, recommendations are made about whether they should continue to get more SE, be referred for therapeutic treatment, or nothing. Three months after the feedback, a follow-up questionnaire is sent to the couple.

CASE STUDY: BILL AND SUSAN

This case was chosen for a number of reasons. First, it provides a look at the use of enrichment with a couple who seemed clinically at risk. Second, this case is illustrative of both the content and process of SE. Third, use of the programs with this couple demonstrates the flexibility which may be achieved with SE in the hands of someone knowledgeable in its application. Finally, this case hopes to capture the flavor of what actually occurs during SE.

Pre-Interview and Pretest Assessment

Bill, aged 24, is an Army veteran. Born and reared in a small South Carolina town, he works in a job which takes him out of town for days at a time. He presented a relaxed, confident appearance.

Susan, aged 24, met Bill while they were both in the Army. She had lived "all over the country" but has not lived anywhere for more than a few years. She also works but does not have to leave town. She presented a rather reserved, thoughtful appearance.

Pretest Assessment

The GSU Couples Battery included the following instruments: Concerning My Family, Feelings Questionnaire, Family Adjustment Scale, Dyadic Adjustment Scale, and the Holmes-Rahe Schedule of Events.

On the Feelings Questionnaire, Susan said Bill's relationship with her family was quite negative. Susan's difficulty with her parents may only have been projected onto Bill.

On the Dyadic Adjustment Scale, both of them checked that they were "happy" with their relationship. Both checked that they occasionally quarrel and that one of them left the house following a quarrel. Bill reported that he had at one time regretted being married and that they frequently disagreed on demonstrations of affection.

The Family Adjustment Scale (FAS) provides space for a couple to write in their own words areas of satisfaction and dissatisfaction. Susan chose to express her dissatisfactions more than Bill. On 9 of 10 specific behaviors, she made self-critical remarks. Of top priority she wrote, "Life . . . generally an observer rather than a participant." She listed her relationship with Bill, with others, and her personal development in negative ratios. On the other hand, Bill ranked Susan as "someone to confide in" (#2) and as "someone to love" (#1).

The FAS suggested that Susan rated high on low self-esteem. In addition, Susan appeared to have some difficulty accepting support. On the other hand, Bill may have offered support to Susan in an ineffective manner. This suggestion about Bill appeared supported in his style of answering on the FAS. He spoke in global terms, which were open to misinterpretation by those reading him, especially someone such as Susan. Susan allowed Bill to make important family decisions, including ones that she should make for herself. Thus, they both agreed to an imbalance of decision making, suggesting inadequate role differentiation and individuation in the marriage.

Discussion

A number of areas appeared open for enrichment. The pretests and interview indicated that Bill and Susan quarrel, and on at least one occasion, conflict was resolved by one of them leaving the house. Bill leaves town frequently (often about once a week for three to four days), suggesting that this "natural" form of conflict resolution may have been used more often than either was consciously aware of. The imbalance in decision making suggested unclear role differentiation. Both agreed to these conclusions. If one attempts to balance this process, he/she may experience resistance from the other. Their affection for each other was unclearly expressed.

This couple had been married three years. Test results suggested that their relationship was barely functional. Trouble areas such as conflict resolution, role differentiation, and affective expression needed to be addressed.

From the intake interview and tests, the following SE programs were suggested: (1) Confronting Change (may be effective to overcome expected resistance); (2) Assertiveness (may help to rebalance the differentiation of marital roles); and (3) Communication (the most gentle of the programs that addresses conflict resolution, consequently, it may be more acceptable and may be usable despite its family orientation).

First Session

After introduction of the three programs, Susan chose the program of Communication and Bill concurred. This program is designed for families but is adaptable for couples.

Lesson 1: Unfair Communication. This lesson revealed a number of communication practices that were blocking the couples' closeness. Susan confided that she used guilt when she felt that her needs were not being met. She would tell Bill when a need was not met and then "*lay on the guilt*" when he complained that task performances were not meeting his expectations. Bill's use of expectation appeared throughout the session. Clearly, this program had something to offer them. They both played the "numbers game" (i.e., they kept a score of wrongs inflicted by their partner). In addition, Bill reported that he used the silent treatment as a way to instill guilt in Susan. Also, when he saw an argument coming or when involved in an argument, he would "clam up." He clammed up to protect the marriage, to squelch an unhappy scene, and to escape an issue he did not want to have brought up again. He maintained that the arguments were usually soon forgotten.

What was evident from this lesson was that Bill and Susan had bountiful insights into their marriage. In this instance, the insight was being used to sustain the dysfunctional dimensions of their marriage. Despite the intellectual awareness of their transactions, no effort was made for changes. Bill's use of the silent treatment served to keep the relationship grounded by keeping Susan confused about what was going on in the relationship. In effect, he was saying, "I am unsatisfied with your dissatisfactions about my showing a lack of affection for your not doing as much for us as I am. To dramatize my point, I will not talk about my dissatisfactions." Bill had the added impetus of being able to leave her and go out of town for three to five days at a time during an average week. These departures could not be avoided, but they did not help the marriage. In view of this sequence of events, it was no wonder that he experienced the arguments as forgotten. The lesson ended with a home work assignment.

Lesson 2: Hurtful Communication. This lesson begins to deal with disagreements and how they are resolved. Following some resistance, Bill and Susan settled into one of their common issues, Bill's lack of expressing affection. When asked about nagging, Susan reeled off a list of her most common naggings. Each issue focused on intimacy and affection. She complained that Bill was often too busy to be affectionate. He replied that when he had been affectionate, she was cold and unresponsive. This clear disparity had gone unresolved despite apparent good intentions.

It became apparent that fear of fighting coupled with a fear of closeness kept this couple in a constant state of stand-off. The intellectualization of insight was used to maintain the imbalance of the marriage.

Lesson 3: Negotiation. Bill and Susan were found to experience more conflict than was previously thought to occur. Consequently, the program was changed from Communication to Negotiation. Negotiation was chosen because it focuses on the use of silent treatment as a form of communication. In addition, the entire program goes into conflict resolution in a more in-depth manner. The couple agreed to the change.

Two lessons (Communication and Hurt) were completed in the same session. Throughout this session a thread of enmeshment became clearer. Bill responded, not to Susan, but at how she fulfilled his expectations of her. Each was afraid of what the other was feeling. Each was afraid to let the other know how he/she was feeling. Afraid to self-disclose, they were unable to get close. In a later exercise, Bill consistently changed statements that were supposed to begin with "I" (self-disclosure) to statements beginning with "I think that you . . . " In addition, Susan played victim in this dialogue. Bill rescued her by preaching to her on one level and blaming on another level. Thus, Bill kept from having to self-disclose.

Lesson 4. Susan reported that when Bill yelled at her, she feared physical violence would occur. She qualified this report by adding that there had been no physical violence. She often tried to second-guess what Bill was thinking and would interrupt what he was trying to convey to her. In short, she tried to do his thinking for him, which was seen as a fear of knowing his real thoughts and an inability to accept their differences. Bill regarded this second-guessing as an invasion of his privacy.

Lesson 5: Trust. Two lessons were also done in one session. Bill and Susan reported having resolved an argument using "I" statements. They did not list their hurts as requested in one exercise. Both were apparently resistant to the exercises of this lesson, occasionally saying that the exercises were irrelevant to them and their marriage. Both claimed that they had a very honest, trusting relationship and that there was little they feared or hid from each other. Susan thought the first exercise was attempting to "open a can of worms" and then withdrew the remark. Bill remained silent.

In the area of dishonesty, Bill said that he did not relate to Susan everything that he did when he went out of town. He used to, but she became so uncomfortable with it that he stopped. The issue went unresolved. Bill then displayed a recognition of himself that he wished to try out. He reported being afraid that feeling expressed to her may not be his real feelings. Because of this fear, he could not be intimate when he did not feel like it.

Lesson 6: Quid Pro Quo. As Bill summarized back to Susan what she wanted to see in him, he interrupted his own recall. He said in a defensive tone that what Susan wanted to see in him were all things directed toward meeting her needs. Susan recanted and said that the things she wants to see in him were things for him, not her. She said that he "completely misunderstood everything I said. I want you to relax and enjoy it for yourself. To do things for *you!*" Bill appeared unable to accept any sort of support.

On the other hand, Susan could voice her needs concretely and plainly. Despite this quality, Bill said that he could not fully understand her. She requested more direct, spontaneous, and verbal support. Bill concluded by saying that he wanted to return to good times together, like they used to have.

Pre-Test and Post-Test Comparison

On the Dyadic Adjustment Scale, Susan made no significant changes. Her score remained about the same. Bill also showed few changes. On the Family Adjustment Scale, Susan ranked as #1 that she needs to be more dependable. This ranking reflected how Bill had conveyed to her that her dependability served to validate him. Bill ranked as #1 and #2 his dissatisfaction with his lack of emotional expression and his lack of spontaneity. He suggested, more than he had done previously, a more specific problem-solving approach to their communication. He assumed more personal ownership of the difficulties. Hopefully, this new-found awareness was more than intellectual insight! On the Feelings Questionnaire, both reported that they were "slightly negative" about how each understood the other. Once again, on this questionnaire as on all pre- and post-test measures, scores were quite high, suggestion that neither was willing to recognize their fusion and polarization. They do appear, however, to be slightly more aware of the problems.

The changes from pre- to post-test were not significant, although there was some movement in a positive direction from one test to another. Probably this marriage might have to get worse before it gets better.

Feedback Session

Bill and Susan were told that their willingness to talk, as well as their trust and determination were greatly appreciated. They were cautioned that their determination might hamper them in efforts to resolve conflict.

The suggestion was made that each continue to take more ownership, as they had done in SE, of their difficulties by using more "I" statements and fewer "you" statements. They were told that their intellectual and verbal skills were of a high quality, but their intellectual awareness and insight without action are meaningless. Finally, they were told that their love for each other was very real and deep. As they really do love each other, they wanted to give the other their very best. In order to give their best, they would have to grow individually as persons and not as each other's mirror images. In short, to be really close, they must be separate.

A future plan was outlined for their marriage. Possible interventions were suggested. Susan, however, resented this suggestion. The door to the various forms of treatment was left open for them.

CONCLUSION

SE provided an introduction to change and did not push them into what they were not ready for, i.e., therapeutic intervention that might be required in the future. In this way, the program may have served an effective outreach and preventative function.

Perhaps the major shortcoming of the entire program was its brevity. The couple was beginning to adopt new negotiation skills in the fifth session. Interestingly, a follow-up questionnaire indicated at least some maintenance of their gain.

REFERENCES

Azrin, N. H., Master, B. H., & Jones, R. (1973). Reciprocity counseling: A rapid learning-based procedure for marital counseling. *Behavior Research and Therapy, 11*, 365–382.

L'Abate. (1985). Structured enrichment (SE) with couples and families. *Family Relations, 34*, 169–175.

L'Abate, L., & associates. (1975a). *Manual: Family enrichment programs*. Atlanta, GA: Social Research Laboratories.

L'Abate, L., & associates. (1975b). *Manual: Enrichment programs for the family life cycle*. Atlanta, GA: Social Research Laboratories.

L'Abate, L., & McHenry, S. (1983). *Handbook of marital interventions*. New York: Grune & Stratton.

L'Abate, L. & Rupp, G. (1981). *Enrichment: Skills training for family life*. Washington, DC: University Press.

L'Abate, L., & Sloan, S. Z. (Eds.). (1981). *Workbook for family enrichment: Development and structural dimensions*. Atlanta, GA: Georgia State University.

Mace, D. R. (Ed.). (1983). *Prevention in family services: Approaches to family wellness*. Beverly Hills, CA: Sage Publications.

Otto, H. A. (Ed.). (1976). *Marriage and family enrichment: New perspectives and programs*. Nashville, TN: Abingdon.

Satir, V. (1967). *Conjoint family therapy*. Palo Alto, CA: Science and Behavior Books.

SECTION IV. TRAINING

Differentiation of Resources in Mental Health Delivery: Implications for Training

The following mental health delivery systems, which include a variety of "movements" or approaches, are briefly differentiated and reviewed: prevention, self-help groups, social-skills training programs, psychotherapeutic interventions, environmental modification, and community resources. The implications of this differentiation for training in clinical psychology are discussed.

Historically, very few options were available to clients with mental or emotional problems (L'Abate, 1964). If medical or psychiatric treatment failed, hospitalization was the ultimate recourse. With the creation of psychotherapeutic approaches, alternatives to hospitals and medical treatment became available. It is the thesis of this article that the greater differentiation of resources in mental health delivery systems poses some questions about traditional training in clinical psychology. Each of the specialized delivery systems is worthy of a doctoral curriculum. Hence, clinical psychology needs to face up to this differentiation of resources and consider whether to abandon the generalist model and adopt, in part, a specialization model. At least six different approaches to service delivery align themselves along a continuum of complexity and perhaps costs (from the least expensive to the most expensive).

The first approach (Approach 1) contains all *preventive programs* available to high- and moderate-risk populations, as well as to the public at large. This is essentially an educational approach to help people learn to recognize stress and to cope with it by asking for help. The second approach (Approach 2) contains the *mutual help groups*, divided by symptomatology (emotional, social, or physical). The third approach (Approach 3) includes *social-skills training programs*. Some of these programs have strong preventive functions that overlap with the first approach. The fourth approach (Approach 4) includes all professionally led *psychotherapies*. The fifth approach (Approach 5) involves *environmental modifications*, exclusive of drug administration and physical treatment, that can be administered on an inpatient or an outpatient basis. The sixth approach, (Approach 6), *community efforts*, returns to the first. The model is essentially circular. Approach 6 differs from Approach 1 in representing the larger context within which prevention as well as other activities can take place.

Review of the Approaches

THE FIRST APPROACH: PREVENTION

The prevention approach has received much attention in the last few years (Apter, 1978; Bloom, 1980; Forgays, 1978) but has not been incorporated ideologically, functionally, and substantively into existing mental health delivery systems. This failure may be due to (a) inadequate training in prevention and preventive activities; (b) low status with therapists, administrators, and policy makers; (c) primacy given to high immediacy mental health concerns and crises; or (d) inadequate ideological and technical preparation in academic and clinical training.

Most views of intervention in the mental health field have been conceptualized in terms of prolonged one-to-one (patient–therapist) relationships (Berger, Hamburg, & Hamburg, 1977). Only recently, especially through the efforts of Albee and his co-workers (Albee, 1979a, 1979b), has the field of prevention come to the fore, with a differentiation of primary, secondary, and tertiary approaches to mental health problems. Primary prevention aims at reducing the incidence of disorders by intervening with supposedly functional populations. In spite of its importance as primary to other delivery systems, prevention lacks educational programs, organized professional associations, and bureaucratic support systems (Herbert, 1979).

Cowen (1977) argued that the scope of primary prevention should emphasize competence training (Approaches 1 and 3) and analysis and modification of social environments (Approaches 5 and 6). Cowen considered resistances to primary prevention not only in terms of the many factors that affect mental health and sense of well-being but also in terms of the lack of training programs that would produce specialists qualified to work in this area. As far as can be determined, no preventive training courses exist at present.

Rappaport and Chinsky (1974) have suggested a model of prevention that includes a conceptual (behavioral) and a style-of-delivery (seeking) component. This model includes extension of services through public education and training of nonprofessionals in behavioral modification techniques and social learning principles.

THE SECOND APPROACH: MUTUAL HELP GROUPS

Major characteristics of mutual help groups (Aschheim, Harman, Quiesser, & Silverman, 1978) are (a) contract between two or more individuals with a common problem, (b) expansion of the identification with another individual into identification with a group sharing the same common problem, and (c) expansion of group identification into active participation in any active program of help.

The recent review of Silverman (1978) provides an apt classification of mutual help groups: (a) groups developed in response to professional failure, like most anonymous groups and groups for developmentally handicapped children; (b) groups developed from technological advances; and (c) groups developed in reaction to social change, like childbirth, bereavement, widowhood, divorce, or childlessness. Silverman also considers that the role of professionals in relating to their group should be to make referrals, serve as consultants or board members, or initiate groups. Therefore,

LUCIANO L'ABATE *is Professor and Director of the Family Psychology Program at Georgia State University. He is a Diplomate of ABEPP and Approved Supervisor of the American Association of Marriage and Family Therapists. He is also engaged in private practice and consultation (part time) in marriage and family therapy.*

M. LYN THAXTON *received her MLn in Library Science from Emory. She is presently Associate Professor and Librarian at Georgia State University and is enrolled in the graduate program in family psychology.*

REQUESTS FOR REPRINTS *should be sent to Luciano L'Abate, Department of Psychology, Georgia State University, Atlanta, GA 30303.*

232

self-help groups can be classified according to Silverman's scheme or according to the nature of the symptomatology, that is, physical, emotional, or social.

THE THIRD APPROACH: SKILL-TRAINING PROGRAMS

L'Abate (1980) has identified a wide range of programs qualifying as social, interpersonal skill programs that have been successfully applied to individuals, couples, families, and groups. Among programs that qualify in this category are (a) assertiveness, (b) communication and conflict resolution, (c) enhancement, (d) encounter, (e) enrichment, (f) effectiveness, (g) fair fighting, (h) mediation, (f) problem solving, and (j) sexuality. These programs involve a time-limited contract over one specific preselected topic for an agreed-upon number of sessions, with clients who clearly understand that skill training is not therapy but under certain conditions may possess certain paratherapeutic qualities.

The structure of these programs varies a great deal from L'Abate's (1977) verbatim instructions to trainers to loosely organized principles that guide the delivery of the program. Paraprofessional intermediaries can learn these methods in a short period of time and can deliver them in a relatively successful mode under supervision. L'Abate uses a step program to train graduate students in enrichment procedures. The students start by working with mock couples and families and simulated real family situations; then, in order, they work with selected nonclinical families drawn from a supposedly nonclinical population (introductory psychology classes, whose students need credits for experimental participation), borderline clinical families who do not show severely impaired behaviors, and families who are in therapy and who need additional skill training.

One of the most problematic areas of training paraprofessionals (Duncan, Korb, & Loesch, 1978) is the effort to train them in acquiring and using professional skills without professional credentials. In spite of Durlak's (1979) results, L'Abate (1969, 1973) maintained that there should be a distinct separation between technical and professional skills, which allows paraprofessional intermediaries to work under the supervision and support of professionals.

The issue, then, becomes one of separating technical from professional skills. In psychodiagnosis, for instance, this separation is easier than in intervention. Test administration and scoring are technical skills; test results, interpretations, and write-ups are professional skills. In intervention we can separate structured skill-training activities, which could be used by paraprofessional intermediaries, from "unstructured" therapeutic activities, which are used by professionals. L'Abate (1980) has suggested an entire curriculum for skill-training programs that would not only lead to the doctoral degree but that would also allow for differentiation within the specialized approach of skill training.

THE FOURTH APPROACH: PSYCHOTHERAPY

A number of prolonged psychotherapeutic interventions by professionals can be identified. However, what is relevant from the viewpoint of delivery and training is that psychotherapeutic techniques are more expensive and less successful than other approaches because they supposedly deal with more dysfunctional populations.

Some critics with a psychoanalytic viewpoint (C. Miller, 1977; J. Miller, 1977) believe that people who fail at skill training reveal the need for more prolonged and professional help than can be provided by this method. These "failures" in no way diminish the value of skill-training programs, however. Persons who do not respond to skill training reveal that they need a different kind of approach that may or may not be provided by prolonged psychotherapeutic relationships.

In the mental health field, no one can assert with confidence that one's favored approach is without dropouts. Most therapy-oriented approaches need to consider that approximately 30% to 60% of psychotherapy patients drop out within the first six sessions, with or without the therapist's consent (Lorion, 1978, p. 921). Hence, various subapproaches within this general approach should be distinguished: (a) crisis therapy; (b) brief or short-term treatment; (c) time-limited therapy; and (d) long-range therapy, reserved for well-motivated patients who show potential to profit by a prolonged intimate relationship. As Strupp (1978) recommended, "Short-term therapy should be the treatment of choice for practically all patients" (p. 18).

THE FIFTH APPROACH: ENVIRONMENTAL MODIFICATIONS

Among various environmental modifications that can be considered under this rubric would be (a) job placement; (b) hospitalization; (c) incarceration; and (d) foster placement in halfway houses, youth villages, or orphanages (Schwartz & Schwartz, 1964). The evaluative work of Ellsworth (1978) and his co-workers (Ellsworth, Foster, Childers, Arthur, & Kroeker, 1968), who compared relative effectiveness of psychiatric settings, seems as essential as the work of Fairweather (1964), who did evaluations within psychiatric settings. The issues brought out by Cometa, Morrison, & Ziskoven (1979) concerning halfway houses and by Rubin (1978) on aftercare also should be considered.

Moos (1973) has been especially instrumental in identifying methods whereby human environments can be conceptualized and assessed. His major areas of concern include (a) ecological dimensions, (b) behavior settings, (c) dimensions or organizational structure, (d) dimensions identifying collective personal and/or behavioral characteristics of the milieu inhabitants, (e) dimensions relating to psychosocial characteristics and organizational climates, and (f) variables relevant to the functional or reinforcement analyses of environments. Moos investigated certain types of social environments, such as community-oriented psychiatric treatment programs, and conceptualized these along various dimensions.

THE SIXTH APPROACH: COMMUNITY EFFORTS

Under this rubric services should be considered that coordinate community mental health programs, which often work independently of each other (Herbert, 1979; Magill, 1979) and will need evaluation (Miskiman, 1979). Goodstein and Sandler (1978) have developed a model to distinguish community health and community psychology, with the latter approach stressing useful changes in social systems of deviance control and of socialization and support. In considering psychology within the community, Heller and Monahan (1977) emphasized three perspectives: (a) case-centered consultation, (b) organization development, and (c) behavioral consultation.

Fields (1980) reviewed some of the most recent developments in what is called the "community mental health empowerment model," in which relationships among various mental health/welfare and neighborhood agencies are considered. Dohren-weld (1978) presented a conceptual model that not only allows bridging the gap between clinical and community psychology but also allows discrimination between etiological determinants of psychopathology and various methods of intervention. Moreover, Dohrenweld distinguished between clinical and community psychology by stressing the roles of supportive social agencies and political action with disadvantaged status groups. Her distinction indicates that there are different kinds of training needed for clinical versus community responsibilities.

Issues Among Delivery Systems

These approaches are not mutually exclusive. Free entry and exit from one approach to another, as well as parallel uses of different approaches, may work synergistically for those who cannot profit by treatment modalities within one approach. Of course, degree of (dys)functionality would be the major independent variable that would determine entry into one specific delivery system. The problem, however, is that a linear relationship between dysfunctionality and type of treatment has not been determined.

If one approach fails, another should be tried, provided clients are interested in receiving services. The major issue here is one of voluntary versus mandated referral. Self-referrals may produce greater benefits than referrals under coercive conditions. On the other hand, when treatment is offered among less attractive and costly alternatives, such as jail or bankruptcy, the greater the chance is for positive outcome. For instance, in Approach 1 most of the populations are supposedly normal, whereas in Approach 2, controls lie in the hands of members of mutual help groups. In Approach 3, the number of variables increases in terms of client populations, programs available, and professionals and semiprofessionals available. The number of variables increases in Approach 4 in terms of the vast range of psychotherapies and professionals available. The addition of variables in Approaches 5 and 6 reaches the level of community where control becomes unyielding. Thus, as the degree of complexity increases, one becomes aware that an underlying aspect of complexity is degree of control and, of course, costs. Controls decrease as approaches progress from prevention to community.

Among major issues for a systematically designed delivery system are consideration of a ladder or lattice system for entry, exit, and reentry into the various available options and service availability. For instance, many rural populations or populations living in relatively small towns do not have access to the wide scale of services available in large cities. Another issue is identification of individuals, problems, and conflict configurations of traits or symptoms that lend themselves to one specific approach rather than to another.

Sank (1979) gave a specific illustration of a multiple approach to crisis and disaster intervention following forcible seizure and holding of hostages by members of a religious sect. Many of these hostages suffered from a variety of emotional after effects following the ordeal. Sank (p. 335) listed how each modality of behavior and its symptomatic manifestation were treated according to a graduate increase of services, depending on the severity of the symptoms. For instance, anxiety attacks and sleep disturbances, among others, were treated with deep muscle relaxation (Approach 3). Others were treated through sharing their experiences with other hostages (Approach 2). More complex cognitions were treated through rational emotional therapy (Approach 4).

More complex marital and familial conflicts were referred to appropriate therapists (Approach 4). Medical follow-ups and physical treatment (Approach 5) were administered where indicated.

Implications for Training

A major question raised by the various "movements" or approaches reviewed here is whether clinical psychology can afford to continue with one general type of training or should it consider the creation of specialized programs at the doctoral level. Until recently, the generalist model prepared everyone similarly and gave them the skills that they needed for further specialization. The more recent differentiation of mental health delivery systems, as considered in this article, raises some questions about the effectiveness of the generalist model and suggests the possibility of a specialist model. The specialist model is present in the clinical program at Georgia State University, where five different doctoral clinical tracks are available: (a) general, (b) psychotherapy, (c) behavior modification, (d) family psychology, and (e) child clinical psychology. In addition a community program exists outside of the clinical program.

Conclusion

As this article illustrates, the mental health field is facing an embarrassment of riches, a variety of approaches, and a divergence of viewpoints and methods about delivery services that need systematic applications requiring specialization. A systematic approach to mental health delivery systems and training may help us use most of our available resources to meet the needs of our consumers in a more flexible and effective fashion than is available in clinical psychology.

REFERENCES

Albee, G. W. Preventing prevention. *APA Monitor*, August 1979, *10*, p. 2. (a)

Albee, G. W. The next revolution: Primary prevention of psychopathology. *Clinical Psychologist*, 1979, *32*, 16–23. (b)

Apter, S. J. (Ed.). *Focus on prevention: The education of children labeled emotionally disturbed.* Syracuse, N.Y.: Division of Special Education and Rehabilitation, Syracuse University, 1978.

Aschheim, B., Harman, E., Quiesser, R., & Silverman, P. *Review of technical assistance materials and related literature concerning mutual help groups.* Cambridge, Mass.: American Institute for Research in Behavioral Sciences, 1978.

Berger, P., Hamburg, B., & Hamburg, D. Mental health: Progress and problems. *Daedalus*, 1977, *106*(1), 261–276.

Bloom, B. L. Social and community interventions. *Annual Review of Psychology*, 1980, *31*, 111–142.

Cometa, M. S., Morrison, J. K., & Ziskoven, M. Halfway to where? A critique of research on psychiatric halfway houses. *Journal of Community Psychology*, 1979, *7*, 23–27.

Cowen, E. L. Baby-steps toward primary prevention. *American Journal of Community Psychology*, 1977, *5*, 1–22.

Dohrenweld, B. S. Social stress and community psychology. *American Journal of Psychology*, 1978, *6*, 1–14.

Duncan, M. V., Korb, M. P., & Loesch, L. C. Competency counselor training for parapro-fessionals. *Counselor Education and Supervision*, 1978, *18*, 223-232.

Durlak, J. A. Comparative effectiveness of paraprofessional and professional helpers. *Psychological Bulletin*, 1979, *86*, 80-92.

Ellsworth, R. B. The comparative effectiveness of community clinic and psychiatric hospital treatment. *Journal of Community Psychology*, 1978, *6*, 103-111.

Ellsworth, R. B., Foster, L., Childers, B., Arthur, G., & Kroeker, D. Hospital and community adjustment as perceived by psychiatric patients, their families, and staff. *Journal of Consulting and Clinical Psychology Monograph*, 1968, *32* (1-41, Pt. 2).

Fairweather, G. W. (Ed.). *Social psychology in treating mental illness: An experimental approach.* New York: Wiley, 1964.

Fields, S. Mental health networks: Extending the circuits of community care. *Innovations*, 1980, *7*, 2-17.

Forgays, D. (Ed.). *Primary prevention of psychopathology* (Vol. 2). Hanover, N. H.: University Press of New England, 1978.

Goodstein, L. D., & Sandler, I. Using psychology to promote human welfare: A conceptual analysis of the role of community psychology. *American Psychologist*, 1978, *33*, 882-892.

Heller, K., & Monahan, J. *Psychology and community change.* Homewood, Ill.: Dorsey, 1977.

Herbert, W. The politics of prevention. *APA Monitor*, August 1979, pp. 7-9.

L'Abate, L. *Principles of clinical psychology.* New York: Grune & Stratton, 1964.

L'Abate, L. The continuum of rehabilitation and laboratory evaluation: Behavior modification and psychotherapy. In C. M. Franks (Ed.), *Behavior therapy: Appraisal and status.* New York: McGraw-Hill, 1969.

L'Abate, L. The laboratory method in clinical child psychology: Three applications. *Journal of Clinical Child Psychology*, 1973, *2*, 8-10.

L'Abate, L. *Enrichment: Structured interventions for couples, families, and groups.* Washington: University Press of America, 1977.

L'Abate, L. Towards a theory and technology for social skills training: Suggestions for curriculum development. *Academic Psychology Bulletin*, 1980, *2*, 207-228.

Lorion, R. P. Research on psychotherapy and behavior change with the disadvantaged. In S. L. Garfield and A. E. Bergin (Eds.), *Handbook of psychotherapy and behavior change.* New York: Wiley, 1978.

Magill, R. *Community decision making for social welfare: Federalism, city and the poor.* New York: Human Sciences Press, 1979.

Miller, C. H. Human-potential movement: Implications for psychoanalysis. *American Journal of Psychoanalysis*, 1977, *37*, 99-109.

Miller, J. Discussion of "The human-potential movement: Implications for psychoanalysis." *American Journal of Psychoanalysis*, 1977, *37*, 111-114.

Miskiman, D. E. An evaluation of a community outreach program. *American Journal of Community Psychology*, 1979, *7*, 71-77.

Moos, R. H. Conceptualization of human environments. *American Psychologist*, 1973, *28*, 652-665.

Rappaport, J., & Chinsky, J. M. Models for delivery of services from a historical and conceptual perspective. *Professional Psychology*, 1974, *5*, 42-50.

Rubin, A. Commitment to community mental health aftercare services: Staffing and structural implications. *Community Mental Health Journal*, 1978, *14*, 199-208.

Sank, L. J. Psychology in action: Community disasters: Primary prevention and treatment in a health maintenance organization. *American Psychologist*, 1979, *34*, 334-338.

Schwartz, M. S., Schwartz, C. G., & Field, M. G. *Social approaches to mental patient care.*

237

New York: Columbia University Press, 1964.

Silverman, P. R. *Mutual help groups: A guide for mental health workers* (DHEW publication No. 78-646). Washington: U.S. Government Printing Office, 1978.

Strupp, H. Psychotherapy research and practice: An overview. In S. Garfield & A. Bergin (Eds.), *Handbook of psychotherapy and behavior change: An empirical analysis.* New York: Wiley, 1978.

Chapter 21

In Favor of Specializations Within Clinical Psychology

Luciano L'Abate

The purpose of this paper is to argue in favor of specializations in clinical psychology and to criticize traditional practices of a uniform, general clinical training. I believe that a traditional monolithic approach (i.e., the generalist model) is counterproductive in that (a) it stifles diversity and pluralism, (b) it limits creativity and uniqueness, (c) it slows flexibility and differentiation, and (d) eventually it retards change and evolution in the profession. How is change to take place if not through specialization? Specialization after the PhD, as some proponents of the generalist model propose, only delays specialization and imposes on trainees additional years of student status.

Uniformity of training maintains the status quo of a bygone era. Clinical psychology could offer myriad specializations. In addition to the most obvious specializations (behavior modification, psychotherapy, and clinical child psychology), clinical psychologists could start specializing in a variety of new areas. The sooner such specialization starts, the better. Furthermore, specialization in clinical psychology has already begun (Rickard & Bernatz, 1983), if nowhere else, in the behavioral-nonbehavioral distinction and in the community-oriented programs (L'Abate & Thaxton, 1981).

Strickland (1983) has described the two major concerns facing Division 12 (Clinical Psychology) of the American Psychological Association as the specialty vs. the generic discipline, or profession, and the linking of "traditional clinical psychology to the growing field of health psychology" (p. 52). Both these concerns are part of the same issue of definition: How shall clinical psychology define itself? As a general discipline or a specialty? In considering this question 20 years ago (L'Abate, 1964), I wrote that the clinical psychologist was a jack-of-all-trades and master of none or a specialist, who has more opportunities to contribute to the discipline.

Rickard and Bernatz (1983) suggested that subspecialty training should identify a body of knowledge and should include the following four parameters: "client populations, services rendered, problems addressed and setting for services" (p. 75). They condensed most criticisms of subspecialty training into (a) too premature, (b) too expensive, and (c) meeting a limited need. Rickard and Bernatz responded to all three criticisms. I might add that the solution need not be either-or but may be both: generalist training for the departments that do not have a specialized faculty and specialty (or subspecialty) training for the departments that do have qualified faculty.

In addition, Rickard and Bernatz submitted a set of six criteria for subspecialty training that they set up in the form of shoulds. Subspecialty training (a) should be clearly subordinate to general-experimental and specialty clinical training; (b) should be clearly defined so that a common corpus of content and skills may be acquired; (c) should include course work, practice, and faculty modeling subspecialization experiences, which (d) should be integrated and programmatic, beginning early and extending throughout training. (e) Internships selected should offer training in that particular subspecialty, and (f) subspecialty training should take place in the practitioner-scientist model. Additional criteria for subspecialty training, according to Rickard and Bernatz, consist of (a) identifying the need for such training, (b) assessing faculty availability and competence in specific subspecialty, (c) identifying a pool of student applicants, (d) developing the training, (e) monitoring it, and (f) evaluating it. As Pottharst (1969) noted:

> Abiding specializations in the psychosocial professions seem to follow the social setting of man's living (school psychologists, industrial psychologists, family therapists, community psychiatry, etc.) or else to follow the stages of psychosocial development (adults and children, adolescent specialties, those who work with older adults, "later maturity," etc.)

> Specialty designations by school or by allegiance to a particular approach or clinical-occupational system, like psychoanalysis or existentialism or behavior therapy, present more of an ideological choice to sophisticated clients than a treatment alternative based on specialization alone. (p. 81)

I tend to agree with Pottharst on the first two points (specialization by setting and by psychosocial stages). His third point is no longer valid. Specialists in either psychotherapy (regardless of school) or behavior therapy would argue that their specialties cannot be lumped together with other specialties. Specialization should take place throughout graduate training from the beginning to the end in the practitioner-scientist model (this criterion is questionable, and a great deal of leeway should be allowed among faculty and students). Internships should be appropriate to the specific subspecialty.

Given such a wide range of possible specialties, the generalist would ask, What are the functions that would be common to all these specialties? In fact, clinical psychology has been founded on the traditional functions of evaluation, treatment, and research. This model, however, fails whenever ideologies clash in reference to major treatment models; that is, a behavioral orientation will provide a vastly different training from a psychodynamic orientation. A supposedly eclectic orientation would require the generalist to become a jack-of-all-trades and a master of none. The concept that specialization should take place after the PhD fails simply because little

240

postdoctoral specialization is available and opportunities are few and far between.

The final criteria for defining any specialty among the array of possibilities are faculty expertise and availability. If one were to simplistically reduce the issue to generalism equals status quo and specialization equals change, one could avoid dealing with the complexities of these issues. Yet, again, the question has to be asked: How is change to be obtained (in any system)? If not through specialization, then through what channels? The obvious question here of course is, Why change? Why not leave things as they are? One would then need to argue that change is desirable if, but only if, clinical psychology can more effectively fulfill human needs and serve the welfare of the society of which it is part. If we want to meet these needs, we need to demonstrate that we are not doing so within the present structure and that a "better" new structure would do what the old structure could not do.

Reasons for Specialization

We need to change because current training models (general) are not relevant to many of the problems we face. Emerging conceptions of mental health and models of treatment have been considered in the past in at least two symposia (Grinker, Albee, Schafer, Garmezy, Thrasher, & Mensh, 1971). Rubinstein and Coelho (1971) raised the question whether psychology can be socially relevant. The answer is that psychology can be socially relevant only to the extent that it mirrors the society it represents (Coelho, 1971). Seeman and Seeman (1973) saw the emerging trends in clinical psychology as including an expansion of goals, increased attention to the ecology of service, and an increased variety of intervention techniques (not to mention evaluation techniques).

We need to change because current training models (general) are obsolete for solving the needs presented to us. Blau (1973) raised the issue of relevant competence in graduate training, and Rice and Gurman (1973) commented on the differences between academic training and clinical internships. Another issue is training for job relevance in the future (Howe & Neimeyer, 1980). Supposedly, the more differentiated a society becomes, the greater the necessity for differentiated services. We can best accommodate such societal differentiation with professional differentiation.

Many articles have been written on the inadequacy of clinical training in the areas of alcoholism (Selin & Soren, 1981), rural mental health delivery (Hargrove & Howe, 1981), and minorities (Green, 1981). One of the many issues in training is of course the definition of competence and the identification and weeding out of incompetence (Clairborn, 1982).

We need to change because most of our students, having learned that specialization pays off, want specialization. Levitt (1974) commented on clinical psychology interns' inadequacies in dealing with acute crises and lower socioeconomic classes because of deficits in their academic training. In a survey of former clinical psychology interns, Steinhelber and Gaynor (1981) found that respondents wanted less testing and administration and more psychotherapy training.

Jobs are becoming more and more differentiated; that is, employers are demanding more specialized skills (compare the want ads of 30 years ago with those of the today).

In general, old models may no longer be as popular or as feasible as new models. Advocating specialization does not mean doing away with generalism. Specialization will speed up the rate of information acquisition in the profession.

The following propositions are submitted for debate and discussion in terms of their validity, relevance, and application.

Even when generalism is necessary, it is still oriented toward urban rather than rural problems (Hargrove, 1982; Hargrove & Howe, 1981), toward white rather than minority populations (Green, 1981), toward the middle class and the affluent rather than the poor (Hollander, 1980).

The issue is whether clinical psychology is sufficiently mature to take the next step in professional differentiation, that is, breaking up into specialty training and relegating the generalist model to programs that do not have specialized faculty. Specialization is possible only when faculty members are sufficiently knowledgeable to ensure adequate training in that specialty. The issue is a moot one for training programs that do not have specialized faculty members.

Perhaps these issues could be divided into issues of rigor versus relevance, narrow gauge versus broad gauge training. Because these issues cannot be considered dichotomies, the plurality of American culture is allowing us to fill in the points along these two main continua. Unfortunately, not enough has been said in favor of specialization in clinical psychology.

Toward an Integrated Model of Specialization

The following classification suggests that specialization can take place along three different routes: (a) the characteristics of professionals, (b) the characteristics of the clients, and (c) the characteristics of physical facilities. Each of these characteristics can be broken down further, as shown.

Classification of Applied Specialties in Clinical Psychology

I.   Characteristics of Professionals

A. By functions desired

    1. administration
    2. research
    3. treatment
    4. prevention
    5. assessment

B. By preferred clientele

    1. individuals
    2. groups
    3. couples
    4. families
    5. communities

C. By preferred treatment modality

    1. behavior modification
    2. biofeedback
    3. psychotherapy
    4. social skills training
    5. family therapy
    6. self-help

II. Characteristics of Clients

A. By disease entity

    1. alcoholics
    2. schizophrenics
    3. neurotics
    4. normals
    5. delinquents

B. By age range

    1. infants
    2. children
    3. adolescents
    4. young adults
    5. adults
    6. geriatric adults

C. By special populations

    1. minorities
    2. women
    3. retardates
    4. other

III. Characteristics of Physical Facilities

    A. By settings

        1. university clinics
        2. hospitals
        3. mental health clinics
        4. rural-urban
        5. halfway houses, etc.
        6. other

    B. By medical specialties

        1. pediatrics
        2. psychiatry
        3. family medicine
        4. other

    C. By judicial specialties

        1. courts
        2. jails and penitentiaries
        3. probation offices
        4. other

At Georgia State University, for instance, in addition to a general track, we have four specializations: child, psychotherapy, behavior modification, and family psychology (L'Abate, 1983). A fourth specialization, medical psychology, is in the planning stage. At GSU, clinical students need to satisfy (a) University residence requirements, (b) College of Arts and Sciences language requirements, (c) departmental requirements, (d) clinical requirements, and (e) subspecialty requirements. The GSU program fulfills the criteria that content and skills should be specific to the subspecialty and that the program should include course work, clinical practice, and faculty modeling.

Conclusion

The need for specialization in clinical psychology is urgent. The evolutionary process of differentiation is inevitable. More specialization in clinical psychology will take place whether some of us like it or not. Clinical psychology is too broad to encompass only general training; we also need specialization. Both kinds of training--general and specialty--are necessary.

References

Blau, T. H. (1973). Exposure to competence: A single standard for graduate training in professional psychology. Professional Psychology,

4, 133-136.

Clairborn, W. L. (1982). The problem of professional incompetence. Professional Psychology, 13, 153-158.

Coelho, G. V. (1971). In conclusion. Professional Psychology, 2, 126-127.

Green, L. (1981). Training psychologists to work with minority clients: A prototypic model with black clients. Professional Psychology, 12, 732-739.

Grinker, R. R., Albee, G. W., Schafer, J., Garmezy, N., Thrasher, R. H., & Mensh, I. N. (1971). Emerging conceptions of mental duress and models of treatment. Professional Psychology, 2, 129-144.

Hargrove, D. S. (1982). The rural psychologist as generalist: A challenge for professional identity. Professional Psychology, 13, 302-308.

Hargrove, D. S., & Howe, H. E., Jr. (1981). Training in rural mental health delivery: A response to prioritized needs. Professional Psychology, 12, 253-260.

Hollander, R. (1980). A new service ideology: The third mental health revolution. Professional Psychology, 11, 561-566.

Howe, H. E., Jr., & Neimeyer, R. A. (1980). Job relevance in clinical training: Is that all there is? Professional Psychology, 11, 305-313.

L'Abate, L. (1964). Principles of clinical psychology. New York: Grune & Stratton.

L'Abate, L. (1983). Family psychology: Theory, therapy, and training. Washington, DC: University Press of America.

L'Abate, L., & Thaxton, M. L. (1981). Differentiation of resources in mental health delivery: Implications for training. Professional Psychology, 12, 761-768.

Levitt, R. (1974). Deficits in the skill development of clinical psychologists. Professional Psychology, 5, 415-421.

Pottharst, K. E. (1969). Role-model and theoretical models. In L. L'Abate (Ed.), Models of clinical psychology (School of Arts and Sciences Research Papers, No. 22, pp. 75-86). Atlanta: Georgia State College.

Rice, D. G., & Gurman, A. S. (1973). Unresolved issues in the clinical psychology internship. <u>Professional Psychology</u>, <u>4</u>, 403-408.

Rickard, H. D., & Bernatz, M. L. (1983). Delimiting subspecialty clinical training. <u>The Clinical Psychologist</u>, <u>36</u>, 75-78.

Rubinstein, E. A., & Coelho, G. V. (1971). Can psychology be socially relevant? <u>Professional Psychology</u>, <u>2</u>, 111-117.

Seeman, J., & Seeman, Z. (1973). Emergent trends in the practice of clinical psychology. <u>Professional Psychology</u>, <u>4</u>, 151-157.

Selin, J. A., & Soren, S. (1981). Alcoholism and substance abuse training: A survey of graduate programs in clinical psychology. <u>Professional Psychology</u>, <u>12</u>, 717-721.

Steinhelber, J., & Gaynor, J. (1981). Attitudes, satisfaction and training recommendations of former clinical psychology interns: 1968 to 1977. <u>Professional Psychology</u>, <u>12</u>, 253-256.

Strickland, B. (1983). Clinical psychology and health concerns. <u>The Clinical Psychologist</u>, <u>36</u>, 52,54.

CHAPTER 22

A TRAINING PROGRAM FOR
FAMILY PSYCHOLOGY:
EVALUATION, PREVENTION AND THERAPY

LUCIANO L'ABATE
Georgia State University

Family psychology differs from family therapy on a variety of dimensions. Philosophically, family psychology emphasizes the relationship of the individual to the family rather than considering the family as a system, deemphasizing the individual, as in systems family therapy. In addition, family psychology is interested in the whole spectrum of functionality-dysfunctionality, while family therapy is interested mainly in dysfunctional families. Substantively, in terms of differences in training, family psychology stresses the importance of theory testing, evaluation of process and outcome of interventions, and prevention with functional or at-risk families. An academic curriculum in family psychology, which has been operational at Georgia State University for the last 10 years, is presented. Clinical training follows a gradual approach, starting with relatively simple Structured Enrichment, progressing to more complex training in Covenant Contracting and Systematic Homework Assignments, and finally family therapy.

The purpose of this paper is to present a training program for family psychologists that has been operational at Georgia State University for the last decade (Ganahl et al., 1985; Kochalka & L'Abate, 1983a, 1983b; L'Abate, 1983a; L'Abate et al., 1979). Personally, the more I hear and read about the field of family therapy, the more I want to retain the label I find more comfortable: I am a family psychologist first and a family therapist second. Theory testing, evaluation, and prevention are just as important as therapy. Hence, when I see family therapists blithely going about their business enthusiastically but uncritically, I retreat into the more skeptical, even cynical position of psychologist. Family therapy is not sufficient without attention to issues of theory testing, evaluation, and prevention.

It follows from the above that I am not interested in training family therapists. At the present time the field of family therapy is growing out of control. I am not interested in helping to produce the normative, run-of-the-mill family therapist.

247

I prefer to train family psychologists and ensure that they will have an abiding interest in issues of theory testing, through outcome and process evaluation, family prevention, and, finally, family therapy. Students from this program have been placed into medical schools and university psychology departments where, I hope, they will continue to practice some of these values.

I think that clinical psychologists who have sold out to the family therapy movement have given up rights of primogeniture by joining the commonplace, the host of inadequately trained individuals who claim to represent family therapy. *Of course, there are many and notable exceptions. There are outstanding family therapists whose standards are in sharp contrast to the run-of-the-mill who represent the majority of the family therapy movement.* My quarrel is *not* with degrees per se but with the overall standards used to train so-called family therapists. It is relatively easy to join many seductive family therapy concepts and practices. It is much more difficult to retain a skeptical position that requires critical restraint, guarded and tentative judgment, and an open mind tempered by questioning doubts.

The major philosophical differences that distinguish family psychology from family therapy deal with 1) the position, function and role of the individual in the family and 2) the need to consider the whole range of functionality-dysfunctionality among individuals in families. While most family therapists emphasize the importance of the family system (seemingly *void* of individuals!), family psychology stresses the importance of *both* the individual *and* the system that is: the individual *with* and *within* the family system and the family as a system of interdependent individuals. By the same token, 3) interest in the whole range of functionality-dysfunctionality in families would translate into an interest in preventive, interventional methods and services that will benefit most families rather than a select sample of clinical families. This interest in individuals *within* their families along the whole spectrum of functionality-dysfunctionality translates clinically in areas usually bypassed by the family therapy community; these are: (a) theory testing, (b) evaluation, and (c) prevention.

ACADEMIC CURRICULUM

The substance of the academic curriculum is contained in Appendix I. An academic curriculum that derives from the three substantive points of difference between family psychologists and family therapists already mentioned, needs to include at least one course on family evaluation that would include the plethora of new and old ways of assessing families (Bagarozzi, 1985; Bagarozzi & L'Abate, in press; Gilbert & Christensen, 1985; L'Abate & Wagner, 1985). In addition it must include at least one course on prevention that includes all of the new ways of intervening with families which are based on education and a skills-training public health model rather than a crisis-oriented private practice model (Bloom, 1980; Guerney et al., 1985; Jessee & L'Abate, 1981; L'Abate, 1983a, 1985, 1986; L'Abate & McHenry, 1983; Murphy, 1979; Roberts & Peterson, 1984; Stolz, 1984). In addition to these courses it is important to include a course on *methods*, rather than theories and techniques (L'Abate et al., in press).

Goals and Purposes of the Program

The academic curriculum has been described above and elsewhere (Ganahl et al., 1985a) in detail. This program was developed with at least three purposes in mind. In the first place, it intends to train family psychologists, *not* family therapists. This differentiation is based on the fact that there is and will be an overabundance of family therapists due to the following reasons: There is an overproduction of therapists of all persuasions and disciplines graduated from hundreds of training programs in psychiatry, clinical psychology, counseling and guidance, marriage and family, pastoral counseling, social work, etc. Many graduates of these programs become "family therapists."

As Lazarus commented on this matter (Aylward, 1984): "The glut of therapists on the market is something to be reckoned with" (p. 10). Haley and Madanes (1984) estimated that there are approximately 200 training programs in family therapy available at the present time. In contrast to these staggering numbers of therapists being produced, how many training programs for family psychologists are there in the country? At last reckoning, less than a handful (Ganahl et al., 1985). As a result of so many training programs, standards of training and practice in family therapy are questionable, as commented repeatedly by Framo (1984). Although his critical comments were directed toward California standards for certification in marriage and family therapy, they generally apply also to training programs that allow the M.A. or its equivalent as the highest level of education necessary to practice, with no full-time internship. AAMFT accepts an M.A. even for its highest status of Approved Supervisor. These criteria are insufficient and unacceptable to psychologists who require the Ph.D. plus one year of full-time internship as the minimal level of acceptable independent practice.

One could also argue that family therapy per se without any larger perspectives, either in empirically based practice or in the larger community, may eventually be limited. As Gianfranco Cecchin and Luigi Boscolo (Harris, 1984) commented on this issue: "Family therapy is a dead-end street. It is dangerous to create a profession out of it" (p. 11). Family therapy is not the province of any specific discipline (at least thus far!), and hopefully never will be.

In the second place, while family therapists are mainly concerned with therapy to the exclusion of theory-testing, evaluation of process and outcome, and prevention, family psychologists are specifically concerned with those very issues (Bagarozzi, 1985; Gilbert & Christensen, 1985; Guerney et al., 1985; L'Abate & Milan, 1985; L'Abate & Wagner, 1985). These are the three activities that differentiate family psychologists from family therapists. Generally family therapists are not trained to evaluate the outcome of their therapy and are not effectively concerned with prevention. Not only are they as a group not interested in theory testing, evaluation, and prevention, but there is practically no training in research and evaluation techniques in most nonacademic family therapy training programs. Research and evaluation must come from psychologists who are trained in these areas.

In the third place, there is an academic market opening up for well-trained family psychologists because psychology and clinical psychology, scientifically and professionally, are finally becoming aware of a need for a family orientation in training and in practice (L'Abate, 1983b). The establishment of an APA Division of Family Psychology in 1984 is an indication of this awareness. Even though this progress has been and will be slow, there is no question that a paradigm shift in psychology is in the making. It is inevitable that this shift will take place (L'Abate, 1983b; L'Abate, 1985). At the present time, there are not enough sufficiently trained students to fill the increasing requests for faculty positions in psychology departments that are interested in opening up to a family-oriented approach.

As shown in Appendix I, the purpose of our academic curriculum is to give students the widest possible knowledge of evaluation, prevention, and intervention strategies with as wide a spectrum of families as possible, starting with functional or semi-functional, nonclinical, families and eventually dealing with families with greater and greater pathology. One must remember that most of the students in our program come with a B.A. degree, and many of them have no experience with families on a professional basis.

It is important to train students to avoid taking mutually antagonistic stances (L'Abate, 1983a). For instance, they need to appreciate working with what are usually considered mutually compatible combinations of: (a) theory *with* practice; (b) research *with* practice; (c) evaluation *with* intervention; and (d) prevention *with* therapy. Out of this background, whatever professional choices students make will be based on information and not on ignorance.

THE IMPORTANCE OF THEORY TESTING

The field of family therapy is rampant with theories and theorettes (Hansen & L'Abate, 1982). However, much of it is vacuous, untestable rhetoric, seductively sterile and without substantive demonstrability. Hence, the field is in dire need of researchers who will distinguish between speculative mumbo jumbo and testable theorizing, leading ideally to specific linkages to methods of intervention.

By the same token, the field of family therapy is also replete with techniques rather than methods (L'Abate et al., in press). Hence a great deal of what goes for therapy in this field is mostly a nonsystematic hodgepodge of personal gimicks, guru-laden, individualized styles rather than repeatable and reproducible methods. As a result, the cult of the guru reaches untold limits, where the personality of the therapists is exalted at the expense of competence and methodology. Of course, there are exceptions to these generalizations, which stand out clearly, but discontinuously, from the norm. They do not seem to affect a field steeped in the cult of individual style at the expense of testable theories and methods.

THE IMPORTANCE OF EVALUATION

If evaluation is not considered in training why should it become important in practice? Hence, the message from many family therapy training centers is very clear: Evaluation is *not* important, and we shall not waste any time teaching or learning it. Let us stick to the fashionable but short-sighted shibboleths of "ecosystemic epistemology" and rely exclusively on the personal and subjective judgment of the therapist. As a result, the importance of the therapist's subjective judgment is proclaimed at the expense of *other*, additional and different sources of information (Hansen & L'Abate, 1982). In other words, evaluation becomes a mutually exclusive position. If I, the therapist, see things as I interpret them, I do not need any additional and different sources of information either to support and verify my impressions or to correct them. This is an unreasonable responsibility to give trainees and therapists alike, teaching them to become the ultimate and absolute arbiters and judges of family functions and dysfunctions, without reliance on objective evidence. In fact, objective evidence seems to be scorned and ridiculed by the rank-and-file representatives of the family therapy profession (Colapinto, 1979).

This cavalier attitude toward evaluation is reflected in the practices of many of the important gurus in the field such as Haley, Modanes, Satir, Whitaker, and others (Hansen & L'Abate, 1982; L'Abate & McHenry, 1983). Most of them bypass completely any type of formal evaluation, and instead show how it is possible to understand families without any formal tools of evaluation. Thus, the accepted practices of evaluation in the field consist of subjective and informal impressions unhampered by any kind of externally objective correction.

This dangerous and irresponsible path, both for training and for the welfare of our families, is based on a position of *exclusion* rather than *inclusion*, relying unduly on the subjective judgment of the therapist. To verify an event in a court of law, it takes at least two separate and independent sources of information. One source could and should be the human observer, *but* the other needs to be one that is relatively free from influence by the observer. I, for one, maintain that it takes *both* sources of information to evaluate families: the personal, subjective, and impressionistic (aesthetic and dialectical) *and* the objective, formal, and demonstrative (pragmatic and empirical). To rely on one source of information alone, at the expense of the other, is irresponsible professional practice. It is also a limited form of training, which ultimately decreases the chances of improving our services to families.

This defective practice is probably due to the fear of evaluation of outcome and of possible critical feedback about one's clinical and therapeutic practices. It is more comfortable to continue therapeutic practices without the possibility of objective feedback that may force changes in them. Evaluation is a form of feedback. By cutting ourselves off from it, we bypass the possibility of improving our therapeutic practices, because without evaluation, critical feedback is impossible, or certainly very difficult.

THE IMPORTANCE OF PREVENTION

Another area that suffers from *exclusive* rather than *inclusive* training and clinical practices is prevention (Bloom, 1980; Kessler & Albee, 1975; L'Abate, 1983, 1986; Murphy, 1979; Roberts & Peterson, 1984; Stolz, 1984; Wright & L'Abate, 1977). Because therapy with critical or chronic families assumes such great importance it is easy to forget that for every clinical family, at least impressionistically, there may be six or seven that could use additional or different sources of help (L'Abate, 1983a). Hence, it is important to extend our services to functional or semifunctional families who risk *future* breakdown. Obviously, this identification cannot take place without evaluation, since we cannot distinguish subjectively which families would need preventive services and which would need therapeutic services. If our perspective is limited strictly to therapy, it follows that we will focus only on clinical families, excluding others who may be as much in need. Yet, the family therapy field has cut itself off from prevention, to the point that preventers do not talk to therapists and vice versa (L'Abate, 1983a). This cutoff only limits the training of students and ultimately the services we can offer to families.

Hence, a serious, responsible, comprehensive training program cannot rely on *exclusive* practices, but needs to *include* practices that, although unpopular to trainees eager to "do therapy" as soon as possible, are important components of training. I submit that these unpopular training components—theory testing, evaluation, and prevention—are just as important as therapy for the family therapist.

TRAINING FOR PREVENTION

The last decade has seen a veritable explosion of preventive, social skills training programs for couples and families (L'Abate & McHenry, 1983; L'Abate & Milan, 1985). If the 70s was the decade of family therapy, the 80s might well

251

become the decade of preventive programs (L'Abate, 1986). Because most family therapy training programs ignore prevention, most therapists are not interested in it. On the other hand, professionals who identify themselves as preventers are not concerned with therapy. Either way, families are shortchanged from needed services. Furthermore, *both* practices are *exclusive* of each other, diminishing the impact on families that could result if both practices were united synergistically (L'Abate, 1985). Fortunately, I am both a preventer (L'Abate, 1986) and a therapist. I abhor mutually exclusive practices, because I feel that each detracts from the other. However, if I had to choose, I would put prevention ahead of therapy because I think the need is greater in this area.

RATIONALE OF THE PROGRAM:
GRADUALNESS, GRADUALNESS, GRADUALNESS!

Gradualness has been the watchword of this program. Instead of allowing students immediately to work therapeutically with clinical families (the sink-or-swim approach), students start with nonclinical couples and families, using relatively easy techniques of intervention that require manuals. They then move gradually to more complex work with clinical families. Some of the stages of their clinical training are described below.

Structured Enrichment. This approach came into being specifically as a way of training students (Jessee & L'Abate, 1981), to minimize their understandable and expectable anxieties in beginning work with families, and to teach them *first* to work with functional and semifunctional couples and families. Once a certain degree of proficiency is achieved, usually after three cases, the student can graduate to the next step, requiring less structure and more responsibility.

Covenant Contracting. This approach has been described in detail in L'Abate and McHenry (1983) and Kochalka et al., (1983). It requires the use of a manual and of some standard forms, but the student no longer needs to rely on verbatim instructions from a manual. From this step, which ideally should require at least three cases, the student can graduate to the next, which requires more complexity and therapy-like analogies.

Systematic Homework Assignments (SHWAs). The rationale and construction of these SHWAs can be found in L'Abate (in press). Briefly, this step involves assigning SHWAs to volunteer couples or adding them to the process of therapy. Again, a minimum of three assignments seems necessary to master this type of intervention. One of the advantages of SHWAs lies in their theory-testing nature. They comprise three distinct and relevant areas: depression, negotiation, and intimacy.

Thus, gradualness need to take place according to: (a) decreasing structure, from more structured to less structured forms of intervention (Kochalka & L'Abate, 1983a, 1983b); (b) increasing complexity, as defined by more difficult problems to deal with; (c) increasing responsibility, in taking initiative and assuming control; and (d) increasing creativity, because the less the structure, the greater the freedom to be creative and original.

Family Therapy. This program does not have anything original to add to the process of training. Students receive supervision from one-way mirrors, from tapes, from notes, and from audiotapes. They are exposed to a wide range of supervisors who provide a variety of theoretical and therapeutic models. From this vast range of choices students work out whatever model is comfortable for them. Typically, during the first year, students are supervised by faculty members. In the second

252

year, they are assigned to various practicum settings under the supervision of the setting supervisors. Advanced third or fourth year students are supervised by adjunct supervisors in private practice. Eventually, each student will go on to an APA approved internship for one full year before receiving the Ph.D., which also requires a dissertation. The major problem here lies in the fact that there are no "pure" family internships in clinical psychology. Consequently, many if not all of our students have to learn traditional child clinical psychology methods of evaluation (intelligence testing, projective techniques, etc.) in order to qualify competitively for admission to these internships. As a result, family psychology students end up taking many more hours of coursework than students in other clinical specialties. The only solution to this problem will take place when "pure" family-oriented internship settings open up for our students. Until then we do not know how to solve this problem, lest students apply for admission to AAMFT approved internships where traditionally individual-oriented testing practices are not used.

DISCUSSION

The greatest resistance to following this gradual sequence of training comes from graduate students with M.A.s and a certain degree of experience in family therapy. At the outset, some of them react negatively to the imposed structure and the seemingly simplistic constraints of manuals with verbatim instructions. Some of these students, however, come around full circle when they recognize the usefulness of learning through a structure, starting with nonclinical couples and families.

The major feature of this training program lies in its reproducibility. At the present time a great deal of clinical family therapy training is based on magical or mystical practices that are based on nonreplicable, individualized techniques rather than methods. In contrast, in our program the clinical usefulness of the approach is first established. It is then, secondly, imparted to the student on the basis of its *established* usefulness, rather than on the whim and will of a supervisor. Since these training components are reproducible, they are also testable. Someone else can take these components and reproduce them to see whether they work, when they work, and with which students and families they work. Without checking on each other, I doubt very much that we can improve our training practices.

CONCLUSION

The outcome of this program is pretty clear. Out of 12 Ph.D.s graduated in the last few years, five have university appointments in medical schools or in psychology departments. Some of them have already distinguished themselves by participating actively in research and publication as well as in various professional meetings from different disciplines. Quality is certainly more important than quantity. We do not need more family therapists. We need leaders in family psychology who can be master therapists in addition to being evaluators and preventers.

REFERENCES

Aylward, J. (1984). The economics of psychotherapy: An interview with Dr. Arnold Lazarus. *The Psychotherapy Newsletter, 2*, 10–15.
Bagarozzi, D. A. (1985). Dimensions of family evaluation. In L. L'Abate (Ed.), *Handbook of family psychology and therapy* (pp. 989–1005). Homewood, IL: Dorsey Press.
Bagarozzi, D. A., & L'Abate, L. (in press). *Marriage and family evaluation: A sourcebook for clinicians and researchers.* New York: Brunner/Mazel.

Bloom, B. L. (1980). Social and community interventions. *Annual Review of Psychology, 31,* 111–142.

Colapinto, J. (1979). The relative value of empirical evidence. *Family Process, 18,* 427–441.

Framo, J. L. (1984). Framo responds. *Family Therapy News, 6,* 2.

Ganahl, G. F., Ferguson, L. R., & L'Abate, L. (1985). Training in family therapy. In L. L'Abate (Ed.), *Handbook of family psychology and therapy* (pp. 1249–1317). Homewood, IL: Dorsey Press.

Gilbert, R., & Christensen, A. (1985). Observational assessment of marital and family interaction: Methodological considerations. In L'Abate (Ed.), *Family psychology and therapy* (pp. 961–988). Homewood, IL: Dorsey Press.

Guerney, B. G., Guerney, L., & Cooney, T. (1985). Marital and family problem prevention and enrichment programs. In L. L'Abate (Ed.), *Handbook of family psychology and therapy* (pp. 1179–1217). Homewood, IL: Dorsey Press.

Haley, J., & Madanes, C. (1984, December 13). Personal communication.

Hansen, J. C., & L'Abate, L. (1982). *Approaches to family therapy.* New York: Macmillan.

Harris, E. G. (1984). The Milan approach in transition. *AFTA Newsletter, 18,* 9–11.

Jessee, E., & L'Abate, L. (1981). Enrichment role-playing as a step in the training of family therapists. *Journal of Marital and Family Therapy, 7,* 507–514.

Kessler, J., & Albee, G. W. (1975). Primary prevention. *Annual Review of Psychology, 30,* 557–591.

Kochalka, J., & L'Abate, L. (1983a). Clinical training in family psychology. In B. F. Okun & S. T. Gladding (Eds.), *Issues in training marriage and family therapists* (pp. 63–71). Ann Arbor, MI: ERIC/CAPS.

Kochalka, J. A., & L'Abate, L. (1983b). Structure and gradualness in the clinical training of family psychologists. In L. L'Abate (Ed.), *Family psychology: Theory, therapy and training* (pp. 287–299). Washington, DC: University Press of America.

Kochalka, J. A., L'Abate, L., Lutz, J., & Metts, J. (1983, October). Covenant contracting: Training functions and treatment outcome. Paper read at the National Council of Family Relations Meeting, St. Paul, MN.

L'Abate, L. (1983a). Prevention as a profession: Towards a new conceptual frame of reference. In D. Mace (Ed.), *Toward family wellness: The need for preventative services* (pp. 49–62). Beverly Hills, CA: Sage Publications.

L'Abate L. (1983b). Training in family psychology. In L. L'Abate (Ed.), *Family psychology: Theory, therapy and training* (pp. 277–285). Washington, DC: University Press of America.

L'Abate, L. (1985). Structured enrichment (SE) with couples and families. *Family Relations, 43,* 169–175.

L'Abate, L. (1986). Prevention of marital and family problems. In B. Edelstein & L. Michalson (Eds.), *Handbook of prevention.* New York: Plenum.

L'Abate, L. (in press). *Systematic family therapy.* New York: Brunner/Mazel.

L'Abate, L., Berger, M., Wright, L., & O'Shea, M. (1979). Training family psychologists: The family studies program at Georgia State University. *Professional Psychology, 10,* 58–64.

L'Abate, L., Ganahl, G., & Hansen, J. C. (in press). *Methods of family therapy.* Englewood, NJ: Prentice-Hall.

L'Abate, L., & McHenry, S. (1983). *Handbook of marital interventions.* New York: Grune & Stratton.

L'Abate, L., & Milan, M. (Eds.). (1985). *Handbook of social skills training and research.* New York: John Wiley & Sons.

L'Abate L., & Wagner, V. (1985). Theory-derived, family-oriented, test batteries. In L. L'Abate (Ed.), *Handbook of family psychology and therapy* (pp. 1006–1031). Homewood, IL: Dorsey Press.

Murphy, L. R. (1979). Prevention: The clinical psychologist. *Annual Review of Psychology, 30,* 73–107.

Roberts, M. C., & Peterson, L. (1984). Prevention models: Theoretical and practical implications. In M. C. Roberts & L. Peterson (Eds.), *Prevention of problems in childhood: Psychological research and applications.* New York: John Wiley & Sons.

Stolz, S. B. (1984). Preventive models: Implications for a technology of practice. In M. C. Roberts & L. Peterson (Eds.), *Prevention of problems in childhood: Psychological research and applications.* New York: John Wiley & Sons.

Wright, L., & L'Abate, L. (1977). Four approaches to family facilitation: Some issues and implications. *The Family Coordinator, 26,* 176–181.

APPENDIX I

GEORGIA STATE UNIVERSITY
FAMILY PSYCHOLOGY PROGRAM

Purpose

The purpose of this specialty is to train Ph.D. students to become leaders in research and training in family psychology in their theoretical, clinical, and professional applications. This specialty prepares students to work with couples and families, using a variety of models of evaluation, intervention, and prevention. Research and research methodology are emphasized as the specific contribution that clinical psychologists can make in this field. Research tests theoretical and practical viewpoints according to responsible and accepted criteria of scientific and professional practice. Hence, this specialty is theoretically eclectic and empirical in application.

Departmental Core and Methodology

In addition to required courses, one on the biological and cognitive-affective bases of behavior and another on professional ethics, family psychology students are required to take the following methodology courses or their equivalents:
Advanced Child Development or Advanced Social Psychology
Statistics II
Statistics III
Research Design or Single-Case Methodology or Observational Methodology

Clinical Core

Introduction to Behavior Modification
Behavior Disorders or Behavioral Disturbances in Children
Proseminar in Child and Family

Family Psychology Core

First year:
Family Evaluation, plus one hour of practicum
Prevention and the Family
Methods of Family Therapy

Second year:
Theories of Family Therapy
Personality Development in Marriage and the Family
Marital Interventions, plus one hour of practicum
Third year:
Human Sexuality
Family Law
Sociology of the Family

Supervised Clinical Training

Enrichment:
Three completed cases, one where role-playing has been done by the student as a client and another two cases with the student as trainer. At least one of these three cases should be a family.
Covenant Contracting:
Three completed cases are required.
Systematic Homework Assignments:
At least three systematic homework assignments are required.
Practicum in Family Therapy:
Students should have continuous, ongoing cases with quarterly credits from three to five hours.
Internship:
Students are expected to apply to nationally ranked clinical facilities with specific training in family therapy. Please note that such a facility is presently not available in the Atlanta area. Consequently, students will need to plan for at least one year of training outside of Atlanta.

M.A. thesis and Ph.D. dissertation should be on areas relevant to the student.

Chapter 23

A Graduate Curriculum in Preventive Psychology*

Luciano L'Abate

More than a generation ago, Sanford (1965) reviewed the field of prevention, as it was then known, and presaged many of the issues that we face today. In the area of training, he concluded:

As we think of the future and of the new roles for the clinical psychologists that are emerging, the deficiencies of present training programs become apparent. To meet the needs and to take advantage of the opportunities the future will present, existing programs must be revised, and totally new programs should be developed. (p. 1397)

The purpose of this paper is to present a rationale and background for a graduate curriculum in preventive psychology and to describe this curriculum. The purpose of such a curriculum is to teach students methods for mental health social practices in general.

The Rise of Preventive Activities

The increased interest in prevention and preventive health-related activities can be traced to at least four sources: (a) effect that has spread from preventive efforts in the field of physical health; (b) increased interest at the federal level, which has spread to the American Psychological Association (APA); (c) impact of the Vermont Conference on Scientific and Professional Attitudes and Interests; and (d) concern and curiosity about prevention at the community level.

Contextual Spread

For instance, the value of prevention in the physical area has been amply demonstrated by the dramatic surges in heart attack prevention, brought about by increased attention to exercise and improved diet. Other drastic changes that illustrate the value of prevention in public health can be found in immunizations, the fluoride treatment of water supplies, and so forth. The enthusiasm resulting from these successes may have attuned us to the value of prevention in mental health as well.

---

*I am indebted to Gregory W. Brock, Bernard Guerney, Jr., Dick Holland, David R. Mace, Kenneth B. Matheny, and Fred Stevens for their thoughtful comments on a draft of this paper.

Federal Contribution

Among the many political considerations is the increased interest in prevention at the federal level (Brandt, 1982), both in the body politic and in the National Institutes of Mental Health (Goldston, 1979), which has established an Office of Prevention. Some of these considerations were recently discussed by Kiesler (1983) in terms of the limitations of psychotherapy in solving pressing national needs, the need for the reduction of stress and for cost-effective methods of evaluation and intervention, the rise of social support and self-support groups. He also acknowledged one of the main issues in prevention—that the public is not interested: "That's been a consistent problem with prevention. You can't even get people to listen, or to read about it." Elsewhere (L'Abate, 1983) a case for prevention has been made on the grounds that it is cheaper, more innovative, easier, happier, cleaner, and takes place before greater dysfunctionality sets in, or worse, before it is too late. As for a new profession of preventers, one needs to keep in mind that at least at this juncture, prevention does not pay (i.e., the merit system has no job classifications for preventers). In comparison to psychotherapy, prevention is not yet glamorous. At least for some individuals, prevention may stifle creativity and may seem too limited. Because of increased interest at the federal level, APA has shown its increased interest by creating a task force on promotion, prevention, and intervention alternatives in psychology (R. H. Price, personal communication, December 2, 1983). The objective of this task force is to "identify workable innovative program approaches. . . particularly in primary prevention." In response to an inquiry directed to APA members, the task force received 297 responses, from which a limited number will be selected as promising examples of preventive intervention strategies (R. H. Price, personal communication, May 9, 1984).

The Vermont Conference

In addition to political considerations, interest in prevention has been spurred by community psychology, an interest that led Albee (1982) to establish the Vermont Conference on Prevention (L'Abate, 1982). This conference and the publications derived from its annual meeting have furnished the bulk of what is known about prevention.

Community Interest

Grass-roots interest is also increasing, as shown in Georgia for instance, by the Georgia Coalition on Consultation, Education, and Prevention.

In addition to these four trends, at least two others have helped strengthen concerns and interest in preventive activities. One trend, the greater differentiation of psychology as a science and as a profession, is indigenous to psychology. The second trend, the rise of the social skills training (SST) movement, has taken place outside psychology, even though a great many psychologists are part of it.

Differentiation in Psychology as a Science and a Profession

Inevitably, the more a profession develops, the more it divides itself into various specialties and subspecialties. In the past decade, psychology has grown from a few divisions to a doubling of divisions to the point that the APA had to declare a moratorium on accepting new divisions. Clinical psychology as a professional representative of mental health practices has also experienced growth.

Among the many schisms in clinical psychology (research vs. practice, evaluation vs. intervention), the most relevant issue in regard to a curriculum in preventive psychology is the split between clinicians and preventers.

Most therapists are not interested in prevention or in preventive activities; most preventers are not interested in most therapeutic activities. One might say that the Weltanshauungs of these two classes of individuals are completely different. One profession, the therapeutic one, follows a private practice model, that is, the most good for the few in need or in crisis. Most preventers, on the other hand, seem more interested in a public health model, that is, the maximum good for the largest number of people. Fox (1982) has supported a public health model. His thesis is as follows:

> Clinical psychology must reorient itself toward general practice that offers services to the many and away from specialty practice that offers services to the few. . . . professional psychology is poorly organized and structured to deliver the services needed by society. We must begin to reconceptualize the nature of our profession, make modifications in our training and delivery systems, and develop a different interface with the rest of the health care system.

> Perhaps the time has come to devote the majority of our efforts (or at least half of them) to the delivery of those services needed by the majority of the population. It is difficult to see how psychology will ever gain access to the major health care market unless we emphasize services other than those distinctly labeled as "mental health."

> Our training programs are not always producing students capable of delivering the services that are most needed. For example, many clinical psychology programs still devote most of the intervention portion of their curricula to teaching students how to do psychotherapy.

But psychotherapy is not the service most needed by the large segment of the mentally disturbed who are confined to hospitals. (pp. 1051, 1052, 1055)

Fox has advocated (among other solutions) the use of therapeutic modules, because of their cost-effectiveness and applicability to the general population rather than a few selected individuals. These modules resemble social skills training programs.

Recently, Levy (1984) proposed that "traditional conceptions of [clinical psychology] centering around the treatment of individuals suffering from mental health problems are no longer adequate." He argued for a clinical psychology focusing on human services "concerned with the promotion of human well-being through the acquisition and application of psychological knowledge about the treatment and prevention of psychological and physical disorders" (p. 486). Levy, essentially, has favored professional specializations in clinical psychology, an issue that is considered in greater detail elsewhere (Craddick, submitted for publication; L'Abate, submitted for publication).

The Rise of the SST Movement

The past decade, especially the past few years, have seen a veritable explosion in publications concerning the use of SST with individuals, groups, couples, and families (Bellack & Hersen, 1979; L'Abate & Milan, 1985; Singleton, Spurgeon, & Stammers, 1979; Spence & Shepherd, 1983; Trower, Bryant, Argyle, & Marzillier, 1978), in a variety of populations at risk, both inside and outside institutions. A different view of psychopathology based on competence rather than abnormality serves as the theoretical background for this movement (Phillips, 1978; Pickett-Rathjen & Foreyt, 1980; Wine & Smye, 1981). Within this movement are other specialties that have focused specifically on the use of social skills with couples and families (Guerney, Vogelsong, & Coufal, 1983; L'Abate, 1983).

In addition to increased programs and publications (Marshall, Kurtz, & Associates, 1982), the formation of a professional association dedicated to uniting trainers from various disciplines would indicate, among other signs, that SST is not a passing fad or a temporary trend.

In terms of health promotion, SST in many of its approaches (L'Abate & Milan, 1985) is devoted to the development of more functional attitudes as well as behaviors that will allow individuals to exhibit behaviors that pay off for them and for others at minimal emotional and interpersonal cost. Examples of this approach are assertiveness training (Curran & Monti, 1982), effectiveness training (L'Abate, 1981), and many others (Bellack & Hersen, 1979; Authier, Gustafson, Fix, & Daughton, 1981). All these approaches work with nonclinical or semiclinical populations, teaching them newer ways of becoming more assertive, more effective, or less shy.

260

By promoting healthier attitudes and behaviors, SST would, I hope (and it does need to be demonstrated), help prevent further breakdowns and the development of conflictful and pathological behavior patterns. This of course is only a hope, because to my knowledge, no one has yet demonstrated the long-range effects of SST to the point that it deserves to be called preventive.

As healthier patterns are promoted and more dysfunctional patterns are prevented, I hope that the level of competence--interpersonal, dyadic, parental, spousal--would increase. By linking SST to competence training, one can trace the whole movement to a new view of pathology, one that is more positive and less stereotyping and dehumanizing than a psychiatric perspective.

The main theme of most preventive literature (Albee, 1982; Hobbs, Dodecki, Hoover-Dempsey, Moroney, Shayne, & Weeks, 1984) is training for competence. As mentioned earlier, the same theme can be found in the SST literature, even though a great many social skills trainers (Guerney, et al., 1983; L'Abate, 1984; L'Abate & Milan, 1985) are very careful to qualify the preventive value of this approach because it lacks qualifying evidence. In addition to training for competence, this form of training would, I hope, possess some preventive function, though it has yet to be demonstrated (L'Abate, 1985). The goals for these presumably different sources are the same: emphasis on the functionally positive aspects of human existence and the crucial importance of interpersonal competence as the main dimension of mental health and healthy functioning.

Broad Versus Narrow Prevention

There are at least two different views of prevention. A broad one, resulting from the community psychology movement, considers prevention in terms of advocacy, liaison with other agencies, and assisting self-help groups. A more narrow definition of prevention focuses on training individuals in groups, couples, and families in interpersonal skills. In an ideal training program, of course, both views would need to be part of the curriculum (I confess to favoring a more narrow view in terms of my specific interests and expertise). The broad views would need to be taught to and implemented by students.

Training for Preventive SST

The schisms between therapists and preventers prompted me (L'Abate, 1981) to conclude that

A whole new profession of "preventers" rather than therapists needs to be built from the ground up. The individuals would have different skills, different perspectives, and different goals from the therapists. . . . [they will need to be] . . . full-time individuals who would become part and parcel of any community mental health program, especially if their employment were to become a requirement for federal and state funding, and if their salaries were to be comparable to those of therapists. . . . Once these conditions were to be obtained, it would not be difficult to train a special corps of preventers. . . . Current mental health practices lack or fail to possess clearly preventive measures. Skill training is first and foremost a preventive intervention. That is where the major issues in mental health lie. (pp. 657, 658)

Yet when one reviews the field of training for prevention (Price, 1983), one finds that outside advocacy training and other community skills, there is very little to indicate what kind of training this field should consist of. Training for prevention seems bare of essentials, lacking a core and a specific direction. Given this lack of substance, I suggest that training for prevention sould consist of training for SST training. Perhaps this equation is misguided, but I would need to be convinced that other directions are indeed possible. For the time being and for the purposes of this proposal, training for prevention will consist of training for SST training. (The pros and cons of this position will need to be discussed later.)

Training for Research

As I have indicated, to avoid committing the same errors made by the mental health professions, we need to make sure that research and practice are combined. To achieve this goal, we will need to train students to view research as a vital ingredient in any intervention, especially prevention (L'Abate, 1981).

Hence, research will need to be viewed as the necessary component of any preventive activity. Without it one should not be allowed to intervene. Issues of testability, verifiability, and accountability, that is, the essence of the scientific approach, will need integration with preventive practices. (L'Abate, 1983)

The Nature of the Curriculum

A curriculum is developed on the basis of faculty expertise and availability, the relevant courses already available, and administrative support. An ideal curriculum for preventive psychology training and research (L'Abate, 1983) cannot be created de novo. One needs to work with whatever is available--and relevant--to such a curriculum.

With these historical and contextual considerations in the background, the following curriculum has been developed from the relevant courses available in the Department of Psychology and the School of Education at Georgia State University. This curriculum

262

consists of the following requirements: (a) University requirements concerning residency (2 consecutive years of full enrollment, two courses per quarter); (b) College of Arts and Sciences requirements concerning foreign languages and grade point average; (c) departmental requirements for a core curriculum to ensure a sufficient background in the historical, empirical, and methodological aspects of psychology as a science and as a profession, including a course in ethics; (d) committee requirements concerning various courses in community, personnel, and methods of evaluation in community psychology; and (e) curriculum requirements consisting of an educational sequence in interpersonal skills, with an optional course in parenting skills, a behavioral sequence, including a course on social skills in children, family enrichment, a dynamic component made up of an experiential course in group interaction, a practicum in one of various outpatient and residential settings in the greater metropolitan area, an advanced seminar on the theory and practice of preventive psychology and research possibly leading to a dissertation proposal, a 1-year internship in a setting where preventive psychology training is practiced and supervision is available from qualified professionals, and finally, a doctoral dissertation in preventive psychology training and research.

Issues and Implications

Employability

One of the thorniest issues in training for a new specialization is, of course, employability. Many jobs and positions will be available only to the extent that the federal government is able to mandate prevention as part of any mental health grant and to the extent specialists in prevention become hard to find, so that mental health clinics will need to create these positions to receive federal support. As Gregory W. Brock (personal communication, December 14, 1983) noted:

> The entitlement for community mental health centers specifies quite clearly that all centers are to have a community consultation/education thrust and centers are to employ people to carry out preventive programming. Community mental health center directors have tended to not keep this dictate in mind when they map out their personnel profiles, so not many centers fulfill the community education/consultation role. Another reason directors have let this part of their programs slide along is that professionals who can identify themselves as psychologists usually do not have the training or the motivation to fill the needs of the education position. Your program could turn out people to occupy these positions.

Another source of prevention is church organizations. Many larger church congregations now employ

263

full-time family, marriage and parenting skills educators whose charge is to provide church members with the full range of preventive, educational, enrichment activities. A third source of positions for graduates is federal, state, and local governments. At these levels, university extension plays an important role in employing family life educators-prevention specialists.

No proposal for change is free from weaknesses and deficits. At least three critical areas in my proposal need consideration.

A justified criticism (M. Milan, personal communication, 1982) is that preventive psychology may not be sufficiently unique and therapeutically inclusive to qualify for specialization status. This criticism also raises a general question facing psychology as a science and as a profession: What are the limits of differentiation? At what point does a profession stop or slow down the progressive breakdown into smaller and smaller parts? As far as SST and research are concerned, the issue can be answered according to a variety of criteria: (a) a substantive body of knowledge, as shown by books, chapters, and journal articles; (b) an acceptably large number of professionals who identify sufficiently with such an enterprise to consider it worthwhile as a life career; (c) a sufficient number of students who wish to be trained in such a specialization, (d) appropriate institutional support in administrative and collegial sources and resources, and (e) job availability. The first four criteria are adequately met by the current proposal. It would not have come about had it not been for the support of friends and colleagues, those in the Interpersonal Skills Training and Research Association (ISTARA) and faculty members in the College of Education, the Department of Psychology, and throughout the administrative structure. Administrative support is easily obtained when no new resources are needed and no funds requested.

Critics of the SST approach (Timnick, 1980) have suggested that its only purpose is to expand the job market for psychologists. If applied mechanically, this approach would produce social robots, not a more civilized society. The question facing us at this juncture is, What else is there? When a technology shows a significant degree of empirical evidence for its usefulness, when should we start to use that technology? If not now, when? What other available approaches would produce the same results at a lower cost?

Conclusion

This proposed curriculum is being implemented at GSU. It will require changes, refinements, and additions. Suggestions and criticisms will be given the utmost attention and consideration. This new profession will have to learn from the mistakes of older professions, particularly the schisms and separations that have characterized the mental health movement. It will be important for this new profession to combine, rather than to separate, research with services, evaluation with intervention, theory with practice, and even combine prevention with therapeutic interventions, using a career lattice in which professionals work with nonprofessional intermediaries.

References

Albee, G. W. (1982). Preventing psychopathology and promoting human potential. American Psychologist, 37, 1043-1050.

Authier, S., Gustafson, K., Fix, A., & Daughton, D. (1981). Social skills training: An initial appraisal. Professional Psychology, 12, 438-445.

Bellack, A. S., & Hersen, M. (Eds.). (1979). Research and practice in social skills training. New York: Plenum.

Brandt, E. N., Jr. (1982). Prevention policy and practice in the 1980s. American Psychologist, 37, 1038-1042.

Curran, J. P., & Monti, P. M. (Eds.). (1982). Social skills training: A practical handbook for assessment and treatment. New York: Guilford.

Fox, R. E. (1982). The need for a reorientation of clinical psychology. American Psychologist, 37, 1051-1057.

Goldston, S. E. (1979). Primary prevention programming from the federal perspective: A progress report. Journal of Clinical Child Psychology, 9, 80-83.

Guerney, B. G., Jr., Vogelsong, E., & Coufal, J. (1983). Relationship enhancement versus a traditional treatment. In D. H. Olson & B. C. Miller (Eds.), Family studies: Review yearbook (Vol. 1). Beverly Hills, CA: Sage.

Hobbs, N., Dodecki, P. R., Hoover-Dempsey, K. V., Moroney, R. M., Shayne, M. W., & Weeks, K. H. (1984). Strengthening families. San Francisco: Jossey-Bass.

Kiesler, C. (1983, September). A "top-down" look at public policy. APA Monitor, p. 5.

L'Abate, L. (1981). Social skills programs with couples and families. In A. S. Gurman & D. P. Kniskern (Eds.), Handbook of family therapy (pp. 631-661). New York: Brunner/Mazel.

L'Abate, L. (1982). Skill training and structured enrichment programs for marriage and family life. In P. A. Keller & L. G. Ritt (Eds.), Innovations in clinical practice: A source book (pp. 299-308). Sarasota, FL: Professional Resource Exchange.

L'Abate, L. (1983). Prevention as a profession: Toward a new conceptual frame of reference. In D. Mace (Ed.), Prevention in family services: Approaches to family wellness (pp. 49-62). Beverly Hills, CA: Sage.

L'Abate, L. (1986). Prevention of marital and family problems. In B. Edelstein & L. Michalson (Eds.), Handbook of prevention (pp. 177-193). New York: Plenum.

L'Abate, L., & Milan, M. (Eds.). (1985). Handbook of social skills training and research. New York: Wiley.

Levy, L. H. (1984). The metamorphosis of clinical psychology: Toward a new charter as human services psychology. American Psychologist, 64, 486-494.

Marshall, E. K., Kurtz, P. D., & Associates. (1982). Interpersonal helping skills. San Francisco: Jossey-Bass.

Phillips, E. L. (1978). The social skills basis of psychopathology: Alternatives to abnormal psychology. New York: Grune & Stratton.

Pickett-Rathjen, D., & Foreyt, J. P. (Eds.). (1980). Social competence: Interventions for children and adults. New York: Pergamon.

Price, R. H. (1983). The education of a prevention psychologist. In R. D. Feiner, L. A. Jason, J. N. Maritsugu, & S. S. Farber (Eds.), Preventive psychology: Theory, research and practice (pp. 290-296). New York: Pergamon.

Sanford, N. (1965). The prevention of mental illness. In B. B. Wolman (Ed.), Handbook of clinical psychology (pp. 1378-1400). New York: McGraw-Hill.

Singleton, W. T., Spurgeon, P., & Stammers, R. B. (Eds.). (1979). The analysis of social skills. New York: Plenum.

Spence, S., & Shepherd, G. (Eds.). (1983). Developments in social skills training. New York: Academic Press.

Timnick, L. (1980). Social skills programs. Psychology Today, 16, 43-49.

Trower, P., Bryant, B., Argyle, M., & Marzillier, J. (1978). Social skills and mental health. Pittsburgh: University of Pittsburgh Press.

Wine, J. D., & Smye, M. D. (Eds.). (1981). Social competence. New York: Guilford.

Chapter 24

Covenant Contracting: Training Functions and Treatment Outcomes

James Kochalka, Luciano L'Abate,
John Lutz, and James Metts

The purpose of this paper is to describe a psychoeducational procedure known as Covenant Contracting (CC) as it is used in the training of family psychologists at Georgia State University. In this paper we describe the framework in which Covenant Contracting is used, then discuss the procedures of Covenant Contracting as a springboard for consideration of its training and service benefits.

Training Context

Since training procedures can only be understood within a particular context, a brief description of the training program is provided. Family Psychology is one of five clinical PhD specialties within the Department of Psychology; the others are General Clinical, Behavior Therapy, Psychotherapy, and Child Clinical. In addition to the didactic coursework in traditional psychology and family-related areas (see L'Abate, Berger, Wright, & O'Shea, 1979) students participate in a sequence of clinical exposure that ranges from the very structured to mostly unstructured. Specifically, four clinical experiences constitute most of the clinical training in this specialization before the 1-year clinical internship. The first is Structured Enrichment (see chapter 17), a highly programmed form of intervention that students complete with nonclinical couples and families during the beginning of the first year. The second experience, Covenant Contracting, is completed during the second half of the first year. Also during the second year, students complete one Intimacy Workshop (see chapter 18), which is a theme-focused one-day group that is conducted with four to six couples. During the second year, students conduct marital and family therapy in the GSU Family Studies Center.

The philosophical underpinnings of this particular clinical sequence may be summarized as follows. First, we believe that family psychologists should, in addition to providing systems-based interventions for dysfunctional couples and families, be able to provide preventive services for couples and families at any point on a continuum of functioning. This analogic model of service delivery challenges the therapy vs. no therapy distinction with the addition of services that may have preventive and enriching value. This belief in a continuum of service delivery justifies the use of nonclinical couples and families at the outset of training because we believe that this population has been underserved by clinicians and can benefit from innovative approaches. We consider it unfair both to trainee and to client to expose them to the erring ways of a novice clinician. We agree with Constantine (1976), who suggested that neither trainees nor clients benefit from the sink-or-swim approach of beginning a clinical training sequence with couples and families in distress.

Second, clinical training should be conducted within a competence-building context. We have attempted this by first providing trainees with a great deal of structure for their initial clinical contacts and gradually reducing the structure as the students experience success (Kochalka & L'Abate, 1983). This gradual reduction in structure allows trainees to experience less anxiety and potentiates their skills.

Rationale

CC is a training procedure that allows observation of and intervention in a couple's interactional processes (see L'Abate & McHenry, 1983). The procedures have been adapted from Sager's (1976) tripartite conceptualization of marital satisfaction based on each spouse's expectations of the marriage. To state Sager's concept briefly—each spouse brings to a relationship expectations and wants in three categories: (a) expectations for marriage, past, present, and future (e.g., a mate who is loyal); (b) biological and psychological needs (e.g., closeness-distance, activity-passivity); and (c) external foci of problems rooted in (a) and (b) (e.g., communication, child-rearing practices). Further, these categories are included in three levels of awareness: (a) conscious and articulated, (b) conscious but not articulated, and (c) unconscious and unspoken. The goal, from Sager's perspective, is to help each spouse determine the components of his or her individual contract, then to help the couple negotiate a mutually satisfying interactional contract. Sager does not specify how he uses the contracting procedure except to say that it is used idiosyncratically throughout therapy, in which other procedures are used. With all due respect to Sager's intrapsychic formulas, we have adapted his notion of contracts as a stimulus for couples to provide interactional grist for study from a communications perspective.

Our adaptation allows the relatively novice trainee to observe and intervene with a couple. The completion of the individual contracts and a joint contract provides the content of the program for trainee and client.

Procedures

We use CC with married or seriously committed couples. Subjects for our work come from a psychology undergraduate pool who have selected this project from several possibilities. Because the average age of undergraduates at GSU is 27, we are assured of having couples who represent a variety of life cycle stages (Carter & McGoldrick, 1980).

CC takes place in eight 1-hour sessions. Session 1 is spent in rapport building and the completion of pretests. Sessions 2 through 7 are spent addressing the content of CC. Session 8 is a feedback session in which trainees and clients discuss the experience and in which trainees offer suggestions for future psychoeducational or psychotherapeutic involvement.

The tasks of the trainee during the sessions are to (a) briefly explain the concepts of contracting, (b) help with the completion of each spouse's individual contract, and (c) foster a context for the negotiation of elements of a mutual contract.

During the first session the trainee must rather quickly establish rapport with the subjects. Trainees, from the outset, state that the experience is not therapy and that they will not allow volatile issues (e.g., sexual difficulties) to be addressed. CC is presented as an educational and skill-building process, whose only purpose is to consider a limited number of issues during the time available.

In Sessions 2 through 4, the trainee helps delineate each partner's individual contract (expectations and wants) on each of Sager's three categories. As the partners go over their lists, one category per session, reading them aloud, the trainee observes the extent to which partners are able to differentiate individual needs and wants through the use of "I" statements versus "we" statements. Partners are encouraged to be slightly selfish during these individual contract sessions in order to draw out individualized dimensions; they are reassured that later they will work toward a joint negotiation of areas of difference. The trainee encourages the partners to specify their needs through clear communication. For example, if the female partner says that she wants more time with the male partner, the trainee might ask her to state when and under what conditions she wants more time.

At the end of the fourth session, the partners are instructed to go over their lists individually, selecting the items that each considers most important, and to generate a prioritized list to be used in negotiating their joint marital contract.

In Sessions 5 through 7 individual needs and wants are negotiated through a series of quid pro quo sessions. The trainee helps the couple list their prioritized needs and wants specifically enough that each partner will know what the other wants and will know when the other's need or want has been met. The trainee also helps each partner to generate what will be given in exchange for getting what he or she wants in the relationship and from the partner. The couple is also helped with negotiation skills (i.e., increasing specificity in wants and needs statements, generating alternatives, and making counterproposals). In this stage the trainee continues to guide the couple away from obviously polarized areas to less problematic issues. (Difficult issues will be noted so that they can be incorporated into the feedback session.) The trainee often actively takes sides during this stage. For example, one husband wanted to pursue 5 more years of education, and his wife was able to ask only that he set the table on the nights that he was home. In this instance coaching and feedback were necessary to help the couple articulate an equitable exchange. Intensification is used to help the partners agree on terms by going beyond the usual communication sequence in which the husband suggests and the wife defers to him.

Finally, it is necessary for the trainee to have helped the couple resolve at least one reasonably significant area of their contract by the end of Session 7.

In Session 8 the partners are congratulated for having increased their skills in articulating contractual concerns, problem areas are noted, and recommendations for future work, if needed, are made.

Treatment Outcome

The comments that have been made by participants suggest that CC helps partners articulate marital concerns and reach solutions on issues of moderate intensity. Our clinical impressions have been positive and have reflected the beneficial effects of participation.

Though we consider the nonclinical populations fair game for psychoeducational interventions, we are still searching for the dimensions that are responsive to the client's perceptions of benefit from participation. At this point we can only present data that suggest that CC is definitely not an iatrogenic procedure (i.e., couples do not report reduced satisfaction as a result of having "stirred up" issues on such a short-term basis). We used the Dyadic Adjustment Scale (Spanier, 1976) for pre- and posttest comparisons on 21 couples who participated in CC through the Family Studies Center: males--pretest 110.66, posttest 114.04; females--pretest 106.71, posttest 111.47; combined scores of males and females (N = 42)--pretest 108.69, posttest 112.76.

Implications for Training

It has been suggested that an initial task in training marital and family therapists is to help the trainee think in terms of interactional or systemic views, as opposed to intrapsychic views of behavior (see Falicov, Constantine, & Breunlin, 1981; Liddle, 1980; Sluzki, 1974). Most of the attempts that have been cited are didactic and lack the educational potency of an experiential approach. We believe that conducting the CC procedure allows the trainee to observe the contrast between the individual contracts and the constraints provided by the need to blend those individual wants into a functioning dyad. The CC procedure allows trainees to elicit data both at the individual and at the interpersonal level. A clear bias in some systems models has been the neglect of the individual subsystem. The use of CC allows the trainee to see the individual cognitions that each partner brings to the marriage as well as the systemic dance that occurs when the partners interact. For example, the partner who verbally requests more time with the other partner may, in the dyadic context, seem to consistently deflect potential solutions to the problem.

Another benefit of CC is that it allows the use of role behaviors that may be considered along a hierarchy of expertise. In recent years GSU has accepted students whose clinical exposure has ranged from having never been in the room with a couple or family to 3 or 4 years of marital and family therapy experience. Given this diversity of skills, CC allows each trainee to find his or her own level of competence. We have defined several skills that cluster around several role categories and that may be viewed on a continuum reflecting the increasing skills demanded of the trainee. Some of the operative roles that we have defined operate at all levels of CC, but they may demand increasing skills at more complex levels.

Educator. As an educator the trainee merely provides structure at the beginning of CC (i.e., not therapy but skill building) and also specifies the dimensions of Sager's categories.

Information Gatherer. In the information-gathering role, the trainee acquires information about the couple. This role continues throughout CC but takes place specifically during the history taking, while assessing the individual contracts, and while observing the couple's interactive patterns on a systemic level.

Gatekeeper. The role of the gatekeeper is to allow and encourage information from the couple that will serve a proactive end (i.e., aid the negotiation of a mutual contract) or to disallow information that is potentially volatile and that may be considered inappropriate within the limited context of CC. Even during the initial sessions of helping the spouses articulate their individual contracts, some information will be minimized. This role assumes that a nonobjective reality (Reamy-Stephenson, 1983) will be created during CC and that the trainee is largely responsible for determining the parameters of this reality.

Coach. The role of coach emerges during the later work on a negotiated contract. It is an active role that requires a sensitivity to the clarity of issues, the appropriateness of the attempts at exchange, and the parity between partners. For example, one partner may become frustrated in attempting to specify an individual need. The trainee may help the partner stay with the issue by encouraging him or her to further specify its features until the other partner understands what is being requested.

Affect Regulator. The role of affect regulator reflects a higher-order skill that requires the trainee to modulate the intensity of the exchange between the partners (e.g., a reduction of the emotionality that prevents the partners from thinking clearly about the issues). If the trainee senses that the partners are colluding to avoid their differences on a particular issue, the trainee may raise the intensity in various ways (e.g., by making slightly provocative remarks such as "You two can do better than that").

Consultant. The consultant role presumes a professional socialization that allows the trainee to respect, when appropriate, the personal boundaries of the partners. This role is also evident during the feedback session when the trainee makes recommendations for the couple's future involvement in therapy. It is also evidenced in the ability to move in and out of the couple subsystem.

Summary

Although CC is only in its formative stages both as a treatment and as a training procedure, we hope that it can be useful for marital therapists in training and also for couples who wish to improve the quality of their relational life. Our efforts at GSU are under way along three tracks: (a) the development of an assessment procedure that will better capture the nature of the change that occurs in CC, (b) the attempt to specify more clearly the skills gained by trainees during the conduct of CC, and (c) the use of CC with couples who are experiencing moderate degrees of marital distress.

References

Carter, E., & McGoldrick, M. (1980). The family life cycle. New York: Gardner Press.

Constantine, L. (1976). Designed experience: A multiple, goal-directed training program in family therapy. Family Process, 15, 373-387.

Falicov, D., Constantine, J., & Breunlin, D. (1981). Teaching family therapy: A program based on training objectives. Journal of Marital and Family Therapy, 7, 497-505.

Kochalka, J. A., & L'Abate, L. (1983). Structure and gradualness in the clinical training of family psychologists. In L. L'Abate, Family psychology: Theory, therapy and training (pp. 287-299). Washington, DC: University Press of America.

L'Abate, L., Berger, M., Wright, L., & O'Shea, M. (1979). Training family psychologists: The Family Studies Program at Georgia State University. Professional Psychology, 10, 58-65.

L'Abate, L., & McHenry, S. (1983). Covenant contracting. In L'Abate, & McHenry, Handbook of methods of marital intervention (pp. 53-61). New York: Grune & Stratton.

Liddle, H. (1980). On teaching a contextual or systemic therapy: Training content, goals and methods. American Journal of Family Therapy, 8, 58-69.

Reamy-Stephenson, M. (1983). The assumption of non-objective reality: A missing link in the training of strategic family therapists. _Journal of Strategic and Systemic Therapies_, 2, 51-67.

Sager, C. J. (1976). Marriage contracts and couple therapy. New York: Brunner/Mazel.

Sluzki, C. (1974). On training to think interactionally. _Social Science and Medicine_, 8, 483-485.

Spanier, G. (1976). Measuring dyadic adjustment: New scales for assessing the quality of marriage and similar dyads. _Journal of Marriage and the Family_, 38, 15-28.

CHAPTER 25

Implications of the Enrichment Model for Research and Training

LUCIANO L'ABATE and

J. BRIEN O'CALLAGHAN*

The enrichment model using structured short-term instructions through the use of manuals shows some definite advantages for process and outcome research, theory testing, applicability to nonclinical families, and comparisons of structured versus unstructured and cognitive versus affective approaches. In training, the enrichment model can be used for a more active approach to undergraduate specialization, and graduate education. Examples of graduate programs using enrichment programs as an integral part of their training are given.

A case has been made recently for the value of "family enrichment" as a new and alternative family intervention model (L'Abate, 1974; L'Abate, et al., 1975a, 1975b). Family enrichment is a broad categorical term for a variety of family programs and experiences which are more structured, short-term, and definable than family counseling or therapy (Otto, 1975) and more experiential and affective than family life education.

Outcome data on the effectiveness of family enrichment is at present virtually nonexistent. Its absence has been noted, and attempts at evaluation are in progress (L'Abate, Wildman, O'Callaghan, Simon, Allison, Kahn, & Rainwater, 1975). Another potential value of the family enrichment model, besides greater specificity of application and of outcome, is its function in family research and in the training of family workers. The present paper is an attempt to outline some of these implications for research and training.

Implications for Research

There are a number of research areas in

which the "family enrichment" approach offers distinctive contributions:

Outcome Research

By more clearly specifying the procedures of intervention, family enrichment lends itself to a clearer explanation of outcome results. By cutting down on the variability in therapist's style, a greater degree of control is established over the entire process of intervention. Enrichment allows to "know" what went on during the intervention, especially if the instructions are contained in a manual. This degree of structure plus the pre-established length of enrichment allow a greater comparability in different types of enrichment and less variability in the length of intervention. As a result of this decreased variability it would be easier to compare outcome across groups, treatments, and length of enrichment (i.e., three versus six versus twelve sessions).

Theory Testing

Defined exercises, lessons, and programs drawn from various theoretical approaches (e.g., Transactional Analysis, Adlerian family counseling) allow for more clear and accurate testing of the effectiveness of those approaches. When a prearranged manual or program is being followed, the independent effectiveness of the leader or helper is easier to parcel out. Successful procedures, as

*Luciano L'Abate is Professor of Psychology and Director of the Family Study Program in the same Department at Georgia State University, University Plaza, Atlanta, GA 30303.

J. Brien O'Callaghan is a Ph.D. candidate in the Family Study Program in the Psychology Department at Georgia State University.

such, are more easy to isolate. The condensation and articulation of theory into specified programs, lessons, and exercises challenges the researcher to separate the wheat from the chaff, to isolate the important components of the approach being tested. This process of particularizing can be extremely valuable in comparing and contrasting among various models of family and general therapeutic intervention as well, a task that is getting increasing attention of late (L'Abate, 1974; 1975a, 1975b, O'Callaghan, in press; Tavormina, 1974, 1975).

Applicability to Nonclinical Families

Another research implication of family enrichment is its applicability to "normal" families. Progress in normal families can be tested without the prohibitive cost of family therapy. Further, comparative data on the therapeutic concerns, process, and outcome of clinical versus nonclinical families can be gathered.

Process Research

Family process in intervention can be observed on a short-term basis. Because of the brevity of intervention, data can be gathered from more families. Students at various levels of training and expertise can benefit from the experience of observing and coding family process in a large variety of families. In the senior author's Family Study Center at Georgia State University, family process is considered through the use of rating sheets completed by families and couples, content analysis of sessions, and content free measures of interaction (Jacob, 1975).

Structured versus Unstructured Intervention

The use of family enrichment in comparison and contrast to other structured and unstructured modalities, e.g., family therapy or counseling of various persuasions allows for the collection of important data on the relative and specific effectiveness, efficacy, and cost of these different modalities.

Instead of one versus the other approach, combinations of both approaches, that is: therapy *plus* enrichment may increase the range of families that could be helped.

(L'Abate, O'Callaghan, Piat, Dunne, Margolis, Prigge, & Soper, 1976).

Cognitive versus Affective Approaches

Totally cognitive approaches to helping and change have come under criticism recently (Hill & Aldous, 1969). The use of more affective and experimental components is recommended. Family enrichment allows for a separation or combination of cognitive and affective ingredients in a more controlled fashion than in approaches thus far available.

Implications for Training

An enrichment model can be especially useful in the beginning phases of training for marriage and family intervention. By going from structured to unstructured intervention, students are able to acquire more skills and a greater variety of responses than they can otherwise. They start to acquire skills directly with families, first nonclinical "normal" and then clinical. The ideal family specialist of the future could and should master at least three areas of specialization: (a) theory, (b) research, and (c) practice, at various levels of expertise, *i.e.*, B.A., M.A., and Ph.D.

Undergraduate Specialization

At the undergraduate level, most of the relevant, generic background could fall under the general subject of family life education. In other words, this degree and level of specialization would prepare the student to teach family life education as intervener and to teach practical courses to groups in community agencies, churches, and schools.

The general field of family life education and its applications could become, as indeed is the case in some departments already, a clinical major, especially if the student is given the opportunity, under faculty supervision, to practice family life education in parent discussion groups, couples groups, and parent-child groups. Individuals trained at this level would be the front soldiers of the whole family health enterprise. They would come in contact with large numbers of families in churches, schools, and agencies and would become the first ones to recognize needs for more specialized help. They would be referral sources to professionals. Even at an undergraduate level, training could be much more experimental than book-oriented, as suggested by Daly and Reeves (1973). This training would provide an experimental base for teaching to discriminate between functional and dysfunctional types of communication, to develop specific interpersonal skills, to learn feedback, and to allow students to practice more effective ways of behaving in a nonthreatening and supportive environment. Family life education courses and experiences would include academic work in child development, developmental psychology, and other courses offered at present in college settings.

In short, a variety of superior academic and successful applied experiences in the general areas of family life would be most appropriate for entrance in graduate "family" programs or in the job market.

Graduate Education

A major emphasis, but by no means the only one, at the graduate level of family training programs might be on training in enrichment programs and procedures. In other words, specialization at this level would, in part, become more specific and structured, and would require a certain degree of initiative, inventiveness, interpersonal competence, and professionalism. Individuals at this level would be selected from the top undergraduate majors in family life education and related disciplines with sufficient and relevant course-work completed, either prior to admission or as a basis for admission. Coursework and applications would go hand in hand in order to relate theory to the practice of the enrichment process in marriage and family.

Master's Level: At this level at least three specialist substracks could be conceived: A major in *marriage enrichment* and a knowledge of its various applications which, as Otto (1975) indicated, will proliferate. The master's thesis in this area could consist of comparisons of various models of enrichment already available, using different groups and combining research with practice. The second subtrack could consist of *family enrichment* and its various and different applications (L'Abate, et al., 1974, 1975a, 1975b). A third

subtrack could consist *sexual enrichment* and its various applications. Again, the master's thesis in any of the three areas of specialization could consist of comparisons between and among various types and models of enrichment in any area. Personnel trained at this level would furnish the bulk of middle-level professionals and intermediaries who could work alone or under the direction and supervision of more experienced, Ph.D.-level supervisors and directors. Fieldwork might consist of one quarter full-time or its equivalent.

Ph.D. Level: The specialist at this level would need to master all three subtracks mentioned above and, in addition, complete substantive coursework in the areas of: (a) marriage and divorce; (b) family functioning and dysfunctioning; (c) sexuality and its deviations; and (d) research methods and statistics. In addition to this and other substantive background, he would acquire, through a one-year internship, skills in unstructured therapy techniques and experience in supervising family life educators and/or marriage, family, and sexuality enrichers. He would be knowledgeable of diagnostic as well as of intervention techniques at various levels and of various types. Part of his time would be spent in direct contact with families, in supervision, and in training. His Ph.D. dissertation could consist of multiple comparisons of two or more techniques of intervention, structured or unstructured.

Some of the above aspects of training have been incorporated into the Ph.D. program in Family Studies at Georgia State University's Department of Psychology. The sequence of training starts with two theory courses: Personality Development in Marriage and Personality Development in the Family. The next course in the sequence covers Family Evaluation—knowledge and application of structured and unstructured techniques of assessment from interview to rating scales to family tests designed to measure family interaction (L'Abate, 1973, 1974). The next course, Family Enrichment, starts to train the student in role-playing with peers, enriching nonclinical families, and eventually, for those adequately prepared and ready, enriching clinical families. Once this sequence is finished, the student is ready to take course work on techniques of family therapy, and afterwards, allowed to see couples and families in therapy under supervision, either alone or in teams of two therapists, preferably of opposite sex.

As students follow this sequence, they are encouraged to follow coursework in behavior modification and psychotherapy. At advanced levels, they start to supervise undergraduates and graduate students who are beginning to enrich families.

The kind of training proposed here would help create a different kind of mental health professional and paraprofessional than traditionally conceived. They could work independently or together with existing mental health specialists, adding a dimension to the whole mental health enterprise that needs bold, corrective, and innovative action. Their professional identity would be functional, that is, dealing with marriage and the family using a range of structured, semi-structured, and unstructured techniques distinct from traditional mental health specialists already in existence. Only if and when manpower is properly trained shall we be able to help families on a large scale. Until this task is done, our impact may be minimal and fragmentary. The specialization described here may help solve some of the mental health needs still unmet by existing and traditional mental health professions. As Axelson (1975, p. 6) suggested, ". . . additional centers for the training of marriage and family counselors should be organized and certified." Hopefully, the present plan could be implemented in marriage and family centers.

Conclusion

The "family enrichment" model does offer some distinct advantages for research and training in the family field not shared by less structured techniques of intervention, like therapy and counseling. Its promise and potential needs to be explored further and fully before it can be adopted alongside already established techniques of family intervention. Its potential for training new specialists in marriage and the family may represent another advantage to be explored

with its range of application to clinical and nonclinical couples and families.

REFERENCES

Axelson, L. Promise or illusion: The future of family studies. *The Family Coordinator*, 1975, **24**, 3-6.

Daly, R. T. & Reeves, J. B. The use of human interaction laboratories in family life. *The Family Coordinator*, 1973, **22**, 413-417.

Hill, R. & Aldous, J. Socialization for marriage and parenthood. In D. A. Goslin (Ed.) *Handbook of socialization theory and research*. Chicago: Rand McNally, 1969. 885-950.

Jacob, T. Family interaction in disturbed and normal families: A methodological and substantive review. *Psychological Bulletin*, 1975, **82**, 33-65.

L'Abate, L. Psychodynamic interventions: A personal statement. In R. H. Woody & J. D. Woody (Eds.) *Sexual, marital and family counseling*. Springfield, Ill: C. C. Thomas, 1973, 122-180.

L'Abate, L. Family enrichment programs. *Journal of Family Counseling*, 1974, **2**, 32-38.

L'Abate, L.; Wildman, R. W., II; O'Callaghan, J. B.; Simon S. J.; Allison, M.; Kahn, G.; & Rainwater, N. The laboratory evaluation and enrichment of couples: Applications and some preliminary results. *Journal of Marriage and Family Counseling*, 1975, 1, 351-358.

L'Abate, L., et. al. *Manual: Family enrichment programs*. Atlanta: Social Research Laboratories, 1975 (a).

L'Abate, L., et al. Manual: Family Enrichment programs for the family life cycle. Atlanta, Ga.: Social Research Laboratories, 1975 (b).

L'Abate, L.; O'Callaghan, J. B.; Plat, J.; Dunne, E. E.; Margolis, R.; Prigge, B.; & Soper, R. Enlarging the scope of intervention with couples and families: Continuation of enrichment and therapy. *Group Therapy: 1976*.

O'Callaghan, J. B. Transactional analysis and behavior modification: Toward a "quid pro quo." *Transactional Analysis Journal*, (in press).

Otto, H. A. Marriage and family enrichment programs in North America: Report and analysis. *The Family Coordinator*, 1975, **24**, 137-142.

Tavormina, J. B. Basic models of parent counseling: A critical review. *Psychological Bulletin*, 1974, **81**, 827-835.

Tavormina, J. B. Relative effectiveness of behavioral and reflective group counseling with parents of mentally retarded children. *Journal of Consulting and Clinical Psychology*, 1975, **43**, 22-31.

Chapter 26

ructured Enrichment: Training and Implementation with Paraprofessionals[*]

James Kochalka, Hilary Buzas, Luciano L'Abate,
Sherry McHenry, and Elaine Gibson

Abstract

A pilot training and implementation program of structured enrichment involving mental health center volunteers and university personnel was conducted. The following components are described: (a) the general content of structured enrichment, (b) the format and procedures of training and supervision, and (c) general outcome. Suggestions for the improvement of future programs are needed.

In the past decade, the demand for mental health service delivery has increased in all sectors of the American population. Unfortunately, the diminishing budgets of numerous mental health treatment facilities throughout the country have made it difficult to meet this increased demand for services because of reductions in professional staff. The burden of reduced manpower is compounded when one considers the often prohibitive costs of treatment. Currently, as a direct result of economic inflation, treatment costs in many mental health settings exceed the average client's ability to pay. Economic constraints have cast into bold relief the imminent need for cost-effective and accountable models of mental health service delivery.

An underutilized, though potentially rich, source of manpower is the increased implementation of service formats in which paraprofessionals work under the supervision of more experienced personnel. The extent and impact of the use of paraprofessionals within the mental health system has been articulated by many others (see, e.g., Balch & Solomon, 1976; Danish & Brock, 1974; Duncan, Korb, & Loesch, 1978; Gartner & Riessman, 1974; Karlsrusher, 1974; Matarazzo, 1971; Nash, Lifton, & Smith, 1978).

The purpose here is to describe a pilot project in which a university graduate family psychology program and a private community counseling center collaborated in a training and implementation program for paraprofessional volunteer conductors of a structured form of marriage and family intervention known as structured enrichment (SE).

---

[*]An earlier version of this paper was presented in an Education and Enrichment Section of the National Council on Family Relations Annual Meeting in Washington, DC, on October 14, 1982.

SE (L'Abate, 1977, 1981; L'Abate & Rupp, 1981; L'Abate & Weinstein, 1987) is a systematic method of intervention made up of structured, planned programs. SE consists of 50 programs for couples and families that address a number of marriage and family issues (e.g., negotiation, fair fighting training, assertiveness, financial management).

Each program consists of three to six lessons. A lesson contains five to six exercises, which the enricher reads to the participants. The exercise instructions range from simple questions (e.g., in the Negotiation Program, exercises range from those that require simple responses, such as, "When did you last make a mistake and admit it openly?") to those that require somewhat more intense interpersonal involvement (e.g., "Are there areas that you do not feel that you can be honest with your partner about?").

Each program is designed to experientially teach couples and families to negotiate specific problem issues in their relationship. Each SE program is usually conducted in eight 1-hour sessions. The first session is to establish rapport with the participants and to administer a battery of pretests. In the second session the participants are presented with three programs from which one will be selected. Sessions 2 through 7 consist of the SE lessons. The participants complete the posttest at the end of Session 7. The eighth and final session is used to solicit feedback from the participants concerning their satisfaction with the program and also to give the participants recommendations. Recommendations may include a therapy referral, continued SE with another program, or no further interventions at the present.

SE was selected as an adjunct to therapy with couples and families for several reasons. First, there is some evidence to suggest that dysfunctional couples and families experience common symptoms, such as lack of negotiation skills, nonassertiveness, and inability to resolve conflicts (L'Abate, 1981; Miller, 1975). Alexander and Barton (1982) have contended that helping couples and families involves crisis intervention through therapy and skill building through education. SE is a process that promotes understanding of various aspects of relationships through participation in theme-focused exercises. The programs address these areas in a structured format and have shown modest effectiveness with clinical populations (Wildman, 1977). Second, the use of SE in the training of graduate students, many of whom had no previous clinical experience, suggests that these very structured procedures can be adequately learned relatively quickly (Jessee & L'Abate, 1981). Third, the literature concerning the effectiveness of paraprofessional helpers implies that results can be obtained using paraprofessional treatment personnel. For example, Durlak (1979), who surveyed 42 studies comparing the effectiveness of professional and paraprofessional helpers, noted, "Paraprofessionals achieve clinical outcomes equal to or significantly better than those obtained by professionals."

Setting and Personnel

The SE training program was implemented at a private, nonprofit, community counseling center in metropolitan Atlanta. The agency offers individual, couple, and family counseling, as well as training for students, professionals, and volunteers.

A volunteer coordinator, who is a professional counselor, supervises approximately 20 volunteers who provide telephone crisis counseling and referral, educational group facilitation, and outreach programs. Volunteers are selected from applicants with a variety of skills and backgrounds. All applicants complete an 8-week basic counseling skills course, after which volunteer staff are selected. Each volunteer staff member is then supervised weekly by a clinical staff member and participates in an ongoing training group.

The SE trainers were two doctoral candidates in clinical psychology in the family psychology program at Georgia State University; the trainers worked under the guidance of the director of the program.

Training Procedures

Format

An initial meeting was held with the volunteers, the volunteer coordinator, the graduate trainers, and the family psychology program director. This meeting was conducted to help establish rapport and to present SE training for the volunteers' consideration. The volunteers met once after this session and agreed to participate in the training as a group; the graduate trainers reserved the right to select the persons who would conduct the SE program with clients.

Training was conducted for six consecutive weekly sessions of approximately 1 1/2 hours each. Attendance at each weekly session was mandatory. To further ensure attendance the volunteers were informed of the number of weeks and hours involved and asked to commit that time. Only the volunteers who agreed to attend all sessions were selected to participate in the program.

Content

The trainers provided an overview of SE to the volunteers in the first two training sessions. Topics included the concept of pre- and posttesting, both as a means of facilitating program selection and as a measure of accountability; an explanation of how programs are divided into lessons and exercises; and a comment on confidentiality. In the third session the trainers modeled enrichers in a role-play in which volunteers acted as a four-member family. One full lesson was completed during the session; comments by trainers and questions from the volunteers were interspersed throughout the lesson. The fourth, fifth, and sixth sessions were devoted to behavioral rehearsal by the volunteers. Four groups of five volunteers (i.e., two "enrichers" and a "family" composed of mother, father, and child per group) selected a lesson to role-play during the training session. This procedure was continued for 3 consecutive weeks until all volunteers had participated both as enrichers and as family members. The trainers circulated among groups during this time to observe and critique the performance of the enrichers and to answer questions about the process of SE.

Several basic guidelines were given to the enrichers concerning their behavior during an actual session. First, to control the stimuli presented to clients, no substantive changes in the program were allowed. Changes were permitted, however, in using language to better suit the clients' level of comprehension. Second, irrelevant and potentially volatile comments by the family members were stopped by the enricher. For example, if a spouse began to deviate from the exercise by complaining about his or her partner, the enricher would tactfully suggest that the clients' therapist should be made aware of the issue during their next session. The enricher would note the issue and report it to the therapist. No attempt would be made to process these comments with couple or family. Third, enrichers were directed to encourage responses by family members without making judgmental comments. Responses were solicited from each participant without prodding or demanding that the participants interact.

As a result of questions generated by the volunteers during the role playing, the seventh training session was devoted to an SE role-play in which the graduate student trainers acted as enrichers for a group of resistant and pathological family members. This session was conducted to demonstrate how to structure a session when children actively quarrel and parents openly blame each other. This session was important in that it helped allay the volunteers' anxiety about performance. Session 8 consisted of a review of all material covered in earlier sessions, with an emphasis on how to conduct the follow-up session after completion of the formal lessons.

Selection of Enrichers and Clients

Upon completion of the training program, enrichers were selected and assigned to work in pairs; the pairings were based on their demonstrated skill in role playing and the compatibility they exhibited during training. The volunteers' skills were assessed, and the final selection of enrichers was made by the graduate trainers, with the approval of their supervisor.

The purpose and the methods of SE were described to the

professional staff as a means of soliciting referrals from their clinical caseload or from other community contacts. SE was presented as an adjunct to the marriage or family therapy being provided by the therapist. It was suggested that the therapist refer clients who could benefit from the acquisition of a particular skill or the reinforcement of a skill that was being obtained during therapy. Although all clients were clinical in the sense that they were being seen in therapy, no clients were included who did not meet the criteria established for inclusion in SE (L'Abate, 1977). That is, no couples or families who were very chaotic or in crisis (e.g., death, suicide, divorce, abandonment) were included. Couples or families who initially seemed uncooperative or resistant were excluded, as were persons who displayed symptomatology that demanded professional intervention (e.g., psychotic, paranoid, or psychosomatic syndromes). Information about the referred clients was gathered from the therapists and the volunteers. After discussing the clients with trainers and the volunteer coordinator, the project supervisor made the final determination whether the clients were suited for SE. Because opinions about client appropriateness for SE can (and did) differ between therapists, volunteers, and trainers, a clear statement about the project supervisor's role in making the final selection of clients was made in an effort to prohibit potential conflict in this area.

Description of Clients

Three couples and one family participated in SE. The family consisted of a mother, father, 10-year-old son, and 8-year-old daughter. The family was Jewish, upper-class, and well educated. The middle-aged parents had been married for 12 years. The father, an obese man, had previously been in treatment with a psychiatrist because of problems presumably generated by his work. Their current family therapist referred them for SE because they were experiencing communication difficulties. One of the couples participating in SE was elderly (aged 69) and retired. SE was suggested to them when they requested help in improving their relationship. Another couple was referred by their therapist to work on negotiation skills. This couple was young (each 23 years old), had been married for 1 1/2 years, and had no children. The third couple (wife aged 31 and husband aged 29) had been married for 6 years and had two children, ages 4 and 2. Both spouses were college graduates and pursuing careers. They were referred for SE to learn to resolve conflict more appropriately and to express their feelings.

Supervision

Two-Tier Format

The goal of supervision was to ensure accountability for the actions of all persons who participated in the project. This goal was achieved through a format in which the enrichers met with two trainers for 1 1/2 hours per week to discuss their cases. The trainers then met weekly with the project supervisor to review various aspects of the preceding supervision session with the volunteers. An important aspect of this format was the trainers' liaison role between the two institutions. This role required the trainers to adequately convey and present information both to their supervisor and to the volunteers. Also, the trainers needed to be aware of maintaining their position of authority in supervising the volunteers, in an atmosphere of congeniality and mutual respect. Finally the project director's role as the "final authority" was made clear both to the agency and to the trainers to ensure the appropriate functioning of this hierarchical format.

Supervision Meetings Between Trainers and Volunteers

Discussion of the cases with volunteers was conducted in a weekly group. The enrichers were required to maintain notes of all sessions. Specifically, the volunteers were instructed to write down the participants' comments during a session. Because all SE was conducted with co-enrichers, the enrichers alternated between presenting an exercise and writing down responses. The focus of supervision was tailoring the programs to the participants' needs; the tailoring was based on the pretest results, the enrichers' subjective reactions to their interaction with the clients, and the changing recommendations of the therapists. The trainers conveyed this information to the supervisor, and the appropriate SE lessons were then selected.

An important issue that was addressed during supervision was the enrichers' desire to intervene in a less structured fashion. The enrichers felt frustrated when an exercise did not allow the closure of an emotional issue. Because the integrity of the structured format would be violated by the enrichers' free responses, the trainers insisted that they refrain from making additional comments. Frequent reminders that SE is not unstructured therapy helped the enrichers meet this goal.

Meetings Between Trainees and Supervisors

The two graduate trainers met with the project supervisor for 1 hour each week. Supervision was concerned with the enrichers' conduct of the cases and with the trainers' function as supervisors. Issues included the trainers' ability to monitor closely the volunteers' performance, program selection, reported family reaction to lessons, and any questions or issues that had arisen during the most recent volunteer supervision session.

Comparison of Pre- and Posttest Results

Two objective instruments were used to facilitate program selection and measure the changes resulting from SE: the Family Environment Scale (Moos & Moos, 1981) and the Family Adaptability and Cohesion Evaluation Scales (FACES) (Olson, Russell, & Sprenkle,

284

1979). These tests measure family characteristics such as cohesion, adaptability, expressiveness, conflict, which provided information about problem areas that could be addressed through specific SE programs; for example, the lesson Sharing One's Feelings may be used with a family whose score indicates difficulty in expressing emotions.

In comparing the pre- and posttest results obtained on the FACES, all four client groups demonstrated slight positive changes from pre- to posttest on the two scales of adaptability and cohesion. Similarly, results obtained by all members on the FES demonstrated slight positive changes from pre- to posttests. Although the results indicate only minimal changes, these findings are encouraging because no family member exhibited highly deviant scores on the pretest. The current design (i.e., SE conducted concurrently with therapy) does not allow one to ferret out the relative effects of the paraprofessionals' interventions. However, the results are noteworthy in light of other research (cited in L'Abate, 1977) that has demonstrated the incremental benefits of SE plus therapy over therapy alone.

Reactions to the Program

Verbal self-report data from all participants was positive. The clients praised both the format and the content of SE. Because attendance was voluntary, their loyal participation in all sessions lends credence to these subjective reports of satisfaction. Reports from the therapists were also positive, and all the therapists were eager to refer other clients for SE. The volunteers were pleased with the training program, supervision, and their participation with clients. It is important to note the volunteers' willingness to participate in this program, which had no tangible reinforcers. The graduate trainers were satisfied with the opportunity to enhance their training experience through the supervision of persons in the community. This experience was considered invaluable in that it provided an opportunity for the students to learn not only clinical skills but also skills in training and supervising others.

The goal of this pilot program was twofold. The first goal was to conduct a structured intervention applicable to clinical clients that could be implemented by paraprofessionals. The second goal was to demonstrate that such a program can be a beneficial adjunct to therapy. According to the participants' positive comments, clinical observations, direct responses during SE, test measures, and the therapists' impressions of their clients' progress, both the initial goals seem to have been met.

Although results of the pilot project are encouraging, a number of deficits emerged, and they will be addressed in subsequent training and implementation programs of SE in community settings. One of these deficits involves the use of a research design to allow the explicit testing of SE in a mental health center. This deficit could be overcome by using matched clinical groups, one group receiving therapy and another group receiving therapy plus SE.

A second major area to be addressed in future programs concerns the ability to monitor the enrichers' work through the use of videotape feedback in training and supervision. This feedback would allow volunteers to more closely examine vocal inflections and nonverbal behavior that might imply undesirable coalitions with particular clients. Videotape would also facilitate supervision sessions by eliminating the social desirability that is inherent in self-report. An integral principle in training paraprofessionals is the accountability provided by closely monitoring the stimuli presented by the paraprofessionals during the SE sessions. By videotaping SE sessions, the trainers can easily validate that the paraprofessional has not gone beyond the boundaries prescribed by the content of a particular lesson.

Conclusions

SE suggests a successive sieves approach, from the least to the most expensive forms of intervention (L'Abate, 1987a, 1987b). SE could be used as one of these sieves with functional and semi-functional couples and families, and even with clinical families after they have been "normalized" by therapy.

References

Alexander, J., & Barton, C. (1982). Functional family therapy. Monterey, CA: Brooks/Cole.

Balch, P., & Solomon, R. (1976). The training of paraprofessionals as behavior modifiers: A review. American Journal of Community Psychology, 4, 167-179.

Danish, S., & Brock, G. (1974). The current status of paraprofessional training. Personnel and Guidance Journal, 53, 299-303.

Duncan, M. V., Korb, M. P., & Loesch, L. C. (1978). Competency counselor training for paraprofessionals. Counselor Education and Supervision, 18, 222-231.

Durlak, J. (1979). Comparative effectiveness of paraprofessional and professional helpers. Psychological Bulletin, 66, 80-92.

Gartner, A., & Riessman, F. (1974). The paraprofessional movement in perspective. Personnel and Guidance Journal, 53, 253-256.

Jessee, E., & L'Abate, L. (1981). Enrichment role playing as a step in the training of family therapists. Journal of Marriage and Family Therapy, 7, 507-514.

Karlsrusher, A. E. (1974). The nonprofessional as a psychotherapeutic agent: A review of the empirical evidence pertaining to his effectiveness. American Journal of Community Psychology, 2, 61-77.

L'Abate, L. (1977). Enrichment: Structured intervention for couples, families, and groups. Washington, DC: University Press of America.

L'Abate, L. (1981). Skill training programs for couples and families: Clinical and non-clinical applications. In A. Gurman & D. Kniskern (Eds.), Handbook of family therapy (pp. 631-661). New York: Brunner/Mazel.

L'Abate, L. (1987a, June). The practice of programmed family therapy. Paper presented at the annual meeting of the American Family Therapy Association, Chicago.

L'Abate, L. (1987b). Programmed therapy: Self-administered interventions for individuals, couples, and families. Manuscript submitted for publication.

L'Abate, L., & Rupp, G. (1981). Enrichment: Skill training for family life. Washington, DC: University Press of America.

L'Abate, L., & Weinstein, S. E. (1987). Structured enrichment programs for couples and families. New York: Brunner/Mazel.

Matarazzo, J. D. (1971). Some national developments in the utilization of nontraditional mental health power. American Psychologist, 26, 363-372.

Miller, S. (Ed.). (1975). Marriage and families: Enrichment through communication. Beverly Hills: Sage.

Moos, R. H., & Moos, B. S. (1981). Family Environment Scale manual. Palo Alto, CA: Consulting Psychologists Press.

Nash, K., Lifton, N., & Smith S. (1978). Paraprofessionals and community mental health. Community Mental Health Review, 3, 1-8.

Olson, D. H., Russell, C. S., & Sprenkle, D. H. (1979). Circumplex model of marital and family systems II: Empirical studies and clinical intervention. In J. P. Vincent (Ed.), Advances in family intervention, assessment, and theory (pp. 129-179). Greenwich, CT: JAI Press.

Wildman, R. W. (1977). Structured vs. unstructured marital intervention. In L. L'Abate, Enrichment: Structured intervention with couples, families, and groups (pp. 154-183). Washington, DC: University Press of America.

Conclusion

Family psychology has come a long way in the past few years. It has a long way to go to achieve a modicum of influence and impact on the science and profession of psychology. Its potential for contributing to the welfare of individuals and families is immense but still largely untapped. Conceivably, it could become one of the most important specialties in psychology, but its contribution to theory, prevention, therapy, and training remains to be explored. Divisive forces within and without its constituency should not be allowed to decrease its momentum. The future indeed belongs to family psychology!

This second volume will, I hope, spark work by other contributors. There is plenty to be done! Perhaps future volumes on family psychology will include the work of many others--a very pleasant prospect. Family psychology needs to reflect the pluralism of American society and to include in its fold academicians, researchers, clinicians, preventers, and therapists (L'Abate, 1985). Only through the contribution of many different viewpoints, even antagonistic and mutually exclusive ones, can creative tension and controversy produce the conflicts and crises that will be the groundwork for growth. Without diversity and controversy, family psychology is destined to remain in the quagmire of the status quo, which can lead only to stagnation and death!

References

L'Abate, L. (1985). The status and future of family psychology. In L. L'Abate (Ed.), Handbook of family psychology and therapy (Vol. 2, pp. 1417-1435). Homewood, IL: Dorsey Press.